P9-CKL-845

# CHICAGO STUDIES IN THE HISTORY OF AMERICAN RELIGION

*Editors*
JERALD C. BRAUER
AND MARTIN E. MARTY

A CARLSON PUBLISHING SERIES

For a complete listing of the titles in this series,
please see the back of this book.

# Your Daughters Shall Prophesy

## REVIVALISM AND FEMINISM IN THE AGE OF FINNEY

Nancy A. Hardesty

PREFACE BY JERALD C. BRAUER

CARLSON
*Publishing Inc*

BROOKLYN, NEW YORK, 1991

Please see the end of this volume for a listing of all the titles in the Carlson Publishing Series *Chicago Studies in the History of American Religion*, edited by Jerald C. Brauer and Martin E. Marty, of which this is Volume 5.



**Library of Congress Cataloging-in-Publication Data**

Hardesty, Nancy.
Your daughters shall prophesy : revivalism and feminism in the age of Finney / Nancy A. Hardesty ; preface by Jerald C. Brauer.
p. cm. — (Chicago studies in the history of American religion ; 5)
Includes bibliographical references and index.
ISBN 0-926019-42-2 (alk. paper)
1. Finney, Charles Grandison, 1792-1875. 2. Revivals—United States—History—19th century. 3. Feminism—Religious aspects--Christianity—History of doctrines—19th century. 4. Women in Christianity—United States—History—19th century. 5. United States—Church history—19th century. I.Title. II. Series.
BX7260.F47H29 1991
277.3'081'082—dc20 91-27975

Typographic design: Julian Waters

Typeface: Bitstream ITC Galliard

Case design: Alison Lew

Index prepared by the author.

Printed on acid-free, 250-year-life paper.

Manufactured in the United States of America.

# Contents

# An Introduction to the Series

The *Chicago Studies in the History of American Religion* is a series of books that deal with topics ranging from the time of Jonathan Edwards to the 1970s. Three or four deal with colonial topics and three or four treat the very recent past. About half of them focus on the decades just before and after 1900. One deals with blacks; two concentrate on women. Revivalists, fundamentalists, theologians, life in the suburbs and life in heaven and hell, the Beecher family of old and a monk of new times, Catholics adapting to America and Protestants fighting one another—all these subjects assure that the series has scope. People of every kind of taste and curiosity about American religion will find some books to suit them. Does anything serve to characterize the series as a whole? What does the stamp of "Chicago studies" mean?

Yale historian Sydney Ahlstrom in *A Religious History of the American People*, as influential as any twentieth-century work in its field, pays respect to the "Chicago School" of American religious historians. William Warren Sweet, the pioneer in such studies (beginning in 1927) at Chicago and, in many ways, in America at large represented the culmination of "the Protestant synthesis" in this field. Ahlstrom went on to name two later generations of Chicagoans, including the seminal Sidney E. Mead and major figures like Robert T. Handy and Winthrop Hudson and ending with the two editors of this series. He saw them as often "openly rebellious" in respect to Sweet and his synthesis.

If, as Ahlstrom says, "a disproportionate number" of historians have some connection with the Chicago School, it must be said that the new generation represented in these twenty-one books carries on both the lineage of Sweet and something of the "openly rebellious" character that scholars at Chicago are encouraged to pursue. This means, for one thing, that the "Protestant synthesis" does not characterize their work. These historians question the canon of historical writing produced in the Protestant era even as many of them continue to pursue themes shaped in a Protestant culture. Few of them concentrate on the old "frontier thesis" that marked the early years of the school. The shift for most has been toward the urban and pluralist scene. They call into question, not in devastating rage but in steady patterns of inquiry, the received wisdom about who matters, and why, in American religion.

So it is that this series of books focuses on blacks, women, dispensationalists, suburbanites, members of "marginal" denominations, "ethnics" and immigrants as readily as it does on white men of progressive urban bent in mainstream denominations and of long standing in America. The authors relish religious diversity and enjoy discovering the power of people once considered weak, the centrality to the American plot of those once regarded as peripheral, and the potency of losers who were once disdained by winners. Thus this series enhances an understanding of an America overlooked by the people of Sweet's era two-thirds of a century ago when it all, or most of it, began.

Rebellion for its own sake would not long hold interest; it might tell more about the psychology of rebels and revisers than about their subject matter. Revision, better than rebellion, characterizes the scholars. Re+vision: that's it. There was an original vision that characterized the Chicago School. This was the contention that in secular America and its universities religion mattered, as a theme in the national past and as a presence in the present. Second, it argued that the study of religious history belonged not only in the seminaries and archives of denominations, but also in the rough-and-tumble of the secular university, where no religious meanings were privileged and where each historian had to make a case for the value of his or her story.

Other assumptions from the earliest days pervade the books in this series. They are uncommonly alert to the environment in which expressions of faith occur. That is, they do not take for granted that religion comes protected in self-evidently important and hermetically sealed packages. Churches and denominations are porous, even when they would be sealed off; they cannot be understood apart from the ways the social environs effect them, but their power to effect change in the environment demands equal and truly unapologetic treatment. These writers do not shuffle and mumble and make excuses for their existence or for the choice of apparently arcane subject matter. They try to present their narrative in such ways that they compel attention.

A fourth characteristic that colors these works is a refusal in most cases to be typed in a fashionable slot labeled, variously, "intellectual" or "institutional" history, "cultural" or "social" history, or whatever. While those which concentrate on magisterial thinkers such as Jonathan Edwards are necessarily busy with and devoted to his intellectual achievement, most of the books deal with figures who cannot be understood only as exemplars in a sequence of studies of "the life of the mind." Instead, their biographies and circumstances come very much into play. On the other hand, none of these writers is a reductionist who sees religion as "nothing but" this or that—"nothing but" the working out of believers' Oedipal urges or expressing the economic and class interests of the subjects. Social history becomes in its way intellectual history, even if the intellects are focused on something other than the theologians in the traditions might like to see.

Some years ago *Look* magazine interviewed leaders in various denominations. One was asked if his fellow believers considered that theirs was the only true faith. Yes, he said, but they did not believe that they were the only ones who held it. The editors of this series of studies and the contributors to it do not believe that the "Chicago School," whenever and whatever it was, is the only true approach to American religious history. And, if they did, they would not hold that Chicagoans alone held it. To do so would imply a strange solipsistic or narcissistic impulse that would be the death of collegiality in the historical field. They have welcomed the chance to be in a climate where their inquiries are given such encouragement, where they find a company of fellow scholars in the Divinity School, the History Department, and the Committee on the History of Culture, whence these studies first emerged, and elsewhere in a university that provides a congenial home for massed and massive concentration of a special sort on American religious history.

While the undersigned have been consistently involved, most often together, in all twenty-one books, we want to single out a third person mentioned in so many acknowledgment sections, historian Arthur Mann. He has been a partner in two or three dozen religious history dissertation projects through the years and has been an influential and decisive contributor to the results. We stand in his debt.

Jerald C. Brauer<br>Martin E. Marty

# Editor's Preface

It is now commonplace to grant that early feminism in American was grounded not only in Enlightenment philosophy but also in revivalistic Christianity. For many years, the emphasis was on the former and the latter was overlooked. As scholars explored the roots of contemporary feminism, they found that there was not a simple, clear line from one tradition to the present. Instead, a number of movements combined to provide an impetus to extend women's rights in American society. At the same time, religion was understood as an essentially conservative force that suppressed the role of women within both the church and society at large. A number of allegedly "clear" passages in Scripture demonstrated that women were inferior within the Christian community. Nineteen hundred years of male domination would not easily give way to female assertions of their rights. Careful scholarship has documented that in spite of that reality there were always countervailing forces at work within Christianity to affirm the role and rights of women in the churches.

Conservative evangelical Christianity, revivalistic in nature, has been understood as the bastion of male domination and female subordination. The role of women was supposedly fixed in Scripture: to be seen and not heard; to be servants and not to be masters; to exhibit the virtues of piety, submission, and domesticity. It was assumed that this picture of the relation of men and women within the revivalistic Christian communities was rooted in the long history of the movement itself. Conservative Protestant Christianity could be compared only with Roman Catholicism in the way that it subordinated women to men. So it was thought.

Nancy Hardesty was one of the first to affirm that history contradicts this easy generalization. She argues that Charles Finney's revivals were one of the major sources that enfranchised women within the Christian community and raised them to a position of equality. Further, she argues that many of the so-called evangelical conservative Protestant groups that today suppress the role of women did not, in fact, originate that way. They are distorting their own heritage.

Hardesty argues that the nature of Finneyite revivalism itself provided a base for setting women free to participate fully and equally in all aspects of the Christian community's work. She grounds her argument in a careful analysis of Charles Finney's revivalism. The strength of her study rests in her effort to search for the resources in this revivalism that helped to account for the emerging importance and role of women. She is not satisfied simply to recount the story of various women who emerged out of this kind of revivalism to preach and minister in nineteenth-century America. She wants to know *why* they emerged.

Finney's emphasis on all human beings, male and female, as free moral agents capable of exercising their wills to respond to God's will in Christ laid the basis, argues Hardesty, for an equality among men and women. Both were free moral agents, both had to decide to accept or to reject Christ, both then had to shape their lives accordingly. In the area of salvation, one was not superior to the other; therefore, in the area of ethics each was as responsible as the other. This is the reason why so many women became involved in Finneyite reform efforts, including the anti-slavery movement. That was not a "men only" club; it was open to all who had freely given themselves to Christ and who were now responsible for the plight of their fellow human beings.

Hardesty goes to great lengths to establish that Finney's use of Scripture avoided all passages that gave comfort to the idea of the suppression of women and the supremacy of men. She is correct. Finney *was* selective in his use of Scripture, as are most theologians and ministers, and it is important to note what is stressed and what is overlooked. Finney's free will theology elevated the role of women and provided them with a solid base on which to build their cause.

Equally important in Charles Finney's revivals was his use of the so-called new measurers. When he prayed for sinners in distress, he specifically mentioned their names. He called them forward to the anxious bench. He encouraged both men and women to pray aloud in meetings. He expected women to testify publicly in the service concerning their sins and their conversion, and he freely called on them to do so. His opponents were appalled. This did not deter Finney. He even encouraged women to preach; his second wife preached on a number of occasions.

For Hardesty, the question is not simply where Finney stood with regard to all these issues, but where his followers carried some of his insights. Hence, she is concerned with Finney's followers and much of her argument rests on an analysis and exposition of the activity of Finneyites such as Theodore Dwight Weld, the Grimké sisters, and Antoinette Brown.

It was the Finneyites' efforts for moral reform that provided the arena in which women could work directly and could exercise leadership and participation. Without female participation, the anti-slavery movement in America would have been a failure. Women provided leadership, example, dedicated work, and financial support. They founded moral reform societies, they published a journal, they hired women to edit the journal, and they hired other women as missionaries to tour the eastern states to win converts to their cause. Hardesty argues, with justification, that many of the leaders in the women's rights movement initially were active in the Finneyite reform societies and its various benevolent enterprises. This activity symbolized the fact that women's responsibilities could not be carried out only within the home; they extended to the total society. These activities honed the skills of women as debaters, organizers, and active participants in social change. They prepared both leaders and troops.

Not only has Nancy Hardesty told an interesting and exciting story about the development of women's rights and feminism in religious sources; she has also engaged in a serious effort to analyze the nature of revivalism as it relates to the rest of feminism. That is the major strength of her effort. Protestantism in America cannot be understood apart from the emergence and predominance of revivalism. Because it was such a vast and complex movement, many things can be traced to its impact. Hardesty is the first to analyze in depth the nature of Finneyite revivalism in order to sketch out how it was related to the emergence of feminism and woman's rights. Her study invites conservative revivalistic groups in America to reevaluate their present practice with regard to women and the ministry and to women in the church. Also, she provides solid ground to modify the generalization that feminism and the woman's rights movement were grounded initially and basically in an Enlightenment philosophy of equal rights.

Jerald C. Brauer

# Preface

I grew up in a fundamentalist milieu in the 1950s. Women were mothers, teachers, nurses, or missionaries. History was the story that around 1910 my maternal grandparents were part of the small band of the righteous who left the Methodist church and began our Christian and Missionary Alliance congregation a block away. Politics meant anticommunism and wearing a "Pat Nixon for First Lady" button. We were afraid of Roman Catholics in the White House and down the street.

Four years at Wheaton College, Wheaton, Illinois, broadened my outlook considerably. Encouraged by a freshman writing teacher, I majored in writing and spent most of my intellectual energy exploring theology and philosophy. My senior year included reading all of Paul Tillich for a class titled "Theism" and researching a variety of existentialist writers from Gabriel Marcel to Jean Genet for an honors paper on Jean Paul Sartre.

Hoping to become a journalist, I spent a year at Northwestern University, Evanston, Illinois, getting a master's degree in newspaper journalism. This gave me the technical skills I needed, but I knew I would also need expertise in religion. At the time that meant, for me, studying theology. Enrolling in seminary was not an option for a woman. So in the spring of 1966 I enrolled at the University of Chicago Divinity School. I enjoyed the study, but I was not ready so soon again for the discipline and poverty of being a student.

Glimmers of feminism began to dawn on me. My first job was as an editorial assistant at *The Christian Century*. Observing staff relationships, I saw firsthand the discrimination against women. In 1966 I accepted a job as an assistant editor with *Eternity* magazine in Philadelphia. The woman who held the job before me was called an "editorial secretary." When management decided to bring in a man with less training at nearly double my salary, my consciousness was raised. They tried to tell me unequal pay was "good stewardship of the Lord's money."

In 1969 I returned to Illinois to teach freshman and creative writing classes at Trinity College in Deerfield. Shortly thereafter, Letha Dawson Scanzoni, a free-lance writer who had often submitted articles to *Eternity*, wrote to ask if I would collaborate on a book about women and the Bible. For the next five years we researched, wrote, and tried to find a publisher for the book. We also began to speak at various churches and colleges. In those days it was very controversial to say that women were not secondary creatures, the source of sin, and condemned forever by God to be in submission to men. It was revolutionary to claim that women and men were created equal in the image of God and intended for mutual partnership in all aspects of life.

*All We're Meant to Be: A Biblical Approach to Women's Liberation* (Waco, Texas: Word Books, 1974) was published at the beginning of the second year of my doctoral program at the University of Chicago.

When I applied to re-enroll at Chicago, I applied in theology. The chair of the theology department did not blink when I told him I was an evangelical and would like to stay that way, but the dean of students tactfully suggested that I might want to switch to history of Christianity if I seriously hoped to get a degree. Since I had worked with Martin E. Marty at *The Christian Century* and valued his intellect and friendship, I agreed. It was a wise move. I found I enjoyed history very much and that, indeed, most of the people who believed as I did were already dead.

At Chicago from 1973 to 1976 there were no women on the faculty. During my final year Anne Carr came as an assistant to the dean, and I was able to do a reading course in theology with her. We studied David Tracy's latest book. Nobody had heard of "women's history" or "feminist theology." At one point when I was very discouraged, I began to list on the cover of my notebook all of the women historians I could find (most of them were British). I wanted to reassure myself that a woman could actually be an historian. In one course on monasticism, the textbook stated explicitly in the introduction that the writer would deal with male monasticism only. In most classes I felt I was having to complete the professor's agenda and then do women's history on my own on the side—with little guidance, occasional opposition, and at best indifference. Yet I was able to devote most of my papers and projects to women's history. With the enormous wealth of women's history now available, it is hard to believe that was only fourteen years ago.

This dissertation emerged out of discussions with my friend Donald W. Dayton, who was already at work on what eventually became *The Theological Roots of Pentecostalism* (Grand Rapids: Zondervan, 1987), and from courses on revivalism we took from Jerald Brauer. Working in these materials gave me a deeper sense of my own religious history and a foundation for my growing feminism.

During my three years at the University of Chicago, 1973 to 1976, I also participated in the founding of the Evangelical Women's Caucus and of the journal *Daughters of Sarah*. Together with the publication of *All We're Meant to Be*, these events formed what has come to be known as "biblical feminism." Both the Caucus and *Daughters of Sarah* continue to nurture a diverse group of women and men who choose to explore the connections between feminism and biblical faith. Even in the twentieth century, religious faith can motivate and empower some people to progressive social reform.

A teaching position at Candler School of Theology, Emory University, Atlanta, Georgia, motivated me to complete my dissertation in 1976, but there was no possibility of immediate publication. Four years of teaching, advising, and supervising ministry practicums at Emory left me no time for additional research, but eventually I was able to expand and rework some of the material for use in my book *Women Called to Witness: Evangelical Feminism in the Nineteenth Century* (Nashville: Abingdon Press, 1984). Using Frances Willard of the Woman's Christian Temperance Union as a model, I traced the influences of Finney and holiness evangelist Phoebe Palmer on the women involved in abolition, moral reform, woman's rights, temperance, and suffrage. Although the book's value to scholars was limited by lack of precise notes, it did provide many with a new sense of their own history and fostered further work on women in holiness, pentecostal, fundamentalist, and evangelical history. Despite the wealth of recent research on women in religion, the dissertation presented here remains the fullest scholarly treatment of these evangelical women to date.

While I have pursued other feminist topics in more recent work, I still am intrigued by these women and men. They had a Christian faith that empowered them to tackle the problems of society, to seek creative solutions, and to do justice. They had such a broad and inclusive vision in comparison with fundamentalist and evangelicals today. I find them inspiring. They have become my own personal pantheon within the communion of saints.

August 1990
Nancy A. Hardesty

# Your Daughters Shall Prophesy

# Introduction

A nineteenth-century writer outlining the history of the woman's rights movement in Massachusetts quoted this observation from the French critic Taine: "In order to be developed, an idea must be in harmony with surrounding civilization, and the whole age must co-operate with it."[1]

From time immemorial women have been protesting their lot in patriarchal Western society. The Bible records the defiance of Queen Vashti, who refused to obey the orders of King Ahasuerus and was banished lest her conduct "become known to all the women and encourage them in a contemptuous attitude towards their husbands" (Esther 1:17 Jerusalem Bible). Aristophanes' play *Lysistrata* portrays the organized protest of Greek women. The New Testament Gospels show Jesus touching, healing, and teaching women—to the astonishment of his male disciples. Isolated women rose to prominence in the next eighteen centuries—Paula of Bethlehem, Abbess Hilda of Whitby, Catherine of Siena, playwright Hrosvitha, Theresa of Avila, Joan of Arc, Queen Elizabeth, Mary Dyer.

In nineteenth-century America, however, one finds not only outstanding individuals but also an organized movement for woman's religious, social, legal, economic, and political rights, a movement that might be designated "feminist." Why then and there? Building on Taine's observation, what factors in the surrounding civilization were in harmony with this movement? What factors in the age cooperated with it?

Sociologist Alice Rossi in *The Feminist Papers* begins with women who were heirs of the eighteenth-century Enlightenment. These radical women—Abigail Adams, Judith Sargent Murray, Mary Wollstonecraft, Frances Wright, Harriet Martineau, and Margaret Fuller—shared the conviction that reason would rout superstition and secure justice and liberty for all, including women. Brilliant in their analysis of woman's condition and articulate in their presentation of woman's case of justice, they assumed that reasonable men would see their plight and remedy their situation. As Abigail learned from John, neither reason nor threats secured women any rights in the United

States Constitution. Nor did any of these women draw a following of other women or found a movement. They were writers and analysts, not actors.

Historian Aileen Kraditor in *The Ideas of the Woman Suffrage Movement 1890-1910* applied similar Enlightenment categories to later women, calling them "natural rights" feminists. She attempted to show that the women who persisted until they secured the franchise were motivated by and based their persuasion on the same arguments used by the nation's founders. The women read the Declaration of Independence and decided that if "We hold these truths to be self-evident, that all men are created equal, that they are endowed by their Creator with certain unalienable Rights, that among these are Life, Liberty and the pursuit of Happiness," then so are women. Kraditor's evidence may accurately portray the thrust of the later movement that narrowed its sights on one political objective, but she failed to account for all of the factors surrounding the movement's beginnings at mid-century.

Nineteenth-century America was undergoing great change. Symbolic of this shift was the transition of government on 20 January 1829. Refusing to attend the ceremonies, aristocrat John Quincy Adams left the White House the day before. Andrew Jackson, hero of the battle of New Orleans, opened it to the common people who had helped to elect him. Colonial society had been stable and stratified, a more or less homogeneous, agricultural society, a society in which women were valued for their skills in a variety of occupations.[2] However, during the first quarter of the nineteenth century, society changed, and became more fluid for men. New occupations opened for them, and an ambitious young man could find success as a merchant, editor, soldier, businessman. Education was becoming more common and professional schools were emerging. A young man from a poor family could aspire to become a lawyer, a doctor, a minister. State constitutions were being revised to extend the franchise to all men, without religious or property qualifications. The church was disestablished in Virginia (1785), Connecticut (1818), New Hampshire (1819), and Massachusetts (1833). The "standing order" was giving way to the common man, property rights to human rights. As the nation expanded westward, trade and industry developed in the East. Men found new avenues for success through education, business, and politics. Individualism, self-reliance, nationalistic optimism abounded. Progress toward perfection was the prospect. For men.

For women, society was changing in less optimistic directions. Poor women were finding the factory even more restrictive than the home. Women of the emerging middle class were finding greater leisure and fewer options for profitable work outside the home. In mapping the boundaries and the government of the new nation, men had also mapped "woman's sphere." Its provinces were two: home and church. According to one college president, "woman's peculiar work" is "that of the wife, the mother, the daughter. . . . The wife becomes the housekeeper, the mother becomes the nurse, and the daughter the hired servant and paid domestic."[3] Of course women were ideally fitted for their station. "Heaven has appointed to one sex the superior, and to the other the subordinate station," said Catharine Beecher.[4] "She is to be the mother of her race. This fixes the sphere of her duties in the Home," according to an eminent divine.[5]

Surveying women's magazines, gift books, cookbooks, tracts and sermons, diaries and memoirs, historian Barbara Welter found four feminine virtues paramount: piety, purity, submissiveness, and domesticity. The weaker sex could not bear the rough-and-tumble of the business world nor the excitement of politics. The corruption of both would besmirch their purity, affront their piety. Religion was to be their outlet, "by divine right, a gift of God and nature."[6] Naturally endowed with more piety than their menfolk, women were to preserve religion's virtues of humility, submission, and meekness in a culture bent on achieving success by any means.[7] Woman's high calling was to preserve all that was decent in civilization: "All the sacred protection of religion, all the general promptings of chivalry, all the poetry of romantic gallantry, depend upon woman's retaining her place as dependent and defenceless, and making no claims, and maintaining no right but what are the gifts of honor, rectitude and love."[8] "Separated from woman's influence, man is narrow, churlish, brutal. Woman is a helper suited for him. With her help he reaches a loftier stature."[9]

Yet some men saw a more radical vision of social equality, and some women found the courage and stamina to break the mold into which society was trying to pour them. Radical abolitionism had roots in the revivalism that Charles Grandison Finney spread from western New York, to New York City, to the Western Reserve. Gilbert Barnes brought this most forcefully to the attention of historians in *The Anti-Slavery Impulse 1830-1844*. John L. Hammond has substantiated it in a statistical study of "Revival Religion and Antislavery Politics" in Ohio.[10] Whitney Cross in *The Burned-over District* traces the wider influences of revivalism in western New York on a variety of reform movements-temperance, antimasonry, communitarian perfectionism.

The connection between Finneyite revivalism and the woman's rights movement has been noted in passing by several people. Alice Rossi declares that "the impulse of these early American feminists was rooted in the revivalist dedication to benevolent reform of society." They were "responsive to the message of these revivals, drawing from them their convictions about the need for the moral reform of society, which they channeled into abolition and woman's-rights activity."[11] Beverly Wildung Harrison in "The Early Feminists and the Clergy" declares that "the 'conservatism' and 'moralism' of many, even most, of the early feminists was of a character which cannot be understood apart from appreciation of the utopic character of a profoundly Christian evangelical impulse." In fact, says Harrison, "the social origins of the woman's rights movement in America will not be fully or adequately understood, nor the early feminists rightly appreciated, until the connection is duly acknowledged between the woman movement and left-wing Reformation evangelicalism in America." She points specifically to the importance of Finney.[12] Donald W. Dayton in *Discovering an Evangelical Heritage* speaks of "the early Evangelical commitment to feminist principles," and declares that historically "it is Evangelicalism that next to Quakerism has given the greatest role to women in the life of the church," a practice that "crested in nineteenth-century revivalism."[13]

This book uncovers the specific ties between the revivalist and feminist camps and suggests some correlates of Finneyite revivalism that seem to have been conducive to widening woman's sphere, factors from which some women derived inspiration in their quest for expanded roles and equal rights. Six suggest themselves: (1) the "arminianizing" trend that Finney represented theologically; (2) his emphasis on "experimental," "experiential" religion; (3) the consequent reinterpretation of Scripture; (4) his innovative "new measures"; (5) his definition of ministers as merely "soul-winners"; and (6) his emphasis on "usefulness" and universal reform.

These roots of the movement have been ignored for a variety of reasons. The women most prominently involved in the organized "movement" during its early stages finally despaired of answering their clerical critics, and those most involved in the religious aspects of the enterprise drifted off toward Unitarianism. Those who struggled more quietly for woman's rights within the churches were by and large ignored in the still-standard history of the movement, the six-volume *History of Woman Suffrage* begun by Elizabeth Cady Stanton and Susan B. Anthony. Although they illustrate the phenomena with which this book deals, they were among the least cordial to religion of the early pioneers and they represent the more radical wing of the later movement. The evidence for the religious foundations of their crusade that they include (and I found much valuable material in their early volumes) has been ignored by subsequent historians more interested in other issues or in the later period.

Today women have many of the rights for which nineteenth-century women were asking: suffrage, married women's property rights, custody of their children, ordination. But many areas of inequality still exist. And women are still asking many of the same fundamental questions their foremothers grappled with a century ago. Religious women are still struggling to find ways of reconciling feminism with their faith, the integrity of their personhood with the interpretation of Scripture. The lives and writings of nineteenth-century women offer not only inspiration but also wisdom for women today. As Abby Kelley Foster declared to the 1851 woman's rights convention at Worcester, Massachusetts, they serve as reminders that, "Bloody feet, sisters, have worn smooth the paths by which you come up hither."[14]

ONE

# The Finneyites

Western New York State was a seedbed and hotbed of innumerable "ultraisms" in the nineteenth century. Whitney Cross titled his study of revivalism and reform along the banks of the Erie Canal *The Burned-over District*.

The people of the district had migrated from Connecticut and Massachusetts; many of them would go on to Ohio, Illinois, Kansas, and California. They worshiped either in the local "Presbygational" churches founded as part of the Presbyterian-Congregational Plan of Union worked out in 1801, or in Methodist churches. They were educated in the academies that flourished in the canal cities, and they took their places in the professions and in the business community. But the passions of their lives were revival and reform.

The man who struck the match that ignited many of their efforts was Charles Grandison Finney. Historian Richard Hofstadter calls him "one of the most compelling figures in the history of American religion," one who "must be reckoned among our great men."[1] This is the story of the man and those he influenced.

## *Charles Grandison Finney*

Charles Finney (1792-1874)[2] was born 29 August 1792 in Warren, Connecticut, but like many of their contemporaries, his family in 1794 migrated to the western frontier, Brothertown, New York, in Oneida County. They later moved to Hanover, near Kirkland, on the shores of Lake Ontario. For two years Finney attended Hamilton Oneida Academy in Clinton, southwest of Utica. In the fall of 1812, after teaching school for a time at Henderson, near Oswego, Finney went off to school in Warren. He taught school again for two years in New Jersey, but returned home to Jefferson

County when his mother became ill. He began to study law with Benjamin Wright in Adams, south of Watertown.

The promising young lawyer began to take his place in Adams's society, courting the local belles, playing cello at the Presbyterian church. Under the revival preaching of Jedediah Burchard, he became concerned about his spiritual welfare. On "the 10th of October, and a very pleasant day," 1821, he said, "I made up my mind that I would settle the question of my soul's salvation at once." After spending the day in Bible reading and prayer in the woods, he found that "all sense of sin, all consciousness of present sin or guilt, had departed." He had "quiet of . . . mind," and his "heart was all liquid."[3]

He immediately renounced law and began studying for the ministry under the tutelage of the local Presbyterian pastor George W. Gale, a Princeton graduate. "His preaching was of the old school type; that is, it was thoroughly Calvinistic . . . what has been called hyper-Calvinism. He was, of course, regarded as highly orthodox," said Finney.[4] The budding young minister was formally admitted to the care of the St. Lawrence Presbytery on 25 June 1823, and was granted a preaching license in December of that year. Gale arranged for him to be commissioned by the Female Missionary Society of the Western District of New York as a missionary to Jefferson County, beginning 17 March 1824. He was ordained on 1 July 1824, despite the committee's apprehensions about his colloquial preaching style. He began his formal ministry in July at the Presbyterian church in Evans Mills, Jefferson County, north of Watertown.

In October he married Lydia Andrews (1794-1847) of Whitestown, Oneida County. A day or two after their marriage he returned to Evans Mills, promising to come back for her and their wedding dowry within the week. But he learned that Perch River needed help in a revival there. Then a similar call came from Brownville, both west of Watertown. Finally, early in the spring of 1825 he left Brownville to go for his wife. It had been six months since their marriage and they had seldom even been able to exchange letters. He stopped in LeRayville to get his horse shod, and revival broke out there. A church elder at last fetched poor Lydia, and Finney kept on preaching, in LeRayville and next door in Rutland.

From there he went to Gouverneur, to the north in Lawrence County. Revivals quickly followed in DeKalb to the north and then back down through Western, Rome, and Utica.

*The Holy Band*

One of Finney's most important converts in the Utica revival, which began in the winter of 1825 and lasted through spring 1826, was Theodore Dwight Weld (1803-1894).[5] He was born in Hampton, Connecticut, on 23 November 1803, heir to four generations of Congregational clergymen. In childhood, Weld moved with his family to Pompey, south of Syracuse, where his father filled the Congregational pulpit and farmed three hundred acres. Weld's academic preparation, like Finney's, was received in Clinton. His uncle, Erastus Clark, was a founder and trustee of Hamilton College. Many of its students were greatly affected by Finney's revival, but Weld ridiculed the excitement. His aunt finally maneuvered him into attending a meeting that he thought would be addressed by Pastor Samuel Aiken. Instead, Finney preached for an hour on the text "One sinner destroyeth much good." Said Weld, "He just held me up on his toasting fork before that audience."[6] Mrs. Clark bent forward in prayer whenever her restless nephew showed signs of wanting to escape. Weld was eventually soundly converted and joined Finney's "holy band" of assistants. News of Finney's revivals had already reached New England and his measures were under fire from such conservative revivalists as Asahel Nettleton. The practice of women testifying publicly in "promiscuous assemblies," which sprang up in the Utica revival, added fuel to the controversy. Although Finney was charged with this "innovation," Weld's correspondence with the Grimké sisters reveals that it was he who instituted the practice immediately upon his conversion.[7]

From Utica, Finney moved on to Auburn, to Dirck Lansing's First Presbyterian Church. A local Presbyterian "of the most pronounced type, a deacon and an elder of his church throughout his long life" was James S. Seymour.[8] Under his guidance and guardianship was the family of his deceased brother Orson, a bank cashier, who had been born in West Hartford, Connecticut. He, a Presbyterian, had married an Episcopalian from New York City and they had set up housekeeping in Canandaigua. There on 12 January 1820 was born Caroline Maria (1820-1914).[9] When she was four, the bereaved family moved to Auburn. At an early age she "came under the spell of" her uncle's "zeal and of the doctrines and customs of that denomination." Among those she remembered were "the revival meetings of the Reverends Burchard and Finney" in the summer of 1826 and again in the spring of 1831, "excitements which recurred as regularly and inevitably as the spring and fall housecleanings of that time, and which were as disturbing to the peace and routine of my homes."[10]

In the autumn of 1826 Finney began services at Nathaniel Beman's church in Troy. One less-than-satisfied convert during the long revival was Elizabeth Cady (1815-1902),[11] daughter of Judge Daniel Cady. Born in November 1815, she was a native of the area. Her family resided in Johnstown, between Utica and Schenectady. When her elder brother died in 1826, her father cried, "Oh, my daughter, I wish you were a boy!" She resolved to prove to him that a daughter was just as valuable a source of pride, but she never succeeded. Encouragement for her inquiring mind came from her next-door neighbor, the local Presbyterian minister, Simon Hosack. One day she confided to him: "My father prefers boys; he wishes I was one, and I intend to be as near like one as possible. I am going to ride on horseback and study Greek. Will you give me a Greek lesson, Doctor?"[12] He took her into his library and they began. Continuing her education at the Johnstown Academy, she added Latin and mathematics to her accomplishments—she had already learned how injustice is written into the laws against women by reading her father's law books. Her ambition was to attend Union College in Schenectady, as the boys in her class were doing. Instead, she was sent to Emma Willard's Troy Female Seminary from 1830-1832.

"The next happening in Troy that seriously influenced my character," she recalled seventy years later, "was the advent of the Rev. Charles G. Finney, a pulpit orator, who, as a terrifier of human souls, proved himself the equal of Savonarola." As "the result of six weeks of untiring effort," Troy experienced "one of those intense revival seasons that swept over the city and thus the seminary like an epidemic, attacking in its worst form the most susceptible. Owing to my gloomy Calvinistic training in the Old Scotch Presbyterian church, and my vivid imagination, I was one of the first victims." She later rid herself of the Calvinist beliefs that she said "haunted my dreams," producing a "mental anguish which prostrated my health." But she concluded the vignette: "He was sincere, so peace to his ashes."[13]

Elizabeth Cady was not the only one alarmed by Finney's revivals. Criticism of his "new measures" had been spreading like wildfire, back and forth between Unitarians and Universalists in New York and conservative Calvinist revivalists such as Nettleton and Lyman Beecher in New England. During his Troy campaign Finney had met with Nettleton in Albany but dialogue proved impossible. Finally in July 1827 equal numbers of Finneyite and eastern pastors met in New Lebanon, New York, near the Massachusetts line.

Discussions lasted for nine days and the two opposing camps managed to reach a compromise consensus on all issues except one: the practice of women praying aloud in mixed assemblies. The Finneyites would not agree to stifle it and the easterners could not countenance it. Beecher argued the point at length, insisting that the practice was "unscriptural and inadmissable." Beman replied, and Finney termed his arguments "manifestly too conclusive to admit of any refutation." In the end, Beecher could only sputter: "Finney, I know your plan, and you know I do; you mean to come to Connecticut, and carry a streak of fire to Boston. But if you attempt it, as the Lord liveth, I'll meet you at the state line, and call out all the artillery-men, and fight every inch of the way to Boston, and then I'll fight you there."[14]

Undaunted, Finney went back to holding revivals. After some time in Stephentown, New York, he accepted an invitation to Wilmington, Delaware, and from there to Philadelphia, where he spent a year and a half. There he served as a catalyst in efforts by New School Presbyterians to wrest control of denominational machinery from dominance by advocates of the Princeton theology. His friend Beman was moderator of the 1831 General Assembly that acquitted Albert Barnes, a Princeton graduate who had become controversial through an 1829 sermon, "The Way of Salvation," in which he had endorsed the views of Yale theologian Nathaniel Taylor. Philadelphians slowly began to realize that Taylor's and Barnes's views on free will were actually the same assumptions that underlay Finney's revival measures. But by then Finney had moved on to Reading and Lancaster, Pennsylvania, and Columbia in Herkimer County, New York. In the summer and fall of 1830 he had held meetings in New York City at the request of philanthropist Anson G. Phelps, a member of the Association of Gentlemen, which included Arthur (1786-1865) and Lewis Tappan (1788-1873).[15] They were born in Northampton, Massachusetts, home of Jonathan Edwards during the First Great Awakening nearly a century before. Their mother Sarah was a pietist of Edwardsean cast, but the sons drifted toward Unitarianism as they sought to make their fortunes in Boston. Arthur eventually moved his family to New Haven, next door to Nathaniel Taylor, and commuted from there to New York City. He became an "orthodox and earnest" Presbyterian and opened a prosperous dry goods business.

He was impressed with Finney's revivals upstate, despite the reports from Unitarian periodicals that Lewis clipped, describing the preacher as a "half-crazed fanatic."[16] Investigating the reports and finding them untrue, Lewis too became a Presbyterian. Dissatisfied with the state of the church in

New York, they proposed to start their own, following a revivalist pattern. So they founded the First Free Presbyterian Church, imported revivalist pastor Joel Parker from Rochester, and funded the *New York Evangelist* to promote revivals and benevolence.

*Revival in Rochester*

Being without a pastor, the elders of the Third Presbyterian Church in Rochester invited Finney to hold meetings, which he did from 10 September 1830 until 6 March 1831. During this climactic revival of his career in some respects, Finney introduced the necessity of reform into his message; he preached for the first time on temperance. In his *Memoirs*, Finney quoted his rival Lyman Beecher as eventually conceding that "this was the greatest work of God, and the greatest revival of religion, that the world has ever seen, in so short a time, . . . unparalleled in the history of the church, and of the progress of religion."[17]

Finney repeatedly notes the number of business and professional people, especially lawyers, converted during his meetings. At Rochester one of the converts was the deputy county clerk, Henry Brewster Stanton (1805-1887).[18] Born 27 June 1805 in Griswold, Connecticut, he had joined the staff of the *Monroe Telegraph* in Rochester in 1826.

Also converted in Rochester were Joseph Brown and several of his children. Brown, too, was a Connecticut Yankee, born in Thompson, but he reared his family in the small village of Henrietta, south of Rochester. His daughter Antoinette (1825-1921)[19] was too young to attend revival meetings, but her mother gathered the younger children around her knee to hear Scripture and to pray. Antoinette publicly confessed her faith 5 May 1834 at the age of nine and joined the orthodox Congregational church where her father had become a deacon.

Paulina Kellogg (1813-1876)[20] was a teenager when Finney arrived in Rochester. Born 7 August 1813 in Bloomfield, near Niagara Falls, she lost both her parents before she was seven. She was sent to live in LeRoy, southwest of Rochester, with a very strict and orthodox Presbyterian aunt. She joined the church at age thirteen, yet "suffered constant torment from her sins, and found comfort only in the religious enthusiasm of recurrent revivals."[21] Her dream was to become a missionary to the Sandwich Islands, but in 1833 she married Francis Wright, a wealthy Utica merchant, and together they plunged into reform activities.

From Rochester Finney returned to Auburn and then spent a month in Buffalo. In the autumn of 1831 he accepted an invitation to hold a "protracted meeting" in Providence. Friends wanted him to come to Boston, but Lyman Beecher, pastor of the Bowdoin Street Congregational Church, was less than enthusiastic. After hearing a report from the pastor of Old South Church, who had been sent to Providence to spy on Finney's meetings, Beecher relented, however, and Finney received an invitation to Park Street Church, where Lyman's son Edward had been ministering. Although Finney's "searching sermons astonished, and even offended" many of Boston's professed Christians,[22] the visit ended in détente between Beecher and Finney.

### *New York City*

Exhausted by ten years' labor as a revivalist and in need of a permanent home for his growing family, Finney left Boston in April 1832 to become pastor of the Second Free Presbyterian Church in New York City. Lewis Tappan had leased the Chatham Street Theatre and outfitted it as a church and as a suitable place to accommodate the anniversary meetings of all of the benevolent societies. It was here in 1835 Finney gave addresses that later became his *Lectures on Revivals of Religion*—in part to boost the circulation of editor Joshua Leavitt's *Evangelist*, which had been sagging due to its abolitionist stance.

Theodore Weld had taken a desk at the office of the *Evangelist* in 1832, from which to carry on his duties as an agent for the Tappans' Society for Promoting Manual Labor in Literary Institutions. Weld had come to Lewis Tappan's attention through his two sons, who were students with Weld at the Oneida Institute. One of Weld's duties was to secure a site for a manual training seminary the Tappans wished to underwrite to offer further training to members of Finney's "holy band" and to promote their favorite reforms. Weld helped them locate Lane Seminary in Cincinnati, with Lyman Beecher as president. After the "Lane Debates" concerning the relative merits of colonization versus immediate abolition split the student body in 1834, Weld moved most of the "rebels" to a new campus near Cleveland—Oberlin Collegiate Institute. He himself abolitionized the Western Reserve,

Pennsylvania, and upstate New York, while his former fellow student Henry Stanton moved into Rhode Island and Connecticut.

By 1836 Weld's body was exhausted, his voice permanently impaired by his devotion to the work of abolition, and so he retired again to New York City to become an agent for the American Anti-Slavery Society. In October and November, he and Stanton held intensive training sessions, following many of Finney's New Measures techniques, for the Seventy—including two women: Angelina (1805-1879) and Sarah (1792-1873) Grimké.[23]

The sisters had been born into an aristocratic, Episcopalian family in South Carolina, but they, too, were influenced by Presbyterian revivalism. Their older brother Thomas had gone off to Yale and, under President Timothy Dwight's influence, had turned from the lures of deism and the Enlightenment to a sound Christian faith during the revivals there. About 1813 Sarah "first responded to the evangelical appeal." She was "deeply stirred by a revival meeting," backslid, went again with a friend to hear Presbyterian evangelist Henry Kolloch, and was reconverted.[24] After her father's death in 1819, Sarah, who had been his devoted nurse, underwent a great depression, turned to religion, and found consolation in a rural Methodist revival meeting. But she was deeply influenced by the Philadelphia Quakers, who had aided her during her father's treatment there, and so she became a Quaker in 1823.

Revivals swept Charleston in 1825-26. In April 1826 Angelina experienced conversion under the ministry of William McDowell, the local Presbyterian pastor. She left the Episcopal church for the Presbyterians on 8 April 1826, and on 23 April 1828 left the Presbyterians for the Quakers, according to her diary of 27 April 1829. For a year or so, she had been happy among the Presbyterians, experiencing "fervent feeling," teaching Sabbath school, establishing a "female prayer-meeting among Baptists, Methodists, Congregationalists and Presbyterians." But then a six-month period of darkness fell on her soul—which Sarah intensified with pressures to become a Quaker, which she finally did.

The two sisters became concerned about slavery and threw themselves into the abolition struggle. After being trained by Weld and Stanton, they began to hold meetings for women in Massachusetts. Men infiltrated the meetings, and suddenly, without design, the Grimkés found themselves addressing "promiscuous assemblies." Conservative Congregational clergymen, already annoyed by their abolitionism, took this as an occasion to denounce them in a *Pastoral Letter*. Weld urged them to ignore the issue and limit their message to antislavery sentiments, but the sisters felt they must defend their rights as women or they would lose their right to speak for the slave. Sarah responded publicly to the controversy by publishing a series of *Letters on the Equality of the Sexes*. Stanton supported their efforts by opening one of their meetings with a "precious" prayer and sitting on the platform with them. They pronounced him "sound on the subject of women's rights."[25] This controversy marked the opening round of the public battle for women's rights in this country.

*Perfection*

In the summer of 1835 the Finney family moved to Oberlin, Ohio. One of the conditions under which the Lane rebels agreed to move from Cincinnati to Oberlin was that Charles Finney would be hired as professor of theology. The students brought with them a president for Oberlin, Asa Mahan (1799-1889),[26] who served until 1850. He had been pastor of the Sixth Presbyterian Church in Cincinnati and a trustee of Lane.

Mahan was also a product of the burned-over district. Born 9 November 1799 in Vernon, near Clinton, he said he was nurtured in strict Calvinism of the Old School, "the straitest sect," but his mother was "one of the greatest female thinkers and readers on religious topics" that he ever knew. In fact, "no minister in all the region . . . was more fully acquainted with the writings of Edwards, Hopkins, Bellamy, and Emmons than she."[27] After listening to revivalists, his theology changed from Old School passivity to New School belief in human ability, and he sought salvation in 1816. After graduation in 1824 from Hamilton College, Weld's alma mater, he studied at Andover Theological Seminary. Licensed by the Oneida Presbytery on 30 May 1827, he pastored the Pittsford Congregational Church southeast of Rochester, which benefitted from Finney's 1830 revival.

As Finney settled into the role of theology professor, he gained some distance from his revivals. "In looking at the state of the Christian church, as it had been revealed to me in my revival labors," he said in his *Memoirs*, he was led "earnestly to inquire whether there was not something higher and more enduring than the Christian church was aware of; whether there were not promises, and means provided in the Gospel for the establishment of Christians in altogether a higher form of Christian life."[28] Copies of John Humphrey Noyes's *Perfectionist* had circulated at Oberlin and Finney had examined them. He could not accept Noyes's views, yet he was drawn by the notion of perfection and the Methodist doctrine of sanctification. Although Finney resigned from the Presbyterian church on 13 March 1836, he took the pastorate of the Sixth Free Church, Broadway Tabernacle, in New York City, which was Congregational. He and Mahan spent the winter of 1836-37 there, studying the historical formulations of the doctrine of perfection and working on their own doctrine, which eventually came to be known as "Oberlin Perfectionism."

Although John Wesley taught a concept of "holiness" or "entire sanctification" in his *Plain Account of Christian Perfection*, the American Methodist church, the fastest-growing denomination in nineteenth-century America, had by and large abandoned the idea. It was being revived by two sisters in New York City: Sarah Worrall Lankford (1806-1896) and Phoebe Worrall Palmer (1807-1874).[29] Their father Henry was born in Yorkshire, England, where he heard Wesley preach. After coming to the United States, he embraced the Methodist faith and an American Methodist named Dorothea Wade married him. Sarah was born 23 April 1806 and Phoebe 18 December 1807. Both experienced conversion at early ages and joined the Methodist church. At age 18 Phoebe married Walter C. Palmer. He was trained as a physician at the New York City College of Physicians and Surgeons, but later practiced homeopathic medicine. Sarah chose merchant Thomas A. Lankford, of Richmond, Virginia, for her husband in 1831.

On 21 May 1835 at 2:30 P.M. Sarah Lankford affirmed that she experienced assurance of entire sanctification. In August she consolidated prayer meetings she had been attending at both the Allen Street and Mulberry Street Methodist Churches into one meeting at the home that the Lankfords and the Palmers shared at 54 Rivington Street. Known round the world as the "Tuesday Meeting," it met for more than sixty years. Although Phoebe was a member of the prayer group, she herself did not experience sanctification until after an experience "on the evening of July 26th, 1837, between the hours of eight and nine o'clock" when "the Lord gave me such a view of my utter pollution and helplessness, apart from the cleansing, energizing influences of the purifying blood of Jesus, and the quickening aids of the Holy Spirit, that I have ever since retained a vivid realization of the fact."[30] Thereafter she became the more famous of the sisters, leading holiness revivals and camp meetings in this country, Canada, and the British Isles. Through the publication of more than half a dozen books, which together sold hundreds of thousands of copies, she substantially changed the concept of holiness.

Until December 1839 the Tuesday Meeting was for women only. In that year Phoebe L. Upham came to the meeting and wished to bring her husband, Congregational theologian Thomas Upham, professor at Bowdoin College in Maine. From then on the meeting was open to anyone and drew regular participants from around the world. It was not unusual for four or five bishops of the Methodist church to be there, along with clergy and laity from a variety of other denominations. Yet usually Sarah or Phoebe presided and every person present, male or female, lay or cleric, was free to give testimony or pray.

*Oberlin*

For a time Finney continued to commute between Oberlin and New York City. Mary Mahan had written to Weld asking if Angelina Grimké might be interested in teaching in the Female Department at Oberlin,[31] but the two decided to marry on 14 May 1838. They settled first in Fort Washington, New York, and then Belleville, New Jersey, whence Weld commuted to his job in the city as the executive of the American Anti-Slavery Society. He resigned the post in May 1840 after abolitionist ranks split, in part over the issue of admitting women to full participation. Later that year Elizabeth Cady, as the young bride of Henry Stanton, met Philadelphia Quaker preacher Lucretia Mott in London at the World's Anti-Slavery Conference, where American women delegates were refused seats.

Rather than returning to New York in the fall of 1842, Finney again held revivals in Boston, Providence, and Rochester. Returning to Boston in the fall of 1843, Finney at last experienced sanctification himself, even though he had been proclaiming the doctrine since 1837. His greatest struggle in submitting to the will of God was to give his wife Lydia, who was in feeble health, up to God.[32] She subsequently died in December of 1847.

Because of Lydia's poor health, Finney spent most of his time in Oberlin from 1843 until her death. During that period he influenced a group of women students who became very active in a variety of reform movements and particularly woman's rights. Oberlin was, of course, the first college to admit women on a par with men—and blacks with whites. Mahan in contemplating his epitaph asked that it read: "The first man, in the history of the race, who conducted woman, in connection with members of the opposite sex, through a full course of liberal education."[33]

One of the first women graduates of Oberlin was Betsey Mix Cowles (1810-1876). Born 9 February 1810 in Bristol, Connecticut, her family moved to Austinburg, Ohio, in 1811 when her father became pastor of the Congregational church there. Professor Henry Cowles of Oberlin was kin to her father and supplied his pulpit from 1830-35. Betsey enrolled in Oberlin in 1838 and completed the ladies' course in 1840. A deeply religious woman, she was one of the instigators of the Ohio Woman's Rights Association.

Antoinette Brown's parents wanted her to become a missionary, but "after two or three years," her "persistant desire to be sent to Oberlin was gratified." She listed two ties that drew her to the school: her older brother William was already a graduate of the theological department, and "our beloved Professor Finney" taught theology there. She admits "there was considerable difference of opinion on the woman question among the faculty, still more among the students. President Mahan was one of the more liberal and Professor Finney thought that exceptional women might be called upon to become religious teachers."[34] Brown arrived at Oberlin in 1846, completed the ladies' course in one year, and, without encouragement, enrolled in the theological course, completing it in 1850, though the school refused to grant her a degree or encourage her ordination.[35]

Her best friend at Oberlin was Lucy Stone (1818-1893)[36] who was enrolled between 1843 and 1847, graduating with honors from the regular course. Born 13 August 1818 in West Brookfield, Massachusetts, Stone joined the orthodox Congregational church there as a child, but was deeply offended shortly thereafter when Deacon Josiah Henshaw was expelled for antislavery activities. She voted six times to support him, but each time her vote was ignored upon orders from the pastor who said that although she was a member in good standing, women were not allowed to vote. Stone was also in the balcony of the West Brookfield Church in 1837 when the clergymen of the General Association of the Congregational Churches of Massachusetts drafted their *Pastoral Letter* against the Grimké sisters. Stone enrolled at Mount Holyoke Seminary in 1839 but stayed only three months because Mary Lyon was upset by her leaving copies of William Garrison's *Liberator* in the reading room and turning her missionary mite box into one for the American Anti-Slavery Society. In 1843, at age 25, she enrolled at Oberlin. "Men came to Oberlin for various reasons," Stone said, "women because they had nowhere else to go."[37]

Another classmate of Brown and Stone was Sallie Holley (1818-1893).[38] Born 17 February 1818 in Canandaigua, Sallie was the daughter of a

Methodist mother from Schenectady and a more liberal father from Salisbury, Connecticut. Sallie herself joined the Unitarian church in Buffalo about 1841. After teaching briefly in Rochester, she came to Oberlin in 1847. Her 1851 graduation speech, "Ideal of Womanhood," included the right of women to vote and to preach.

Another classmate was Hannah Conant Tracy (1815-1896).[39] Born in Becket, Massachusetts, on Christmas Day 1815, Hannah moved with her family to Rochester, Ohio, in 1831. When she heard about Oberlin opening its doors to women she determined to go, but her father forbade her. Instead, in 1834 she married John Tracy, a theology student who soon became an antislavery lecturer. Hannah read theology with her husband and then law. Shortly before the birth of their third child, her husband died in August 1844 as a result of injuries sustained while aiding escaped slaves. Left to support herself and her children, Hannah wrote for newspapers and taught school. Free to reach for her dream, she enrolled at Oberlin for the year 1847-48. She participated with Stone and Brown in the debating society that met in the woods and in the home of an elderly black woman because college officials would not allow women to participate in such activities on campus. In 1848 Mrs. Tracy became matron of the Ohio Deaf and Dumb Asylum in Columbus.

The first woman's rights convention was called in 1848 by Elizabeth Cady Stanton and Lucretia Mott, among others. It was held on 19 July in the Wesleyan Methodist Church in Seneca Falls, New York. News of the event quickly spread to Ohio. On 19 April 1850 a woman's rights convention was held in the Second Baptist Church at Salem with Betsey Mix Cowles as president. It was the first meeting at which men were totally denied a voice. "*Never did men so suffer*," comments the *History of Woman Suffrage*.[40] At the closing banquet men were allowed to purchase tickets that entitled them to sit in a balcony and smell the food and hear the speeches.

In 1851 the women of Ohio held a convention in Akron 28 May and in the Christian church at Mt. Gilead in December. In May 1852 they convened again in a Baptist church in Massilon to organize the Ohio Woman's Rights Association. Hannah Tracy, who had attended the Akron convention, was named president. In May 1853 the Ohio association met in Ravenna. Caroline Seymour, who had married Ohio banker Theodoric Cordenio Severance, presided, and Antoinette Brown addressed the group. Later that year, in October, the fourth annual national woman's rights convention was held in Cleveland. Asa Mahan was among those attending, along with Brown, Stone, Severance, and other Oberlin women.

### *An International Team*

Finney's own concept of woman's role expanded with his marriage on 13 November 1848 to Elizabeth Ford Atkinson, a widow from Rochester. In November 1849 they made their first trip to England and found that Mrs. Finney was also welcome as a speaker. Her ministry began at a tea-meeting for poor women in a church founded by Methodist revivalist George Whitefield. Thereafter she continued to minister among women wherever they traveled.[41] They remained in England until May 1851.

After returning to Oberlin for the term, they held meetings in New York City in the fall of 1851. From there they moved on to Hartford, where Finney preached in several churches, including Horace Bushnell's.

The next winter the Finneys ministered in Syracuse. "Here again Mrs. Finney established her ladies' meetings with great success," Finney reported. "She generally held them in the lecture room of the First Presbyterian church, I think, a commodious and convenient room for such meetings."[42] He spoke of several outstanding Christian women who emerged as leaders during the meetings.

The third national woman's rights convention was held in Syracuse from 8-10 September 1852. Paulina Kellogg Wright Davis was chair of the convening committee. Antoinette Brown was among the participants. Another was Matilda Joslyn Gage (1826-1898). Her father, another native of Connecticut, had settled in Cicero, New York, where she was born 25 March 1826. The Joslyn home was a gathering place for revivalists and reformers and a stop on the Underground Railroad. From her physician father Matilda learned Greek, mathematics, and physiology, among other studies. At fifteen she went to the Clinton Liberal Institute to complete her formal education. At eighteen she married Henry H. Gage, a Cicero merchant. After several moves in the same area, they settled down in Fayetteville, east of Syracuse, where they were lifelong members of the Baptist church.

One of the local pastors most sympathetic to woman's rights and to revivalism was Luther Lee (1800-1889)[43] of the Wesleyan Methodist church. Lee was born in Schoharie, west of Schenectady, into a pious Methodist family. Though virtually illiterate, he was licensed to preach in 1821 and admitted to the Genesee Conference. His marriage to schoolteacher Mary Miller in 1825 contributed greatly to his education. He was ordained an elder in 1831. In the 1820s and 1830s the Genesee area was the scene of heated antimasonic and abolition controversies, which were factors in the formation of the Wesleyan Methodist Connection, an offshoot of the Methodist Episcopal church. Lee, who had been an agent for an antislavery organization, was elected the denomination's first president at their general conference in Cleveland in 1844. For eight years he edited *The True Wesleyan*. Returning to the pastorate in Syracuse in 1852, he was immediately involved in local controversy. When Susan B. Anthony (1820-1906),[44] a Quaker from Rochester, and Amelia Jenks Bloomer (1818-1895),[45] from Seneca Falls and editor of a temperance and woman's rights paper called *Lily*, were refused seats at a state temperance convention, Lee welcomed their protest meeting in his church. In September 1853 he was called on to preach the ordination sermon in South Butler for Antoinette Brown.

In November 1853 a woman's rights convention was held in Rochester. In the chair was Samuel J. May (1797-1871),[46] a Syracuse Unitarian pastor who had prayed at the Syracuse convention in 1852. A close friend of Brown and Lee, he had hosted the Grimké sisters in his South Scituate, Massachusetts, parsonage and parish in October 1837. They converted him to feminism: "I have never heard from other lips, male or female, such eloquence as that of her [Angelina's] closing appeal. The experience of that week dispelled my Pauline prejudice. I could not believe, that God gave them such talents as they evinced to be buried in a napkin."[47] Bloomer, Brown, and Gage were among the convention's vice presidents; Anthony served as secretary.

While Finney was holding revival meetings during the winter of 1854-55 in Western and Rome, New York, a woman's rights convention met in Albany. This time Elizabeth Cady Stanton was president; May was one of the vice presidents, Brown was on the business committee, and Anthony was secretary. In March 1854 Brown addressed the New York State legislature on the biblical basis for woman's rights, arguments that she had worked out at Oberlin and defended at all of the woman's rights conventions of this period. Finney spent the winter of 1855-56 holding another revival in Rochester, and in the fall of 1856 the seventh national woman's rights convention met in New York City, in his old church, Broadway Tabernacle.

During the "lay revival" of 1857-58, which originally began in New York holiness circles around the Palmers, Finney was holding a series of winter meetings in Boston, at Park Street Church. Mrs. Finney's meetings "became so crowded, that the ladies would fill the room, and then stand about the door on the outside, as far as they could hear on every side."[48] Finney credited the efforts of laypeople, men and women, with the conversion of no less than 500,000 souls during this awakening, which "became almost universal throughout the Northern states" but not in the South where "slavery seemed to shut it out."[49]

In December 1858 the Finneys were off again for England, where they ministered until August 1860. It was their last major trip. On 15 June 1859 the Palmers arrived in England to spend *Four Years in the Old World*, as they titled their account of the revivals that followed. A woman in the pulpit still aroused some ire among British Methodists and Phoebe was verbally attacked by certain ministers. She was defended by Catherine Mumford Booth, who wrote a pamphlet titled *Female Ministry*.[50] Phoebe herself had written a defense of woman's right to preach in *The Promise of the Father*, which was published in late 1859. Although Palmer was never publicly identified with the organized woman's rights movement, many of the Methodist ministers and bishops who defended such rights were her friends.[51]

Finney's health was beginning to fail. He resigned the presidency of Oberlin in 1865, but continued to pastor the First Congregational Church in Oberlin until 1872. In June 1867 the Palmers visited the Finneys at Oberlin and were asked to speak twice in chapel and in the ladies' hall. They also visited Asa Mahan at his home in Palmyra, Michigan.[52]

In 1869 the woman's rights movement split between the more radical National Woman Suffrage Association of Stanton and Anthony and the more inclusive American Woman Suffrage Association headed by Lucy Stone. The latter organization was formed at a convention in Cleveland on 24-25 November. Caroline Seymour Severance was one of its conveners. Those present included Antoinette Brown, Hannah Tracy Cutler, Methodist editor Gilbert Haven, Methodist preacher Amanda Way, Universalist reformer Mary Livermore, and Lyman's son Henry Ward Beecher.[53] The Oberlin community was well represented.

Finney died at Oberlin on 16 August 1875. He had completed his last course of seminary lectures less than a month before and had preached in local churches until two weeks before his death.

### *Conclusion*

Reading the lives of these people whom I label "Finneyites," one finds a pattern emerging, a pattern of Western migration—Yankees turned Yorkers turned Buckeyes. The majority were rooted in Presbygationalism — with a few Methodists, Quakers, and Baptists interspersed. All were immersed in reform—most often temperance and abolition, but also in benevolent societies of various sorts, peace groups, millennial movements, missions, and health concerns such as the Graham diet. When one follows them into the last half of the century, one finds many of them clustered around New York City and then Boston. They attended Unitarian churches, if any. And they flirted with such things as socialism, theosophy, and spiritualism—radicals to the end.

TWO

# Arminianizing the Old Calvinism

Lucy Aiken analyzed the theological situation in 1828 and concluded: "They have gradually and almost imperceptibly quitted Calvinism for Arminianism."[1] Although this observation would not perhaps have corresponded to the Finneyites' own perception of their stance, it had a certain accuracy. In the period between the First and Second Great Awakenings in America, traditional Calvinism took at least a ninety-degree turn.

"Arminianism" was named for the sixteenth-century Dutch theologian Jacobus Arminius (1560-1609), who became concerned that the Calvinists were making God the author of sin and human condemnation with their talk about "eternal decrees." Arminius preached that God's offer of grace was universal and that people possessed the freedom of will to respond in faith. His views were codified by his successors in the Remonstrance of 1610: (1) human election and reprobation are based on God's foreknowledge of human faith or unbelief; (2) Christ died for all humankind, although only believers enjoy God's forgiveness; (3) fallen sinners are unable to do any good or to achieve saving faith apart from the regenerative power of the Holy Spirit; (4) grace is indispensable to all human good, but it is not irresistible; and (5) though God's grace is sufficient to preserve believers in every trial, nothing in Scripture says that they cannot fall from grace.[2]

The views of the Remonstrants were condemned at the Synod of Dort in 1618-19. This meeting of Reformed divines reaffirmed the major tenets of Calvinism: (1) humanity is totally depraved due to an innate sinfulness that is conveyed to all people by natural generation, as a result of our first parents' original sin; (2) God has unconditionally elected both the redeemed and the reprobate; (3) the atonement was limited to the elect; (4) the elect are saved by grace alone, a grace that is a free gift of God and irresistible in its working; and (5) election guarantees perseverance; one can never fall from grace.

Grotius, a follower of Arminius, developed the governmental theory of the atonement. He emphasized the love of God in the atonement rather than God's wrath and justice. In his *Satisfaction of Christ* Grotius argued that Christ, as a substitute for the sinner, satisfied the judicial penalty levied against the sinner. According to Grotius, God's central concern was human happiness.

In England the assault on Puritan Calvinism was more ecclesiastical than theological, though it was also labeled "Arminian." Holland's Arminians attacked the Calvinists' doctrine of predestination. The episcopalians in England attacked the Calvinists' doctrine of the presbytery. Archbishop of Canterbury William Laud, elevated to the see in 1633 by Charles I, defended the Book of Common Prayer and episcopal polity against their Puritan critics. Through the use of secular authority, he rigorously enforced obedience and uniformity in liturgy. His measures were so stern that Puritans were forced to flee to Holland and thence to America. Although some Laudians did in fact reject the doctrines of Calvinism, their differences were more matters of devotion. Classic works of the period were not doctrinal treatises, but Lancelot Andrewes's *Manual of Private Devotions* and John Donne's sermons. They sought to recover the catholic elements of the church.

The Puritans struck back in the "Long Parliament," which abolished the episcopacy, executed Laud, approved the Calvinist Westminster Confession, and rejoiced in the king's death. However, in 1660 the Laudian church was restored under Charles II.[3]

In the next century, two strands of Arminianism diverged. One thread within Anglicanism, which came to be called "Latitudinarian," tended toward a questioning of Christ's divinity and an optimistic rationalism concerning human ability. This trend was symbolized in 1787 when Boston's King's Chapel, "the first Episcopal church in New England, became the first Unitarian church in America."[4] It was this form of Arminianism that drew the fire of Jonathan Edwards in 1734. His sermons on the doctrinal cornerstone of the Reformation, justification by faith, precipitated the First Great Awakening in America.

A reading of Edwards's *A Faithful Narrative of the Surprising Work of God in the Conversion of Many Hundred Souls in Northampton, and Neighboring Towns and Villages* (1737) was an important factor in John Wesley's theological development. Wesley's parents had been reared in Puritan dissent; both of his grandfathers were deprived of their livings on Saint Bartholomew's Day 1662. But Susanna and Samuel Wesley had returned to the Established Church and its Arminianism. Susanna had even for a time been attracted by

Socinian (Unitarian) doctrines.[5] However, Wesley was reared in Trinitarian orthodoxy, in a home life still shaped by Puritanism. He did not share the optimism of British and Boston liberals; he was thoroughly Calvinist in his belief in human depravity. But he was convinced that Christ's atonement was free to all and that prevenient grace freely gave all the power to respond to God's offer of salvation. He also spoke of Christian perfection, of the possibility of sanctification in addition to justification. He believed that God not only gave one assurance of salvation but also power to overcome all willful sin.

In addition to attacks from Unitarianism and Methodism, the doctrines of Puritan Calvinism were also being eroded from within. John Taylor, in a 1740 tract titled *Scripture Doctrine of Original Sin*, argued against the "federal" concept that humanity participated in original sin because Adam was its "federal head," its appointed representative. Humankind suffers because Adam and Eve transgressed God's command, but not because all are guilty of their sin or because their sins are imputed to all of their descendants. Nor did Taylor believe in innate depravity imparted at conception, because this would make sin "*natural* to us; and if *natural*, then *necessary*; and if necessary, then no sin."[6] Taylor argued that we become sinful by making evil choices in response to our natural appetites.

Jonathan Edwards had a copy of Taylor's tract by 1848 and was writing a reply to it at his death. It was printed as *The Great Christian Doctrine of Original Sin Defended*. Although Edwards did not actually speak of the "federal" concept of sin, he argued in detail that God considered Adam the head or root of the race, and thus all people participated in Adam's sin because of a corporate unity with humankind's original parents. In *Freedom of the Will* (1754) Edwards declared that people exercise their wills as God inclines. His critic Charles Chauncy agreed more fully with Taylor. He argued that Adam's sin was not imputed to everyone, though we all inherit such results as mortality and a nature much less perfect than that with which Adam began. He bitterly attacked Edwards's idea of Adam's headship and denied that people are born with depraved natures inherited from their parents. He declared that all freely choose to sin. Chauncy was Arminian in his emphasis on people's role in their own salvation. Edwards maintained an orthodox Calvinism, but his belief that certain means might be used to bring people to the place where the Spirit could deal with them did tend in the direction of human responsibility.

The divisions opened by the First Great Awakening—Edwardsean Congregational New Divinity versus the Old Divinity, Baptist New Lights versus Old Lights, Presbyterian New School versus Old School—proliferated in the ensuing years. Revolutions (American and French), rationalism (French, English, and German), and revivals (Cane Ridge and Yale) took their toll on scholastic orthodoxy and ecclesiastical structure. Individualism, self-confidence, reliance on common sense, nationalistic optimism were flowering. By Finney's time there were a variety of parties in American religious life, divided by both theology and methodology.

To the left (and to the north in Boston) Unitarianism had broken entirely with Congregationalism. When the liberals succeeded in electing Henry Ware as Hollis professor of divinity at Harvard in 1805, Jedediah Morse and Leonard Woods pulled out and formed Andover Theological Seminary in 1808. William Ellery Channing, in his speech "Unitarian Christianity" in 1819, declared that the Calvinist doctrine of the natural depravity of children denied the moral perfection of God's character. Ware added fuel by saying that human beings are by nature innocent and pure, free from either corruption or holiness, until their character is formed by their choices. Moses Stuart, another Andover faculty member, took Channing to task, and was answered by Harvard scholar Andrews Norton, who forced the issues of the Trinity and Christ's divinity, articulating a distinctive theological stance that rallied a party within Congregationalism, leading to the 1825 formation of the American Unitarian Society. Unitarianism became the faith of the rich, the cultured, the New England liberals—and eventually a good number of disillusioned evangelicals.

While railing against the forces of infidelity on the left, those who claimed to be the lineal descendants of the Puritans were an extremely divided lot. In 1801, assuming that they agreed on the Calvinism of the Westminster Confession and on the goal of spreading it among the Yankees turned Yorkers on the frontiers, the Connecticut Congregational Association and Presbyterians combined in a Plan of Union, further refined in the 1808 Plan of Accommodation. Presbyterians benefited most and Congregationalists accommodated most. Polity tended to be Presbyterian; theology the liberalized Calvinism of the New Haven Congregationalists.[7] Churches founded on the frontier were served by pastors of either denomination.

Conservatives in both denominations were unhappy with the marriage. Congregational conservatives congregated in two bastions: Andover Theological Seminary and later Hartford Seminary (1834). The Presbyterian citadel of conservatism was Princeton Seminary. Charles Hodge, resident of the chair of exegetical, didactic, and polemic theology, bragged that during his fifty-year tenure, no new idea or concept had been permitted to originate there.[8] From Princeton emanated the most virulent criticism of Finney and eventually the forces that wrecked the Plan of Union in 1837.[9] But despite the conservatives' railing at the 1816 Presbyterian General Assembly against "Arian, Socinian, Arminian, and Hopkinsian heresies,"[10] they could not hold back the tide of theological change sweeping from New England to the new western frontiers.

*The New Divinity*

Many men claimed the mantle of Jonathan Edwards: Samuel Hopkins, Nathaniel Emmons, Joseph Bellamy, Timothy Dwight, and Nathaniel Taylor. Each modified Calvinism in his own way. Hopkins attacked the central triangle of Calvinistic ideas: original sin, human inability, and the limited atonement. Hopkins agreed that everyone begins life as a sinner, but he denied that humanity, as Adam's offspring, participated in Adam's original sin. He saw sin more as present rebelliousness than as inherited flaw, more constitutional than original. Hopkinsianism was, however, popularly caricatured as a belief "that man ought to be willing to be damned for the glory of God and that God was the author of sin."[11]

Emmons abandoned entirely the old federal notion that God entered into covenant with Adam, but still declared that since Adam sinned, every human being has a "constitution" to be sinful and cannot will his or her own redemption. By an act of sovereignty, Emmons held, God made Adam the "public head" of the race, and when it comes right down to it, God produced in Adam's heart, and in every person's since, an "inclination to do evil," a natural corollary of Edwards's analysis of the will. He was such a staunch believer in the sovereignty of God that he declared that unregenerate people should not even pray for salvation since such action would be blasphemous presumption if they were not among the elect.

Timothy Dwight disagreed with Emmons, though he felt there must be some causal connection between Adam's sin and humanity's. Dwight, a grandson of Edwards and president of Yale 1795-1817, was concerned that students there find a renewed faith. He accepted human agency and declared that no Christian who "learns and performs his duty to the utmost of his power . . . will fail of being finally accepted."[12] Like Edwards, Dwight believed in using means, like revivals, to stir Christians to perform their duty. As a result of his efforts, the Second Great Awakening broke out at Yale in 1801 and students flocked back to the Christian faith.

One of Dwight's protégés was Nathaniel William Taylor, revival preacher at New Haven's Center Church and professor of theology at Yale Divinity School from 1822-57. More than anyone else, Taylor was responsible for what came to be called the "New Haven theology" or the "New Divinity." In an 1818 pamphlet, *Man, a Free Agent Without the Aids of Divine Grace*, Taylor argued that free agency was inherent in human persons who possess understanding, conscience, will. This free agency was not lost in the Fall. However, each person comes into the world in such a state that without the grace of God, everyone voluntarily commits sinful acts as he or she becomes a moral agent. Taylor's 1828 sermon, *Concio ad Clerum*, declared that moral depravity is "man's own act, consisting in a free choice of some object rather than God, as his chief good;—or a free preference of the world and of worldly good, to the will and glory of God."[13] All sin is thus voluntary, said Taylor. "Arminian," cried his accusers.

The New Haven theology was frankly more Arminian in tone.[14] Rather than inherited and imputed sinfulness, it stressed individual guilt for one's own sin. It defined sin as selfishness. It declared that human beings have the power to choose selfishly or unselfishly. God's redemptive work was complete at the cross, so a penitent sinner need not wait for God to initiate it. Forgiveness is immediately available. Nothing pleases God, said the New Divinity, other than instant submission and the exercise of disinterested and universal benevolence. At redemption, God restores to the Christian the power to make such unselfish choices.

At least in part, the New Haven theology attempted to modify Calvinism to fit a revivalist methodology. Revivalism is essentially an American propaganda technique necessary in a society where religion has been disestablished and religious options are numerous. In eighteenth-century Puritan Massachusetts, where all competing sects were banished to Rhode Island, church fathers could wait for people to get converted while still collecting their tithes. But in nineteenth-century America, churches had to attract members through excitements such as revivals, promising salvation for sure if they simply acted at once.[15] As Lyman Beecher, another protégé of Dwight and the pastor of a church in Litchfield, Connecticut, once said, what was needed was not "high-toned Calvinism on the point of dependence . . . but a vigorous prescription of free-agency."[16]

Central to New Haven theology was a belief that God is the moral governor of the world. All persons have the intelligence and freedom to choose—they are free moral agents. And thus they are under moral obligation. God has endowed all human beings with a physical nature and a moral nature, making them capable of choosing good and condemning evil. The choice is voluntary. The highest good is the glory of God, the well-being of the moral governor. Choice of this insures an individual's own best interests and the happiness of the universe.

### *Finney's Theology*

Charles Grandison Finney claimed to be a part of none of these theological schools, though the concept of moral government eventually became crucial to his theology.[17] Yet he too was a product of the evolution of doctrine that was taking place.[18]

Finney's theology initially grew out of his own experience of conversion. He found justification and regeneration as the climax of a process characterized by a concern for his own spiritual state, conviction by the Holy Spirit, a striving after salvation, and a free volitional act of acceptance. He felt responsible to appropriate the provisions of atonement rather than waiting for God to apply them. He was not converted through any of the accepted means of the church, nor through the guidance of any minister. He understood his plight and resolved to do something about it. By an act of the will he chose God.

His theological training supposedly took place under the guidance of William Boardman of Watertown and his own pastor George Gale in Adams. When asked by the St. Lawrence Presbytery whether or not he accepted the Westminster Confession, he tactfully affirmed that he did to the best of his understanding of it. He later claimed that he had not read it before his examination, and when he did he was appalled. "Theological fiction" was his assessment of the work of the Westminster divines. It is hard to believe that he had not received a thorough exposition of the document from Gale because Finney said that "his preaching was of the old school type; that is, it was thoroughly Calvinistic; and whenever he came out with the doctrines, which he seldom did, he would preach what was called hyper-calvinism." But Finney was always a critical listener:

> As I sometimes told him, he seemed to me to begin in the middle of his discourse, and to assume many things which to my mind needed to be proved. He seemed to take it for granted that his hearers were theologians, and therefore that he might assume all the great and fundamental doctrines of the Gospel.[19]

Soon after his conversion, Finney argued half a day with Gale concerning the idea of a "limited atonement," Finney telling Gale that it was absurd to argue that Jesus suffered only the penalties of sin for the elect. Throughout their course of study together Gale "felt the greatest desire to keep [Finney] within the strict lines of Princeton theology." He warned that God would not bless his ministry with the conversion of souls unless he preached the truth, the orthodox faith. Finney agreed that this was so, but he also learned in another conversation that Gale was not sure anyone had ever really been converted under his own ministry!

Finney always insisted that he formed his own theological ideas on the basis of his reading of Scripture. As a law student he had developed an independent approach to problems. He was drawn into a serious study of Scripture originally through the references he found to it in law books. His study of law shaped his hermeneutic. He insisted that theology, like law, should be clear and unified (rather than ambiguous and haphazard, as it appeared to be), supported by orderly, logical argumentation.[20] Finney was a firm believer in the abilities of human reason. He insisted that ministers "should understand the philosophy of the human mind. . . . They should have the Bible in one hand, and the map of the human mind in the other, and know how to use the truth for the salvation of men."[21]

However, Finney may have imbibed at least some of his ideas indirectly from Joseph Bellamy, the Connecticut pastor who studied theology with Jonathan Edwards. Bellamy was the mentor of Peter Starr, a Yale graduate, under whose ministry Finney sat for four years (1812-1816) in the East Greenwich meetinghouse while attending the Warren Academy. Bellamy and Starr stressed the "governmental" rather than the "satisfaction" theory of the atonement in order to avoid the onus of a limited atonement. Bellamy argued that God had to allow sin into the world in order to establish a moral, rather than mechanical, universe. For Bellamy and Starr, both sin and holiness are the result of voluntary acts.[22]

At the root of Finney's theology was the concept of free will. While this may have come from Bellamy and Starr, it may also have been a result of his study of the law. The foundation of Blackstone's definition of "crime" lies in "free will."[23] To say that human beings do not have a free will, are not able to respond to the gospel, "slanders God . . . , charging him with infinite tyranny, in commanding man to do that which they have no power to do."[24] If sinners are unable to respond, if they must be given the Holy Spirit to enable them to obey the gospel, then common justice would compel God to give that Spirit to all before God could justly require repentance. In other words, "when God commands us to do a thing, it is the highest possible evidence that we can do it . . . . equivalent to an oath that we can do it. He has no right to command, unless we have power to obey." God has commanded us to repent; ipso facto we must have the ability to do so. "Conversion consists in the right employment of the sinner's own agency."[25] In conversion the sinner apprehends the truth and wills to obey it, turns from selfishness to benevolence, from willing his or her own self-gratification to willing the highest good for all.

Finney affirmed that he did indeed believe in total depravity, but it certainly was not the traditional Calvinist interpretation of that doctrine. He defined it not as a "disease" of transmitted guilt, nor any constitutional inability to obey God, nor any inherited fault that predisposed all to sinful choices, but a hatred of God. Infants possess the original nature of Adam, Finney believed. They all sin because the temptations to selfishness are so great in the world. Children become sinners the moment they make their first selfish choice. Infants are "neither sinful or holy, until they are moral agents, and render themselves so by obedience or disobedience to the moral law."[26] Total depravity then for Finney is a moral depravity based on a voluntary act over which people have complete control, and for which they are completely responsible: "God has put these states of mind just as absolutely under your control, as the motions of your limbs."[27]

Thus Finney repudiated the traditional idea that it was useless to strive for knowledge of salvation. He ridiculed those who told sinners just to "wait on God," to wait and see if they were among the elect. "Religion is something to *do*, not something to *wait for*," he declared. "*Religion is the work of man*. It is something for man to do." One of his most famous sermons was titled "Sinners Bound to Change Their Own Hearts." He told sinners that their "cannot" consists in their unwillingness and not in their inability. We, as moral agents have the power to obey God, and are perfectly bound to obey, and the reason we do not, is that we are unwilling." A sinner's problem is not hardness of heart but stubbornness of will. "It is not a question of *feeling* but of *willing* and *acting*. . . . WILLING to obey Christ is to be a Christian."[28] Sinners "are called upon to choose . . . whether they will serve God or the world. Let them be made to understand what is to be chosen, and then if the thing is done from the heart, they will be saved."[29]

Finney did not intend to be Arminian, nor did he consider himself to be, but his theology at times borders on a Pelagian optimism about human ability to effect our own salvation. His commitment to saving souls, using a revivalist methodology, forced him to emphasize human ability to make immediate choices. Finney's earliest biographer suggests that "Finney's system preserves all the advantages of Arminianism in the pulpit, and all the strength of Calvinism in the [prayer] closet, and so has been one of the most efficient means looking to that doctrinal agreement" which he saw "rapidly approaching."[30] Finney did much to reconcile the two views of conversion; he also tried to reconcile them concerning sanctification.

### *Perfection*

During a revival meeting for "prayer, praise, and inquiry" at Oberlin during October 1836, a recent graduate, S. W. Streeter, arose to ask President Mahan and Professor Finney: "When we look to Christ for sanctification, what degree of sanctification may we expect from him? May we look to him to be sanctified wholly, or not?"[31] President Mahan replied that they would have to give the question "prayerful and careful attention," and "in due time" he promised the student body a "full and specific answer."[32]

Various forms of perfectionism, the belief that human beings can attain some form of perfection of life, flourished in the 1830s and 1840s. It was an inherent part of the idealism that inspired national optimism and a sense of messianic destiny. Both the Mormons and Shakers had perfectionist tendencies, as did the Swedish colony at Bishop Hill, Illinois, though the movement seemed to be centered in Albany, New York, and to spread east and west along the Erie Canal. Most famous, of course, were the "antinomian perfectionists" who congregated around John Humphrey Noyes, first in Putney, Vermont, and finally in Oneida, New York. Noyes experienced conversion in a Finney revival in 1831 and felt called to the ministry, so he spent a year at Andover, two years at Yale. When he began preaching perfectionism, his preaching license was revoked and when he elaborated his ideas in the *Perfectionist*, a journal he published 1834-36, he was denied ordination. Noyes is most famous for the facts that his community at Oneida after 1848 practiced a form of sexual promiscuity called "complex marriage" and that in 1880 they became a corporation that still manufactures silver flatware.

Noyes taught that it was scriptural for Christians to expect to be able to live a totally sinless life. He believed that God indeed commanded Christians to be as perfect as angels. He argued that this was the logical outcome of New Haven Calvinist theology. If one believed in election by grace and the perseverance of the saints, then perfection should be a natural result. If, as Taylor taught, sin lies wholly in the will and we have the ability to obey the moral law, then through Christ people should be able to attain perfection. To profess holiness is only to acknowledge God's gift, said Noyes. In order to be holy, one simply has to claim it. If one is perfect, then all one does is holy; true Christians cannot sin, according to Noyes.

News of his ideas quickly reached Oberlin. In fact, articles from the *Perfectionist* were being reprinted in Cincinnati newspapers and debated at Lane before the Finneyite students left there. Two questions concerned perfectionists, according to Barbara Zikmund: (1) whether total sinlessness is possible—a doctrinal, theological question; and (2) whether "perfect" Christians are bound by conventional ethical constraints—a practical, ethical question.[33] Noyes was concerned primarily about the second question and thus devoted his energies to elaborating *Bible Communism* (1848) with its practical manifestations in the life of the Oneida community. Mahan and Finney were much more concerned with the first question.

They spent the winter of 1836-37 in New York City, pondering Streeter's question, struggling with such Scriptures as "the very God of peace sanctify you wholly; and I pray God your whole spirit and soul and body be preserved blameless unto the coming of our Lord Jesus Christ" (1 Thess. 5:23). During that winter Mahan felt that he experienced a second work of grace in which Christ "filled and occupied the entire compass of his being."[34] Finney did not enter into the same experience until 1843,[35] but he began preaching their conclusions about Christian perfection almost immediately. His first two sermons on the topic were given at Broadway Tabernacle and reprinted in his *Letters to Professing Christians*. His text was Matthew 5:48: "Be ye therefore perfect, even as your Father which is in Heaven is perfect."

Upon their return to Oberlin, both Finney and Mahan began to explain the doctrine to their students. As word spread, controversy raged. To explain their views in contradiction to the rumors that linked them with antinomian perfectionism, the faculty began to publish the *Oberlin Evangelist*, founded 1

November 1838.[36] The first issue contained a sermon by Mahan, "Is Perfection in Holiness Attainable in This Life?" which became a chapter in *The Scripture Doctrine of Christian Perfection*, published in 1839.[37] His answer to the question was affirmative.

Some opponents, particularly Old School Calvinists (Princeton's Benjamin Warfield in his critique of *Perfectionism* is a prime example) charged that Oberlin Perfectionism as it came to be called (Oberlin people preferred to speak of the "doctrine of Christian Perfection") was simply a logical extension of Taylor's New Divinity. And certainly it was an extension of the modified Calvinism they had been preaching before. They sought a way to give their converts the power and motivation to lead a full Christian life.

With Taylor, Finney and Mahan distinguished between a sinful, depraved nature (all human beings do inevitably sin) and depravity of the will (human beings do have free, undepraved wills and thus they do not sin by necessity). Thus a person can will to be perfect, just as he or she can will to be converted. People are morally depraved because they freely will things that are contrary to the will of God.[38] Perfection as the Finneyites saw it was not perfect living but right willing. It was not like God's perfection (omnipotence, eternity, immutability) or perfect knowledge or freedom from temptation or sinless ethical and moral behavior. Rather it was "perfect obedience to the law of God, . . . perfect disinterested, impartial benevolence, love to God and love to neighbor."[39] Since our will is free of any innate limitations on our moral ability, we can receive instantaneous power from Christ to will correctly. As Zikmund says, "Noyes preached freedom from the law in sinless living, Mahan preached power to follow the law in sinless willing."[40] Many New Divinity Calvinists agreed that morality was based on free will and that therefore perfection was a logical possibility, "attainable," but they refused to admit that anyone ever actually achieved it. Finney lashed out at this equivocation in the same way he had at their hesitation to use means to claim salvation.[41]

But the Oberlin theologians drew on other sources as well as the New Divinity.[42] In the winter of 1836-37 both Finney and Mahan read Wesley's *Plain Account of Christian Perfection* and James Brainerd Taylor's *Life*. When Mahan's book appeared, a review of it by George Peck, editor of the *Methodist Quarterly Review* and author of his own classic *Christian Perfection*, concluded that "though it is not to be maintained that he expresses himself Methodistically upon all the points of this great doctrine, we are satisfied that the thing which we mean by *Christian Perfection* is truly set forth in that work."[43] Old School critic Benjamin Warfield agreed, calling the first half dozen years of Oberlin Perfectionism its "Wesleyan" period and describing Finney's thought in the same years as his "Mahan" period. Zikmund argues that Mahan's presentation of the doctrine was always the more balanced because he maintained the Wesleyan emphasis that sanctification, like salvation, was a gift of God's grace and not something one can attain by human effort. At first Mahan rejected Wesley's emphasis on perfection as a process of growth and declared that sanctification was meant to be an instantaneous experience and was not to be attained through "works," which is what he understood Wesley to be saying. Later he come to see that Wesley's emphasis did not mean "works," and began to teach that perfection involved growth as well as an initial experience.

Attacked by both Old and New School Calvinists, Finney modified his statements in such a way that it not only weakened his doctrine but actually made it more vulnerable to Calvinist attacks, according to Zikmund. Finney upset Mahan's careful balance between Calvinist "ability" and Wesleyan "grace" with his principle of the "simplicity of moral action." Although both Finney and Mahan used this idea, Finney explained it to mean an almost absolute reliance on human ability. Finney also stressed perfection as "perfect obedience to the moral law," which Peck called "legal perfection." Finney spoke of perfection as meeting all of the requirements of the law. Methodists denied that anyone could perfectly conform to the law. Finney seemed to reduce the role of grace to moral suasion, whereas Mahan followed Wesley more closely in declaring grace essential to enable anyone to attain perfection. Finney also seemed to say that the state of Christian perfection was necessary for salvation, which led to an absurdity in speaking to two experiences at all, as Peck pointed out.

### *Holiness*

At least the Methodist formulation of Christian Perfection clearly empowered women. Almost everyone who explored the teaching at all eventually read the testimonies of Hester Ann Rogers, Mary Bosanquet Fletcher, Madame Guyon, and others. And the leading Methodist exponent of the concept in mid-century America and the British Isles was Phoebe Palmer. Through the Tuesday Meeting for the Promotion of Holiness, she influenced a generation of ecclesiastical and intellectual leaders. She herself preached to hundreds of thousands. And her books ***The Way of Holiness***, ***Faith and its Effects***, and ***Entire Devotion*** were read by millions.

She, like Mahan, argued that her belief in the idea of Christian Perfection, or "holiness," was based entirely on Scripture: "Not Wesley, not Fletcher, not Finney, not Mahan, not Upham, but the Bible, the holy Bible, is the first and last, and in the midst always. The Bible is the standard, the groundwork, the platform, the creed."[44] As she said in a letter to the ***Beauty of Holiness***:

> it has been my aim to avoid most carefully, anything like a display of theological technicalities. Inasmuch as the Bible is not a sectarian book, or holiness the mere doctrine of a sect, it has been my aim to present it as the absolute requirement of the Bible. . . . I have aimed to follow the simple Bible mode of teaching.[45]

Claiming clear scriptural teaching and unmistakable experiential verification, she taught what she believed to be simply traditional Methodist belief. But in teaming it up with American revivalist methodology (as Finney had done with Calvinism) she certainly clarified some of the ambiguities in Wesley's formulation, and, in typical American fashion, reduced it to a compact formula.

Palmer saw holiness as a second crisis experience, the beginning of full Christian commitment (which parallels Finney's emphasis on conversion as the beginning of the Christian life and not the end, as had earlier Calvinists). Wesley saw holiness as the possible culmination of the Christian life, the goal toward which one strove. Palmer outlined three steps in the process: first, the entire consecration of one's all; second, an act of faith that God had promised sanctification and would honor that promise based on the work of Christ already completed (again very similar to Finney's doctrine of conversion); and third, immediate public confession that one had received the blessing, regardless of one's feelings (Finney was often criticized for his "immediatism" and for taking converts into the church too quickly, merely on public testimony of their faith). The testimonies recorded in the ***Guide to Holiness***, accounts of the Tuesday Meeting, and Palmer's own reports from her campaigns almost always bear this design. Usually in the first phase people felt compelled to renounce their attachment to their possessions, their children, their spouse, in that ascending order, and sometimes to their own reputation or pride. Once they had dedicated all to God, then they would be exhorted to have faith that once they had done their part, God would do God's part on the basis of Christ's work and would account them holy and give them power to live a holy life. They were then asked publicly to affirm their holy state. In her writings Palmer continually stressed that this experience did not depend on feelings, but upon God's promise. Therefore, one should not wait until one had some sort of mystical experience or tingly feeling before one gave testimony to sanctification. Often persons experienced such feelings only after they had testified.

Considerable controversy was generated by the language that Palmer began to use in the late 1840s. She argued that it came straight from Scripture, but Methodists called it un-Wesleyan and non-Methodists called it confusing. Palmer described the first step as "laying one's all on the altar." From Exodus 29:37, Matthew 23:19, and Romans 12:1-2, she deduced that Christ was the altar and that the altar sanctified the gift. Thus once one determined "to consecrate all upon the altar of sacrifice to God, with the resolve to 'enter into the bonds of an everlasting covenant to be wholly the Lord's for time and eternity,' and then acting in conformity with this decision, actually laying all upon the altar," then, "by the most unequivocal Scripture testimony," they were obliged to "*believe that the sacrifice became the Lord's property; and by virtue of the altar upon which the offering was laid*, became 'holy' and 'acceptable'!"[46] Wesley had emphasized that one was assured of sanctification by the witness of the Spirit. Like Finney, Palmer argued that one did not need to wait. If one has met the conditions, then one could simply claim the promised blessing.

Palmer, like Finney and the New School Presbyterians, emphasized the individual will. According to another woman evangelist, Palmer "would say so often, 'God *wills* that you should be holy. This is the will of God, even your sanctification; is it your will?' She was Arminian to the core. 'Your *choice*—what is it?' "[47] And she stressed human ability to activate the will: "Is God unreasonable in his requirements? Hath he given the command 'Be ye holy,' and not given the ability, with the command, for the performance of it?"[48] During the Palmers' visit to the Old World, an elderly man told her he was "waiting these thirty years for a special call." She asked if he believed the Bible and he said yes. To which she replied: "Now, act on the principle that you really do believe what you profess to believe; that is, that the Bible is the word of God to you, because he has been saying to you ever since your childhood, 'Son, give me thy heart.' Resolve you will do it NOW. It is not knowledge you need, but ACTION."[49]

### *"Holiness Is Power"*

The call to personal perfection, holiness, rang true for many people. While she was still a Presbyterian, Angelina Grimké mentioned reading Fletcher and Wesley on perfection and declared:

> I think I can set my seal to this doctrine—truly it exhibits the plan of Salvation in a far more glorious light than I had conceived of it before—Is not the hope of attaining this a most powerful incentive to press forward—I cannot think with Methodists that the latter part of 7 Rom. describes the feelings of an awakened sinner they are too much like what I daily experience for me to doubt that he was converted at the time he felt them. May not this be that conflict between sin & holiness before he had attained to Sanctification.[50]

In her Sabbath school and prayer meetings she had come in contact with a Methodist woman who became "a helper of my joy and encouraged me to go unto perfection nothing doubting."[51] To her diary of 23 February 1828 she confessed, "I do feel astonished that so many Christians reject the doctrine of Perfection. I am more and more convinced of it from reading the Bible."[52] Letters to her friend Jane Smith in the 1840s continued to discuss the subject:

> I am fully convinced of the doctrine of perfection—of the *absolute* necessity of it before we can be prepared to die, (for this is not the work of *death* but of *life* in its full vigor) & yet Jane *I have not* that faith in Christ which *purifies* the heart—I am still in bondage to my own corruptions, tho' often groaning to be delivered from the pride & impatience of my heart, which overcome me in time of temptation *every* day.[53]

In an 1843 letter, she thanked Jane for a tract of Wesley's on the subject and noted that "the *practical* part is excellent but the theory false I think." She diagnosed his error as

> supposing human nature in itself corrupt. . . . If you read Finney on Sanctification you will find that he has built his theory of Perfection on a different system of Philosophy, the only true one. He makes the nature of man & the requirements of God to harmonise & proves that God is not a hard master gathering, where he has not sowed, or in other words requiring what man from his very constitution is unable to perform. Finney has done a great work in clearing up this great difficulty. The Churches will see & acknowledge it: & the world be blessed abundantly thro' it. It has been mens *false Philosophy* which has made them run into infidelity of falsify the simple truths of the bible.[54]

About the same time, before enrolling in Oberlin, Lucy Stone was "examining the doctrine of Christian Perfection" and declared, "I cannot avoid the conclusion that it is attainable in this life."[55]

The doctrine attracted women's attention for several reasons. As Palmer declared repeatedly, "HOLINESS is POWER."[56] It promised women the power to live an uncompromisingly Christian life, a power that transcended oppressive ecclesiastical structures and even cultural norms. It strengthened one's own direct, personal relationship with God. Both Finney and Palmer spoke of perfection as the attainment of a perfect, harmonious, unbroken fellowship with Christ. And it pointed to the restoration of the Edenic state both in individual lives and by extension in society.

### *The Millennium*

Perfectionism was not understood as merely a personal experience (though the later Holiness Movement came to stress only that aspect), but it was also a social philosophy. As Palmer's biographer explains, "Entire sanctification, as a moral condition, involves, and that necessarily, an inherent operative energy, to be divinely guided in seeking to glorify God, and to meliorate society in the mass, and also as to the individuals which compose it."[57]

Like many revivalists before and since, Charles Finney believed that the conversion of individuals would create a better society. He continually stressed the necessity for committed Christians to involve themselves in the reforms of his day. Imbibing the mood of optimism, he and others assumed that their efforts in revival and reform would usher in the millennium, the thousand years' reign of the Kingdom of God on earth. For example, Lyman Beecher once declared his task to be "the promotion of revivals of religion . . . as a prominent instrumentality for the conversion of the world, and the speedy introduction of the millennial reign to our Lord Jesus Christ."[58]

Revivals were the beginning, perfection the second step. In the initial issue of the *Oberlin Evangelist* the editors declared that one reason for its publication was "to call the attention of Christians to the fact the Millennium is to consist in the entire sanctification of the church."[59] The *Beauty of Holiness* saw a similar vision: "Are not these meetings for holiness . . . the germs, the dawnings of millennial glory? Are they not strikingly imitative of the pentecostal? . . . Is not this the baptism now called for, . . . ere the world blossoms as a rose?"[60] In a series of Finney's letters to "Ministers of the Gospel of All Denominations," originally published in the *Oberlin Evangelist* and reprinted by the *Guide to Holiness*, Finney replied to critics who charged that he had not always preached perfection. He answered that the more he read Scripture the more he learned, and as he grew in the faith, he preached his discoveries. Such "innovation," he considered God-ordained:

> It is as certain as that the world stands, that there must be great innovation, and an almost universal turning of the world upside down, before it is consecrated to God. . . . Why, it is time the world should know that innovation is the thing needed, and that God has commenced a system of innovation by which he intends to change the whole moral condition of the world.[61]

Angelina Grimké saw the same vision from another angle. In an 1855 manuscript on marriage she discussed the woes of women who bear so many children only to see them die. She called for family planning and limitation in a farsighted solution to what has become an increasing world problem. Then she declared:

> It is absurd to expect sudden transformation. Nature's laws are as slow as they are sure. The Millennium is not coming to us thro' Revivals or any miraculous interposition, but by "due process of law" and man must and will work out his salvation from evil by the Divine energy of his own nature. "God working in him to will and to do his own good pleasure" for "his will is our sanctification" thro' individual conflict and conquest. As Christ was made perfect thro' *suffering*, so must *all* be made perfect. This is the Divine Law for the individual and the Race.[62]

Some women saw the increase of attention to woman's rights as a sign of the approaching millennium. The call for the first national woman's rights convention in Worcester, Massachusetts, in 1850 contained this declaration as its second paragraph:

> The upward-tending spirit of the age, busy in a hundred forms of effort for the world's redemption from the sins and sufferings which oppress it, has brought this one, which yields to none in importance and urgency, into distinguished prominence. One half of the race are its immediate objects, and the other half are as deeply involved, by that absolute unity of interest and destiny which nature has established between them.

The call goes on to state that

> by the inspiration of the Almighty, the beneficent spirit of reform is roused to the redress of these wrongs. . . . It is the spirit of reviving truth and righteousness which has moved upon the great deep of the public heart, and roused its redressing justice; and through it, the Providence of God is vindicating the order and appointments of his creation.[63]

Angelina Grimké, in a letter to her friend Jane Smith, declared, "I am persuaded that woman is not to be as she has been, a mere secondhand agent in the regeneration of a fallen world, but the acknowledged equal and coworker with man in this glorious work."[64]

Phoebe Palmer's book arguing for the right of women to preach was titled *The Promise of the Father; or, a Neglected Speciality of the Last Days*. She and many other holiness writers, who almost uniformly supported freedom for women at least within the church, saw that "one of the results of God's great work which is now going on in the world will be to raise and perfect woman's position and character." "The recognition of the labors of females is characteristic of the Spirit's dispensation," said Palmer. "And when the reception of the gift of prophecy is thus recognized in all the disciples of the Saviour, whether male or female, the last act in the great drama of man's redemption will have opened."[65] After listing Methodist "mothers in Israel," an article in the *Guide to Holiness* noted that "the restoration of that golden age of female agency in religion will mark the incoming of a new and promising era in the Church."[66]

The spirit of these ideas was contained succinctly in an 1863 "Letter from Marengo," written to the *Guide to Holiness* by Mother Eunice Cobb, a woman who lived out their feminist implications but saw them in the issue of abolition: "I believe that the hour is near when master and slave shall together rejoice in God and when Jesus shall reign king of nations as he now reigns king of saints."[67]

THREE

# The Force of Experience

The theological shifts in the nineteenth century profoundly affected the roles of women in church and society. Women were freed within the church and encouraged to fill larger roles in society by the revivalist impulse.

The majority of the women in this study, and particularly those active in the woman suffrage movement, were reared in a Calvinist milieu. Most of them experienced conversion. Elizabeth Cady Stanton described her experience vividly, and although writing nearly seventy years after the events and having rejected almost all Christian theology, she could still describe Finney's theology with some accuracy:

> The revival fairly started, the most excitable were soon on the anxious seat. There we learned the total depravity of human nature and the sinner's awful danger of everlasting punishment. This was enlarged upon until the most innocent girl believed herself a monster of iniquity and felt certain of eternal damnation. Then God's hatred of sin was emphasized and his irreconcilable position toward the sinner so justified that one felt like a miserable, helpless, forsaken worm of the dust in trying to approach him, even in prayer.
>
> Having brought you into a condition of profound humility, the only cardinal virtue for one under conviction, in the depths of your despair you were told that it required no herculean effort on your part to be transformed into an angel, to be reconciled to God, to escape endless perdition. The way to salvation was short and simple. We had naught to do but to repent and believe and give our hearts to Jesus, who was ever ready to receive them. How to do all this was the puzzling question. Talking with Dr. Finney one day, I said:
>
> "I cannot understand what I am to do. If you should tell me to go to the top of the church steeple and jump off, I would readily do it, if thereby I could save my soul; but I do not know how to go to Jesus."
>
> "Repent and believe," said he, "that is all you have to do to be happy here and hereafter."[1]

Caroline Severance, like Stanton, was impressed as a child with the negative emphases in the revival preaching of Burchard and Finney:

> My father's early death and my mother's constant mourning for him had made me a serious and super-sensitive child, naturally reverential to the authority of the home and the church. I was thus always under torture for my sins. . . .I was in this state by day and by night, constantly haunted by the torture of the doom, to eternal punishment, so vividly pictured in sermon, exhortation and prayer, for those whose sins were not confessed and forsaken. I had brief intervals of exaltation from a comforting sense of safety in having, at times, found forgiveness and made my "peace with God," as it was termed. . . .
>
> I was under bondage to authority, dogmas and conservative ideas until I married into a family of strong anti-slavery convictions, who had the courage to stand for these convictions in an unsympathetic community and time. . . .
>
> With many others, our family seceded from the old Presbyterian church of the town, because we could no longer sit conscientiously under a preacher, or in a fellowship, where the golden rule of Christianity was not recognized as applicable to all men, whatever the color of their skin, or crinkle, or non-crinkle, of their hair. We afterward formed a new church.[2]

Antoinette Brown's father and older siblings experienced conversion under the ministry of Finney; she was converted within the family circle and joined the Congregational church on profession of faith. The revivals in which Paulina Wright Davis "found comfort" may well have been Finneyite, since she was living at the time near Rochester. The Grimké sisters both experienced conversion under the auspices of Presbyterian revivalists in Charleston, South Carolina. Phoebe Palmer and Sarah Lankford experienced conversion in the Methodist Episcopal Church in New York City. Mary Livermore, a later leader in the woman suffrage associations, experienced conversion but was never sure she was among the elect. Other women such as Lucy Stone and Matilda Gage, Hannah Cutler and Betsey Cowles were members of churches in which testimony to conversion was usually a membership requirement.

### *A Democratic Tendency*

Traditional Calvinist theology with its predestined elect and damned encouraged a rigidly stratified society. Its view of conversion demanded passivity. It emphasized right doctrine, a theology whose nuances could be fully understood and appreciated only by the ministerial elite. Revivalism stressed experience, not doctrine—a very democratizing shift. Finney rebuked his audiences for passivity and urged them to activity. He spoke in terms readily understandable to all.

Antoinette Brown said that her father "had accepted the Calvinistic idea that it was God who must convert him in his own time and had waited years for that time to come." Then he went to one of Finney's meetings and learned that "Prof. Finney laid the whole stress of his preaching on the duty of the sinner himself to work actively for his own conversion. Although a partial Calvinist, he had in that matter taken a new departure."[3] Palmer stressed the same activism and immediacy in regard to Christian perfection: "Resolve that you WILL HAVE IT NOW, and it may be yours at once."[4]

The formula was the same for all; all were sinners in need of salvation, sanctification. Lyman Beecher was particularly appalled over this aspect of Finneyite revivalism. He had heard that in Finney revivals "all men, because sinners, are therefore to be treated alike by ministers of the gospel without respect to age or station in society." He feared that this attitude, particularly in regard to "those who rule over men," would result in a "levelling of all distinctions of society" and "would be the sure presage of anarchy and absolute destruction."[5] As I show in Chapter 5, Beecher and Nettleton were well aware of the implications of this leveling for women. The shift is clearly evident in Finney's sermons and writing. Ronald W. Hogeland has commented on Charles Hodge's "masculine predisposition," which today might be termed a "patriarchal style." Accustomed to an all-male seminary and college audience, he lectured parish congregations on the same theological abstractions: law, grace, authority, justice, obedience, order.[6] Finney had little patience with this kind of doctrinal lecturing.[7] His sermons treated more practical subjects and contained a balance of examples of clergy and laity, men and women. His sermons often closed with an explicit appeal to both men and women to act.

His use of language and examples was illustrative of his basic theological belief that all human beings are free moral agents, fully responsible for their own lives, fully able to exercise free will to change their lives—eternally and temporally. This message came through loud and clear to the women of his day and they repeated it at every turn. The women of the Boston Female Anti-Slavery Society stated it perhaps most explicitly after their confrontation with some of Boston's leading citizens: "What is the sphere and duty of woman, it rests with each one for herself to determine; and to do this, she is aided by a revelation which it rests with each one for herself to interpret!"[8] Sarah Grimké in the first of her *Letters on the Equality of the Sexes* declared: "God created us equal;—he created us free agents;—he is our Lawgiver, our

King and our Judge, and to him alone is woman bound to be in subjection, and to him alone is she accountable for the use of those talents with which her Heavenly Father has entrusted her. One is her Master even Christ."[9] And reflecting Taylor's understanding of original sin, she noted that fallen humanity has "fallen from their original loveliness, but still bearing on their foreheads the image and superscription of Jehovah; still invested with high moral responsibilities, intellectual powers and immortal souls."[10] In another letter she quoted from a contemporary, probably her sister Angelina, the basic outline of pure Finneyite theology:

> Woman's rights and man's rights are *both* contained in the *same* charter, and held by the *same* tenure. *All rights* spring out of the *moral* nature: they are both the root and the offspring of *responsibilities*. The physical constitution is the mere *instrument* of the *moral* nature; sex is a mere *incident* of this constitution, a provision necessary to this *form* of existence; its *only* design, not to give, nor to take away, nor in any respect to modify or even *touch* rights or responsibilities in any sense . . . but merely to continue and enlarge the human department of God's government. Consequently, I know nothing of *man's* rights, or *woman's* rights; *human* rights are all I recognize. The doctrine, that the *sex of the body* presides over and administers upon the rights and responsibilities of the moral, immortal nature, is to my mind a doctrine kindred to blasphemy, *when seen in its intrinsic nature*. It breaks up utterly the *relations* of the two natures, and reverses their functions; exalting the animal nature into a monarch, and humbling the moral into a slave.[11]

Angelina, in her *Letters to Catherine E. Beecher*, put it this way:

> Human beings have *rights*, because they are *moral* beings: the rights of *all* men grow out of their moral nature; and as all men have the same moral nature; they have essentially the same rights. These rights may be wrested from the slave, but they cannot be alienated. . . . Now if rights are founded in the nature of our moral being, then the *mere circumstance of sex* does not give to man higher rights and responsibilities, than to woman. To suppose that it does, would be to deny the self-evident truth, that the "physical constitution is the mere instrument of the moral nature." . . . When human beings are regarded as *moral* beings, *sex*, instead of being enthroned upon the summit, administering upon rights and responsibilities, sinks into insignificance and nothingness. My doctrine then is, that whatever it is morally right for man to do, it is morally right for woman to do. Our duties originate, not from difference of sex, but from the diversity of our relations in life, the various gifts and talents committed to our care, and the different areas in which we live. . . .

> I recognize no rights but *human* rights—I know nothing of men's rights and women's rights, for in Christ Jesus, there is neither male nor female.[12]

When Finney declared that "revivals are hindered when ministers and *churches take wrong ground in regard to any question involving human rights*,"[13] even though he specifically referred to slavery, women, themselves active in abolition, immediately understood their rights to be included as "human rights." Slaves' human rights "cannot be alienated," neither can women's rights. They "blend like colors of the rainbow," said Angelina Grimké. After all, does not Galatians 3:28 state "there is neither Jew nor Greek, there is neither bond nor free, there is neither male nor female: for ye are all one in Christ Jesus"? Antoinette Brown, schooled in the revivals and classrooms of Finney, struck the same note at the 1853 national woman's rights convention in Cleveland:

> Is God the impartial Father of humanity? Is He no respector of persons? Is it true that there is known neither male nor female, in Christ Jesus? In my heart of hearts, I believe it is all true. . . . That which is right, is right eternally, both for men and for women. Where God has given ability, to act in any direction, he has given the right to act.[14]

And such logic did change women's minds and actions. Said the women of Boston:

> we cannot . . . believe that this garment of womanhood wherewith our souls are invested, debars us from the privileges or absolves us from the duties of a spiritual existence. Such a belief is in effect, Mahometanism. . . .
>
> We once verily believed we were in the way of duty when we carefully eschewed every enlarged and comprehensive purpose, as masculine, and unsuited to our sex. Our eyes [are] opened to our error. . . .
>
> Human nature in all its modifications, is made for moral conflict.[15]

Finney's theology also made a shift in regard to sin that profoundly affected the Finneyites' view of women and thus the women's view of themselves. Because the concept of original sin really played no determinative role in Finney's theology, he seldom mentioned the early chapters of Genesis. When he did, his emphasis on free moral agency led him to speak in very general and nonsexist ways. His comments on Genesis and the Fall are much more palatable to feminists than are Augustine's, Luther's, Calvin's, or Barth's. The vast majority of theologians use the occasion to heap abuse on women, commenting not only on Eve's far greater culpability in the situation and multiplying her sins far beyond any that Scripture attributes to her, but also generalizing on women's inferiority through the ages. There is not one trace of such material in Finney's writings. Although his example was certainly not uniformly followed in his age, and some Old School ministers did occasionally bring up such arguments in early woman's rights conventions, by and large the women were spared the necessity of expending energy dealing with such accusations. In their biblical defenses of woman's rights they dealt with Genesis in the positive manner made possible by the Finneyite approach (all human beings are created in God's image as free moral agents with responsibilities to obey God's moral government and implement that government on earth), and spent most of their time talking about outstanding Old Testament women who made significant contributions and about the women and principles of the New Testament.

### *Elect or Damned?*

Finney also shifted the emphasis away from questions of sin, election, damnation, eternity, to questions of salvation, sanctification, regeneration in this life and this world. Traditional Calvinists had concentrated on the inevitability of sin and the uncertainty of salvation. The majority of the human race was already predestined to damnation; the atonement was limited to the elect, and one could never be quite certain this side of the grave whether one was among that number. Equally agonizing, one could never know the status of those who had crossed beyond the grave. One finds this dilemma expressed time and time again by women. Mary Livermore, one of the later leaders of the American Woman Suffrage Association, declared that her strict Calvinist upbringing kept her perpetually overwhelmed by the possibility of damnation even though she felt she had experienced conversion. Her younger sister suggested she "serve God with gladness and not with fear," but she could not. When that sister died at age fifteen, Mary was in despair wondering if she were among the elect.[16] Caroline Severance suffered similar anguish concerning her dead father. Paulina Wright Davis reportedly "suffered constant torment about her own sins, and those of her neighbors."[17]

For Finney the concepts of damnation and eternal punishment were simply necessary correlates of the moral government of God and ideal threats to motivate persons to act immediately in regard to conversion. Stanton admits that he presented the way of salvation from such awful prospects as extremely easy, but she still thought that "such preaching worked incalculable harm to the very souls he sought to save." She for one was terrified: "Fear of the judgment seized my soul. Visions of the lost haunted my dreams. Mental anguish prostrated my health. . . . Returning home, I often at night roused my father from his slumbers to pray for me, lest I should be cast into the bottomless pit before morning."[18] Elsewhere she says:

> all the cares and anxieties, the trials and disappointments of my whole life, are light, when balanced with my sufferings in childhood and youth from the theological dogmas which I sincerely believed, and the gloom connected with everything associated with the name of religion, the church, the parsonage, the graveyard, and the solemn, tolling bell.

She is speaking of the old Scotch Presbyterian church in Johnstown. "Years later," she reported, "the introduction of stoves, a violincello, Wesley's hymns, and a choir split the church in twain."[19] Others reacted similarly to Finney's preaching. Brown says that at Oberlin "Professor Finney's preaching, often of the most extreme revival type, both vexed and interested" Sallie Holley. "His pictures of the condition of sinners in the next world were fearfully vivid, artistic and realistic to an intense degree. He was a man of remarkable eloquence."[20] "Lucy [Stone] had become a Unitarian through listening to Professor Finney's lectures on theology—a result which the professor had certainly not meant to produce!"[21] Another biographer says she was "reacting against Finney's violent and narrow-minded doctrines."[22]

Antoinette Brown, because of her theological education and interests, saw the issues and the shift in emphasis, though it still became an existential struggle for her. In her childhood, she said,

> Our family always belonged to the more liberal type of orthodox Congregationalists. The terrors of future punishment were not largely dwelt upon either in church or at home. To me from a child the whole matter of endless punishment seemed so terrible that I put it out of my mind as far as possible, falling back upon the comfortable assurance that God was always just as well as merciful and that no wrong could or would be done.[23]

At the first woman's rights conventions in the early 1850s Antoinette was always described as "orthodox" and at several conventions Stone was quoted as lamenting the fact that

> when Antoinette Brown has studied Theology, the Orthodox world, with whom she believes, and believes, too, that the majority of men are going to Hell to burn eternally with Devils and damned spirits, should assume to say to her, that rather than that she as a woman should teach them the path to Heaven, they may all go to Hell together.[24]

But the parish ministry proved a trial. Brown could no longer put the issues of sin and punishment out of her mind; her parishioners demanded answers, and their own answers. Brown reported, "before I had been many months at South Butler I began to be assailed by theological doubts." Her biographers report two incidents that may have contributed to those doubts. In the first case, Roger, a fifteen-year-old boy of her congregation, was dying. His mother insisted that she try to frighten him into a conversion experience with descriptions like those she had heard Finney so vividly give. Instead Antoinette assured him of the love of God. He died peacefully, but his mother was so upset that she asked Baptist Elder Coons to preach his funeral. In the second case, Antoinette offered a eulogy of comfort at the graveside of an illegitimate child who died because its mother and grandmother were too ashamed to seek medical help. Roger's mother protested that Brown should have preached on the wages of sin and the doctrine of infant damnation. In a later account of her loss of an "orthodox" faith and her movement toward Unitarianism, Brown said nothing of these cases, but she did comment that "finally a complex wave of difficulties swept me utterly from my moorings, with a present wreck of all positive beliefs. I could not honestly continue to teach religious truth in any form of confident assurance." After resigning the pastorate and retreating for a time into home duties, she declared, "I have found again assurance which seems to me too firm ever to be again shaken, of a personal God, an immortality to men, of an absolute right which is concentrated in that love to God and men which was taught by Jesus and illustrated in his life and in his sublime death." Then she could return to preaching.[25]

One cannot help but ask whether the doctrines of eternal punishment and infant damnation were more distressing to women than to men, and whether this was a factor in the drift of women such as Brown, Stone, the Grimkés, Anthony, and Severance into Unitarianism. In contrasting the attitudes of those women reared in a Calvinist milieu with those of their Methodist sisters, one finds an interesting difference. Methodist women grieved for the loss of their children but they never seemed to doubt that their children were waiting for them in heaven. Palmer lost several children. One was burned to death when a nurse held a candle too close to the infant's bed coverings. Palmer consoled herself and other mothers repeatedly with the idea that, "Surely, God takes our treasures to heaven that our hearts may be there also."[26] Mother Cobb consoled another Methodist evangelist, Mrs. H. A. Coon, who had lost a fifteen-month-old daughter, with a similar thought: "Dear sister, the angels have only taken her to call you to the skies. Oh, do get ready and follow her there."[27] Woman in the holiness tradition such as Amanda Smith and Hannah Whitall Smith, author of the classic *The Christian's Secret of a Happy Life*, leaned toward a belief in "universalism," but they seemed to be able to do so without renouncing their tradition.

### *The Power to Challenge*

Participation in revivalism and in the conversion experience led to questioning traditional ways and thinking. Matilda Joslyn Gage said that "sitting up until midnight listening to the discussions" carried on by her parents and "a large number of clergymen, who yearly held 'protracted meetings' in the place" concerning "baptism, original sin, predestination, and other doctrinal points" early turned her thought to religious questions.[28] Paulina Wright Davis

> was roused to thought on woman's position by a discussion in the church as to whether women should be permitted to speak and pray in promiscuous assemblies. Some of the deacons protested against a practice, in ordinary times, that might be tolerated during seasons of revival. But those who had discovered their gifts in times of excitement were not so easily remanded to silence; and thus the Church was distracted then as now with the troublesome question of woman's rights.[29]

Appalled by the proslavery attitude of the Old School Presbyterians, the Wrights withdrew from the church and "henceforth their religious zeal was concentrated on the antislavery, temperance and woman's rights reforms."

The Christian experience of salvation and sanctification was, and was intended to be, one of power, empowering. In a series of editorials on "Model Revival" in the *Guide to Holiness*, Palmer noted:

> there is ever one standing in their midst, who baptizeth with the Holy Ghost and with fire. The gift is truly for the Marys and the Susannas as for the Peters and Johns. When the Holy Ghost descended, it fell alike upon them all. . . .

> There was a great work to be done, and therefore they *all* . . . spoke as the Spirit gave utterance. . . .
> And who would dare to say that Christianity has lost any of its power. Spirit-beings men and women are still mighty in their sayings and doings.[30]

Those on whom the fire had fallen had little need for external authorities and the women in the nineteenth century began unhesitatingly to challenge authority. Had not Finney felt free to question those elements in George Gale's theology that did not correspond to Finney's experience? His example inspired emulation. Said Antoinette Brown:

> Mrs. [Lydia] Finney, having heard that I intended to study theology appealed to me not to do so, at least not to become a public speaker or minister. When she had brought many stereotyped arguments her last appeal was, "You will never feel yourself wise enough to go directly against the opinions of all the great men of the past." As that was exactly what her husband had done and was doing, it was necessary for me to reply, "That is exactly what Professor Finney is doing, and we all feel that he is making a great advance of thought.[31]

Women in the woman's rights conventions continued to go directly against the opinions of great men past and present. Challenges by clerical critics did not go unanswered. Stanton reported that she and Elizabeth McClintock attended a series of sermons on "Woman's Sphere" that a Pastor Bogue preached at a Presbyterian church, took notes, and proceeded to answer him in Horace Greeley's *New York Tribune*.

### *The Power to Speak and Act*

"Dear Darling, get the blessing of holiness, and it will be a gift of power," Sarah Lankford advised Martha Inskip.[32] Phoebe Palmer declared that, "Holiness is a gift of power, and, when understandingly received by either old or young disciples, nerves for holy achievement."[33] She spoke of her own daily experience of the power of the Spirit "inspiring my thought and nerving me for action."[34] The power manifested in the lives of Lankford and Palmer, Brown and Stone, Stanton and Anthony, served to inspire other women.

This power encouraged, indeed, compelled women to burst the cocoon of "woman's sphere" as it was portrayed for them in pulpit and press. Palmer's biographer recounted one example: "In Tully [New York] Mrs. Palmer's loving instructions were blest, to the entire sanctification of a minister's wife, who was changed from a timid, shrinking, silent Christian, into one of tearful, modest, but pentecostal power, and who afterwards spoke in public, with remarkable effect."[35] For Catherine Booth the transformation was even more radical. From childhood she had advocated woman's rights, and she convinced William of woman's right to preach before she would marry him, but she had not felt herself called to the pulpit ministry until after the birth of her daughter Emma. Just before the birth she had written *Female Ministry*; during her confinement God applied its principles to her own heart. Three months later she confessed to her husband's congregation that while they thought her a devoted, properly demure, bashful, and timid pastor's wife, she had been sinning against God in her silence. She preached in the chapel that night on "Be filled with the Spirit" and after that "was never allowed to have another quiet Sabbath, when [she] was well enough to stand and speak."[36] She preached to millions and with her husband founded the Salvation Army.

Such behavior should not have surprised Finney because it was certainly in keeping with his warning,

> You will be called eccentric; and probably you will deserve it. . . . I never knew a person who was filled with the Spirit, that was not called eccentric. And the reason is, that they are unlike other people. . . . They act under different influences, take different views, are moved by different motives, led by a different spirit.[37]

Can one imagine a broader permission for behavior considered socially deviant? Perhaps it was this type of encouragement that gave women like Stanton, Stone, Anthony, and Bloomer the fortitude to endure the jeers they received for the several years they wore the bloomer costume.[38] It certainly was part of the ethos that gave them and many others the courage to preach abolition and woman's rights in the face of angry mobs.

Preach they must. Finney declared it the duty of all Christians to testify to their faith, "by *precept and example*, on every proper occasion, by their lips, but mainly by their lives. Christians have no rights to be silent with their lips; they should rebuke, exhort, and entreat with all longsuffering and doctrine."[39] Revivalist churches admitted members only on testimony to experience. Said Phoebe Upham in "Woman's Freedom in Worship" in the *Guide to Holiness*: "To *impart* what one receives from God, is the out-going life of the new Christ-nature. . . . How opposed then to the new Christ-nature, and to God's Word, is the sealing of woman's lips in the public exercises of the Church."

She went on to point a finger directly at the "Puritan and Presbyterian Churches."[40]

Giving one's testimony was not simply a virtuous act but indeed essential to retention of one's experience of holiness. Later suffragist and outstanding leader of the Woman's Christian Temperance Union, Frances Willard, confessed that she lost the experience of sanctification gained under Palmer's ministry when she failed to testify to it. Shortly after the experience in Evanston, Illinois, in 1886, she took up teaching duties at the Genesee, New York, Female Academy, and since the area had recently been agitated by the formulation of the Free Methodist Church partly because of their affinity for holiness teaching, several of Willard's male friends advised her to keep quiet.[41] Melvin Dieter has commented that

> It was the theology of the [holiness] movement and the essential nature of the place of public testimony in the holiness experience which gave many an otherwise timid woman the authority and the power to speak out "as the Holy Spirit led her." . . . To those who allowed the theology, the logic was irrefutable.[42]

In her diary for 26 February 1873 Palmer mentioned receiving a letter from a Presbyterian woman asking why women are not allowed to testify in her Presbyterian church. Palmer mused on the question:

> Is it not passing strange that persons of intelligence should allow themselves to be thus bound, when they know it is contrary to the conscious urgings of the Spirit, and above all, to the direct and implied teaching of the WORD. Surely, in Christ Jesus, it is neither male nor female, bond nor free. To all who are made recipients of the free, boundless grace of God, the voice of the all-bounteous Giver sounds forth, "Ye are my witnesses," "*You* know what I have done for *you*, therefore testify for *Me*." Alas! for individuals or church authorities, that would gainsay the Head of the Church and grieve the Holy Spirit by retarding its operations in the hearts of Christ's little ones.[43]

In "Fragments from my Portfolio," Palmer quotes a Christian woman who declared, "My experience is not my own. God has given it, and I do not feel at liberty to withhold it."[44] An article in the *Guide* in 1868, "Speaking in Meeting," points out that "the New Testament includes male and female as brethren, and that which applies to the one in Christian fellowship, applies to both." Both have a duty to share their experience for the "edification of the brethren."[45] The holiness journals were founded to give outlet to testimonies and the first issue of the *Guide to Christian Perfection* contained a special notice on the last page:

> A WORD to the Female Members of the CHURCH.—Many of you have experienced the grace of sanctification. Should you not then, as a thank-offering to God, give an account of this gracious dealing with your souls, that others may be partakers of this grace also? *Sisters in Christ*, may we not expect that you will assist us both with your prayers and pens?[46]

### *Power to Overcome Prejudice*

The experience of conversion and sanctification unleashed a power within Christian society that potentially and in some lives eradicated racial and sexual prejudices, a necessary step for those who were to advocate significant social change. Finney's record is not unblemished. Though his opponents called him an "amalgamationist" in matters of race, he was not. He welcomed blacks into his churches and at Oberlin, but he still seems to have favored social separation. His followers went much further. What really disturbed the citizens of Cincinnati about the abolitionist students at Lane was that they practiced what they preached. They mixed socially with black families, and started schools and other social services for the free blacks of the city. The Finneyite abolitionists were often the more radical in their social views, able to view blacks more nearly as equals. When the Grimké sisters learned that two black young men were in reality their nephews, they made them welcome in their home and paid for their education.[47] The power of Christian experience to overcome prejudices also worked from blacks toward whites. Black evangelist Amanda Smith reported that on the same day she was sanctified, her fear of whites was removed:

> Somehow I always had a fear of white people—that is, I was not afraid of them in the sense of doing me harm, or anything of that kind—but a kind of fear because they were white, and were there, and I was black and here! But that morning on Green Street, . . . I heard these words distinctly. . . . "There is neither Jew nor Greek, there is neither bond nor free, there is neither male nor female, for ye are all one in Christ Jesus." (Galatians 3:28) I never understood that text before. But now the Holy Ghost had made it clear to me. And as I looked at white people that I had always seemed to be afraid of, now they looked so small. The great mountain had become a mole-hill. "Therefore, if the Son shall make you free, then are you free, indeed."[48]

In her public ministry in this country and around the world, she found, however, that "some people don't get enough of the blessing to take prejudice out of them, even after they are sanctified."[49] Still she offered several examples of people who found their prejudices gone with their other sins. Palmer testified to similar results in regard to prejudice against women. Rejoicing in her reception by ministers in Newark, she said: "What a mighty change has a practical reception of the doctrine produced. But a short time since, and the most of them would have condemned as fanatical, and perhaps as almost heretical, a female that would dare give in a testimony for God, before the Church. Now, they invite and urge such testimonies."[50]

The experiences of conversion and sanctification were a powerful force in the lives of nineteenth-century Christians. They optimistically believed they could change the world, but first they must change themselves. Women heartily agreed and felt themselves empowered by their religious experiences. As Angelina Grimké told the Moral Reform Society of Boston: "*This* reformation *must begin with our selves*."[51]

FOUR

# Directly to the Bible

Revivalists checked their experience by Scripture and Scripture by their experience. Reason and common sense provided all the help they felt they needed to reach conclusions just as theologically valid as those of the eminent divines of their own and previous ages.

### *Like a Lawbook*

Even prior to his conversion, Finney was comparing his own readings of the Bible with the preaching of George Gale and finding the pastor wrong. In his *Memoirs* he reported that soon after his conversion he called on the pastor to discuss the nature of the atonement, which Gale, good Princeton alumnus that he was, believed was limited to the elect. Finney said he "objected that this was absurd!" He admitted:

> I was however but a child in theology. I was but a novice in religion and in Biblical learning; but I thought he did not sustain his views from the Bible, and told him so. I had read nothing on the subject except my Bible; and what I had there found upon the subject, I had interpreted as I would have understood the same or like passages in a law book. I thought he had evidently interpreted those texts in conformity with an established theory of the atonement.[1]

Thus Finney outlined his hermeneutic. He certainly did not begin his thinking or study of Scripture from the standpoint of any predetermined system of theology. Indeed, long afterward, after his ordination, when he finally read the Westminster Confession, he confessed:

> I was absolutely ashamed of it. I could not feel any respect for a document that would undertake to impose on mankind such dogmas as those, sustained for the most part by passages of Scripture that were totally irrelevant and not in a single instance sustained by passages which, in a court of law, would have been considered at all conclusive.[2]

As he said in both passages, he read Scripture as he would have read a lawbook. Antoinette Brown confessed that in her early years, when she was heavily involved in woman's rights conventions, it would never have occurred to her that the Bible could have been written like any other book.[3] But Finney approached the Bible with less awe. He considered it inspired and authoritative, but he did not see it as some ahistorical, supernatural document to be laid over present experience. The Old School Princeton theology tended ever more decidedly in that direction.[4] For Finney, the Bible, like the law, represented the condensed wisdom of the past, but it could also be flexibly applied and its interpretation changed to fit present circumstances. As another writer once declared in the *Oberlin Quarterly*, "The Bible is eminently a reasonable book."[5]

Scripture was a source (not a measure) of wisdom to those who took time to apply their minds to it. Finney drew constantly from the Bible in his training for the ministry. He reported that,

> Often when I left Mr. Gale, I would go to my room and spend a long time on my knees over my Bible. Indeed I read my Bible on my knees a great deal during those days of conflict, beseeching the Lord to teach me his own mind on those points. I had nowhere to go but directly to the Bible, and to the philosophy or workings of my own mind, as revealed in consciousness.

He "gradually formed views of my own in opposition to them, which appeared to me to be unequivocally taught in the Bible."[6]

Finney believed that anyone could go directly to the Bible; "plain common sense" would lead them to understand the Scriptures and to "believe that they mean just as they say."[7] In his *Lectures on Revivals*, speaking of the prayer of faith, he noted that "many individuals, who have set themselves to examine the Bible on this subject" have found his views correct: "They found that God meant by his promise just what a plain, common sense man would understand them to mean. I advise you to try it."[8] If people approach Scripture in a spirit of prayer for illumination, Finney held that all converted persons could rightly interpret the Bible:

> they are competent witnesses to this, for they have experience of its truth. The experimental Christian has no more need of external evidence to prove the truth of the Bible to his mind, than he has to prove his own existence. . . .
>
> . . . The Christian is conscious that the Bible is true. The veriest child in religion knows by his own experience the truth of the Bible.[9]

Finney's belief in the authority of Scripture rested on a very pragmatic base, as did the rest of his theology and methodology: "It answers every condition perfectly; it must therefore come from God."[10] Antoinette Brown shared this view of Scripture. At the 1853 woman's rights convention in Cleveland she told clerical opponents of her biblical arguments that if she believed the Bible taught what they said it did, "much as I love and reverence that Book, I could not believe in such a Bible." Instead,

> I should believe the light and the testimony in my own soul, rather. God knows he has given me reason and intellect, and soul, and heart; and I believe his law written upon these, is eternally one with the law written everywhere.
>
> One great aim of my life has been, to show that the God of the Bible, is the God everywhere; and that the revelations of his will do not conflict. . . . And so far as I have studied the Scriptures, they do all blend together in harmony in the one great Golden Rule. "God is no respecter of persons." "There is neither male nor female, for both are one in Christ Jesus"; and I have no hesitation in planting my feet upon the Bible, and feeling that I can harmonize it all with these sublime truths.
>
> While our Biblical expositors make the Bible contradict itself, they need not wonder that infidels arise; for they are the handiwork of such interpretation as theirs.[11]

Brown believed that,

> God is the Author of Nature, including all moral and intellectual natures. . . . This universal Nature, rightly understood, can never falsify; it enfolds the truth; it must be *one* ultimate standard of truth. If the Bible is yet another standard, the two must agree. The written truth must be tested by truth revealed in things and beings.

Actually, "for a long time this theory worked extremely well" for her; "doctrine after doctrine was adjusted in the light of these two standards, the parts slipping into each other's niches like the cogs of two companion wheels." But during her pastorate at South Butler this enterprise ran into some rocks. Her difficulties appear to have been not the issue of woman's rights but

Calvinist doctrines, which she could not reconcile with Scripture. She felt that honesty compelled her to give up the parish.[12]

*The Bible Only*

Finney's approach to Scripture was not lost on other women either. When his disciple Theodore Weld and others of the American Anti-Slavery Society sought to counsel the Grimké sisters against bringing the issue of woman's rights into their presentations, Angelina Grimké in particular answered with an approach very similar to Finney's. Weld had suggested that they needed only to plead their Quakerism as an excuse for their boldness in speaking publicly in front of men as well as women. Angelina replied heatedly, "We are actuated by the full conviction that if we are to do any good in the Anti Slavery cause, our *right* to labor in it *must* be firmly established; *not* on the ground of Quakerism, but on the only firm basis of human rights, the Bible."[13] Sarah sent a similar message to their booking agent at the time, Henry C. Wright:

> I cannot consent to make my Quakerism an excuse for my exercising the rights and performing the duties of a rational and responsible being, because I claim nothing in virtue of my connection with the Society of Friends; all I claim is as woman and for any woman whom God qualifies and commands to preach his blessed Gospel. I claim the Bible not Quakerism as my sanction and I wish this fully understood.[14]

Angelina pleaded with Weld to stand with them on the same ground:

> Now we want thee to sustain us on the high ground of MORAL RIGHT, *not* of Quaker peculiarity. This question must be met now; let us do it as *moral* beings, and not try to turn a SECTARIAN *peculiarity* to the best account for the benefit of Abolitionism. WE do not stand on Quaker ground, but on Bible ground and *moral right*. What we claim for ourselves, we claim for every woman whom God has called and qualified with gifts and graces.[15]

They explained that although Quakers did allow women to speak under certain conditions, they were not advocates of woman's rights nor did they have an entirely pure record on abolition.[16]

In the first of her 1837 *Letters on the Equality of the Sexes*, written in answer to their clerical critics and especially the *Pastoral Letter*, Sarah declared the Bible to be her authority:

> In examining this important subject, I shall depend solely on the Bible to designate the sphere of woman, because I believe almost everything that has been written on this subject, has been the result of a misconception of the simple truths revealed in the Scriptures, in consequence of the false translation of many passages of Holy Writ. My mind is entirely delivered from the superstitious reverence which is attached to the English version of the Bible. King James's translators certainly were not inspired. I therefore claim the original as my standard, *believing that to have been inspired*, and I also claim to judge for myself what is the meaning of the inspired writers, because I believe it to be the solemn duty of every individual to search the Scriptures for themselves, with the aid of the Holy Spirit, and not be governed by the views of any man, or set of men.[17]

Later, speaking of Paul's alleged instructions regarding marriage, Sarah declared:

> I shall proceed to examine those passages, premising 1st, that the antiquity of the opinions based on the false construction of those passages, has no weight with me: they are the opinions of interested judges, and I have no particular reverence for them, *merely* because they have been regarded with veneration from generation to generation. . . . I was educated to think for myself, and it is a privilege I shall always claim to exercise.[18]

And again in her conclusions she wrote, "I am aware, they contain some new views; but I believe they are based on the immutable truths of the Bible."[19]

Phoebe Palmer also displayed what Melvin Dieter has termed "Biblicism," "Biblio-centricity."[20] She said of herself, "My highest and all-consuming desire was to be a Bible Christian."[21] In almost every work by or about her, some variation of the following quotation appears: "THE BIBLE, THE BLESSED BIBLE, IS THE TEXT BOOK. Not Wesley, not Fletcher, not Finney, not Mahan, not Upham, not Mrs. Phoebe Palmer, but the Bible—the holy BIBLE, is the first and last, and in the midst always. The BIBLE is the standard, the groundwork, the platform, the creed."[22] Again and again, Palmer contended that "Holiness is not the distinguishing doctrine of any sect, but the crowning doctrine of the Bible."[23] Concerning the Tuesday Meeting, "the text-book has not been Wesley or Calvin or any human author, but always and everywhere the Bible."[24] In the *Guide to Holiness*, Palmer as editor counseled a letter writer:

> I fear that my dear friend has been hindered, in his Christian course, by an undue attention to the technicalities in theology. The Bible is a wonderfully

> simple book; and, if you had taken the naked Word of God as . . . your counsel, instead of taking the opinions of men in regard to that *Word*, you might have been a more enlightened, simple, happy and useful Christian.[25]

"I speak from experience," she declared. "I was, for years hindered in spiritual progress by theological hair-splitting and technicalities."[26] Therefore, she noted, "It has been my aim to avoid most carefully, anything like a display of theological technicalities. . . . In all my various presentations of truth, I have aimed to follow the simple Bible mode of teaching."[27]

One sees the same approach to Scripture in Finney and Palmer. Both rejected the theological past in favor of their own commonsense, subjective, experiential readings. Both claimed that their theology was grounded in the Bible alone. And both maintained a check and balance between the Bible and experience. Palmer stated this clearly in several places. On the one hand, she told readers of the *Guide*, "You cannot illustrate scriptural truth more instructively or more inspiringly, than by your *personal* realizations."[28] On the other hand, in a letter to the Uphams, she noted, "Surely, the excellency of a religious experience, is only to be tested by its conformity to the Word of God." In fact, "when I hear an experience, for which an explicit 'Thus saith the Lord,' may not be given, my heart is always sad, for I know it must have originated in error." Contrary to the Quaker doctrine of the Inner Light, Palmer believed that "the Holy Spirit never takes us beyond the written word, neither does it take us aside from it."[29] Sarah Cooke, the Chicago exhorter who led D. L. Moody into the experience of holiness, quoted Palmer as once declaring, "Were I to live to be as old as Methuselah, and to be brought into the most perplexing circumstances any one could be brought into, I should ever find the light and guidance I need in the Bible."[30] *Guide* editor George Hughes's eulogy for Sarah Lankford Palmer could just as easily apply to her sister: "The fact is, this holy woman luxuriated upon the Living Word. She had no trouble about 'higher' or 'lower criticism.' She accepted the Holy Bible in its entirety, from Genesis to Revelation, and recognized that it was her high vocation to distribute it to hungry souls."[31] Yet theirs was not a rank literalism. Palmer in *The Promise of the Father* noted that Protestants do not take literally the words of Jesus, "This is my body broken for you," and she found it odd that they become so literal about the phrase, "Let your women keep silence." Both she denounced as "relics of Popery."

This emphasis on the Bible and lay, commonsense interpretation was an important ingredient in the ecumenical base needed for the Finneyite revivals, the holiness movement, and the woman's movement. Time and time again leaders would stress that theirs was not a sectarian movement, that they were bound by no creeds, no doctrinal confessions. They simply read the Bible for themselves and adhered to its teachings, obvious to all.

## *In the Original*

Yet even Luther with his affirmation of *sola scriptura* did not have in mind the independent, subjective interpretation of Scripture apart from the guidance of the church that these nineteenth-century Christians practiced. One must also remember that men and women of the nineteenth century were reared and educated in a different atmosphere from what prevails in most homes today. The Rice family was probably typical. Mary Rice Livermore said in her autobiography that prayer and Bible reading opened and closed every day in their home.

> Every child in the family from the age of seven was expected to read the Bible through once a year, according to a plan marked out by my father. I observed this custom until I was 23 years of age, so that the good book has become ingrained in my memory, a part of my very self. To this day I am saluted in my home as "The Family Concordance."[32]

When the death of her fifteen-year-old sister exacerbated her own anxiety over the doctrine of election, she determined to read the Bible in the original, so she obtained a tutor and studied the Greek New Testament until she was satisfied that it did not teach eternal punishment.[33]

Lucy Stone reported a similar experience, Once while reading her Bible as a child, she discovered Genesis 3:16, which states that a woman's desire shall be for her husband and he will rule over her. As her daughter and biographer Alice Stone Blackwell comments, "She knew that the laws and customs were against the women, but it had never occurred to her that God could be against them." She went to her mother and asked very seriously if there were anything she could take to make her die. When her mother found out the reason her child was contemplating suicide, she consoled her by pointing out other Scriptures that appear to have the same message and told her that women are supposed to submit. "My mother always tried to submit. I never could," Stone later commented. Instead she vowed to go to college, study Greek and Hebrew until she could read the original text, and thus see for herself if in translation "men had falsified the text."[34] Blackwell comments that in later life the texts were of little importance to her but that "she always believed and maintained that the Bible, rightly interpreted, was on the side of equal rights for women."[35] Once on a speaking tour she was sharing an Ohio riverboat with some Kentuckians. A minister began to argue with her about women's head coverings. Losing the argument, he told her she should study Scripture more diligently, particularly those passages about women speaking in public. She shocked him into silence by saying, "I have studied them in their original. I have read them in Greek and can translate them for you." She went on to explain the meanings of the pertinent Greek words and by the time they landed she had proved that the reverend was utterly ignorant of Greek himself and knew but little of the English Bible.[36]

Elizabeth Cady Stanton studied Greek with the Presbyterian minister in Johnstown. At his death he willed her his Greek lexicon, New Testament, grammar book, and four volumes of Scott's Bible commentaries.[37]

Antoinette Brown studied her Bible under the guidance of Finney, Mahan, Cowles, and Morgan at Oberlin. In an 18 March 1848 letter to Stone, she mentioned that "I have been examining the Bible position of woman a good deal this winter reading various commentaries, comparing them with each other and with the Bible and hunting up every passage in the Scriptures that have any bearing on the subject either near or remote."[38] Eventually she put down her thoughts in a paper for Morgan's class. In her diary she reported: "Professor Morgan occupied one entire class period discussing my paper, although the members of the class said they could not see that either of us has made the matter plainer or settled the question."[39] Evidently the paper became the talk of the school because in her own reminiscences of Oberlin, she reported:

> President Mahan was in office for two years after I entered college. He was liberal; and criticized on that account. I used to air my pet opinions in my compositions and one of them was an exegesis on S. Pauls teachings—Suffer not women to speak in the Church. President Mahan heard of it and sent for it and had it printed in the next edition of the *Oberlin Review*. . . . Prof. Fairchild rather objected and wrote an article on the other side. It was printed in the same number.[40]

Actually, by the end of her education Antoinette Brown, and many of the other women in the early woman's rights movement, were at least as well versed in the Scriptures, and in the original languages, as was Finney. He admits that he "acquired some knowledge of Latin, Greek and Hebrew" but "was never a classical scholar, and never possessed so much knowledge of the ancient languages as to think myself capable of independently criticising our English translation of the Bible."[41] Sarah Grimké was much less timid on that score. Replying to the *Pastoral Letter*, she said:

> The New Testament has been referred to, and I am willing to abide by its decisions, but must enter my protest against the false translation of some passages by the MEN who did that work, and against the perverted interpretation by the MEN who undertook to write commentaries thereon. I am inclined to think, when we are admitted to the honor of studying Greek and Hebrew, we shall produce some various readings of the Bible a little different from those we now have.[42]

The women were always comparing notes concerning Scripture, requesting advice from others, correcting one another, developing their arguments. They had good examples to draw upon in the abolitionists' biblical arguments used to meet proslavery arguments in many churches. Theodore Weld's *The Bible Against Slavery* (1837) was the classic. Schooled in its arguments as members of the seventy, the Grimké sisters developed their own woman's rights arguments.[43] Sarah Grimké signed her *Letters on the Equality of the Sexes* "Thine in the bonds of womanhood" and noted that women were "much in the situation of the slave. Man has asserted and assumed authority over us." In speaking of women's legal rights, particularly those of wives, she noted, "the very being of a woman, like that of a slave, is absorbed in her master."[44]

Opponents of both abolition and woman's rights saw clearly the connection between the two. Princeton theologian Charles Hodge, in a review of three books concerning West Indian emancipation, set forth his disagreements with the abolitionists. His first objection was to their principles, to their contention that slaveholding was a sin, because "the advocates of this doctrine are brought into direct collision with the scriptures. . . . One of the most dangerous evils connected with the whole system," said Hodge, was its "disregard of the authority of the word of God, a setting up a different and higher standard of truth and duty, and a proud and confident wresting of scripture to suit their own purposes." His prime example was their "anarchical opinions" on the rights of women. These opinions were but "the legitimate consequences of their own principles. Their women do but apply their own method of dealing with scripture to another case. This no inconsiderable portion of the party have candour enough to acknowledge; and are therefore prepared to abide the result."[45]

*Answering the Clerical Critics*

The women certainly had ample opportunity to make use of their knowledge of Scripture and the arguments they had developed from it. Early woman's rights conventions were open to all comers and local ministers felt compelled to come to set the women straight. They would take the floor and harangue the women for hours. A refrain seems to run through accounts of those early meetings:

> Antoinette Louisa Brown, a graduate of Oberlin College, and a student in Theology, made a logical argument on woman's position in the Bible, claiming her complete equality with man, the simultaneous creation of the sexes, and their moral responsibilities as individual and imperative.[46]

> During the proceedings, Miss Brown, in a long speech on the Bible, had expounded many doctrines and passages of Scripture in regard to woman's position, in direct opposition to the truths generally promulgated by General Assemblies, and the lesser lights of the Church.[47]

> Antoinette Brown was called on as usual to meet the Bible argument. A clergyman accused her of misapplying texts. . . . Miss Brown maintained her position.[48]

> Antoinette Louisa Brown had formed her idea of Woman's Rights from the Bible, and some of her friends thought that she was wasting her time in writing a treatise on Woman's Rights deduced from Scripture. She was an orthodox Congregational minister.[49]

But Brown did not carry the load alone. At the first national convention in Worcester, Abby H. Price of Hopedale, Massachusetts, gave a lengthy speech on biblical support for woman's rights.[50] The convention also received a letter from Jane Cowen of Logansport, Indiana, in which she declared:

> After studying on woman's position for 15 years, without divulging my thoughts to any person, taking the Bible for my guide, I have come to the conclusion that this great evil has its original root in the Church of God. . . . I am of the opinion, that if the Church would allow women the privileges that God has

given her, in both the Old and New Testaments, and education equal with the male sex, and every right that belongs to her, would follow.[51]

At Philadelphia in 1854 Hannah Tracy Cutler debated biblical questions with the Rev. Henry Grew:

> The time has come for woman to read and interpret Scripture for herself; too long have we learned God's will from the lips of man and closed our eyes on the great book of nature, and the safer teaching of our own souls. It is a pity that those who would recommend the Bible as the revealed will of the all-wise and benevolent Creator, should uniformly quote it on the side of tyranny and oppression. I think we owe it to our religion and ourselves to wrest it from such hands, and proclaim the beautiful spirit breathed through all its commands and precepts, instead of dwelling so much on isolated texts that have no application in our day and generation.[52]

No matter what their religious views, nearly all of the early feminists were called on to meet the biblical objections to their aspirations and all did so at one time or another. Caroline Cowles, a Canandaigua schoolgirl, heard Susan B. Anthony speak in 1854 and recorded in her diary:

> When I told Grandmother about it, she said she guessed Susan B. Anthony had forgotten that St. Paul said women should keep silence. I told her, no, she didn't for she spoke particularly about St. Paul and said if he had lived in these times . . . he would have been as anxious to have women at the head of the government as she was. I could not make Grandmother agree with her at all.[53]

At an 1869 convention in Milwaukee Elizabeth Cady Stanton had both aid and opposition from the clergy:

> The platform . . . was graced with several reverend gentlemen . . . all of whom maintained woman's equality with eloquence and fervor. The Bible was discussed from Genesis to Revelation, in all its bearings on the question under consideration. By special request I gave my Bible argument which was published in full in the daily papers. A Rev. Mr. Love, who took the opposite view, maintained that the Bible was opposed to woman's equality. He criticized some of my Hebrew translations, and scientific expositions, but as the rest of the learned D.D.s sustained my views, I shall rest in the belief that bro. Love, with time and thought, will come to the same conclusions.[54]

Some, however, did not find their conclusions convincing. The *Syracuse Star* commented in 1852: "The women of the Tomfoolery Convention, now being held in this city, talk as fluently of the Bible and God's teachings in their speeches as if they could draw an argument from inspiration in maintenance of their woman's rights stuff."[55]

## *A Time for Reinterpretation*

Throughout the nineteenth century, Christian women and men wrote innumerable works questioning traditional Christian definitions of woman's role, offering quite different interpretations of the relevant biblical material and pointing out new material that had not previously been considered relevant to the determination of "woman's sphere." In addition to Sarah Grimké's ***Letters on the Equality of the Sexes***, Antoinette Brown's article on 1 Corinthians 14:34-35 and 1 Timothy 2:11-12 in the ***Oberlin Review***, Phoebe Palmer's ***The Promise of the Father***, and Catherine Booth's ***Female Ministry***, there were other works, ranging from letters sent to be read at conventions, speeches given, and articles in journals to full-length books.[56] To cite just one example, the Worcester convention received a letter from Elizabeth Wilson of Cadiz, Ohio, commenting on Scripture. She had been a delegate to the Cleveland convention in 1853 and authored a two-hundred-page book, ***A Scriptural View of Woman's Rights and Duties***, published in 1849.[57]

The early nineteenth century was a time for biblical reinterpretation. Higher criticism was capturing the imaginations of German scholars, though outside of a few Harvard and Andover faculty members and Boston Unitarians who had studied in Europe, few Americans knew anything of such findings.[58] Still, reinterpretation was being done by many people on a variety of subjects within the framework of traditional understandings of Scripture.

For one thing, the shifts in theological understanding going on among New School thinkers correlated with a shift in biblical understandings that benefitted women. For example, the shift away from a concentration on original sin liberated women from the tyranny of past accusations against women. If Adam was no longer responsible for human sinfulness, then neither was Eve.

The support that Finneyite revivalists gave various social reforms also led to reinterpretation of Scripture. Although scriptural arguments were not a major issue in the temperance movement, reformers certainly emphasized a different reading from that of such men as Martin Luther, who saw nothing wrong with having a few beers. At first temperance workers asked only that people abandon the use of hard liquor; early "pledges" exempted beer, wine, and hard cider. But when Arthur Tappan began to advocate unfermented grape juice instead of wine at Holy Communion, he was going against a literal reading of the New Testament. More important for feminists was the reinterpretation undertaken by abolitionists because the passages dealing with slavery often also dealt with the role of women (Ephesians 5:21-6:9; Colossians 3:18-4:1; 1 Peter 2:13-3:7, and on the other side, Galatians 3:28). Against a literal, ahistorical understanding of Scripture that declared that whatever the Bible displayed and declared was divine decree for all time, the abolitionists saw the Bible as a document of its times, inaugurating a new age, implementing social change as best it could in the ancient social milieu but offering guidelines for increasing social change that those with all the advantages of nineteenth-century democratic American culture were supposed to implement. Rather than as shoring up the status quo, St. Paul was read by abolitionists as recognizing it but undermining it. Obviously this type of thinking had great potential for application to the woman's issue, as Antoinette Brown often demonstrated:

> If we believe the Bible to endorse the institutions of patriarchal times, must we therefore suppose those institutions to be obligatory, or even right, for the present age? Not if we believe Christ, for he told us that things such as polygamy, were permitted on account of the hardness of their hearts. . . . God's will comes to us progressively, and light increases as we are ready to receive it.[59]

## *Scriptural Defenses*

The women developed several different arguments, both defensive and offensive, based on the Bible to use against their critics, clerical and lay. Defensively, they became expert in listing women who played prominent roles in spiritual and political life in Bible times: Deborah, Miriam, Huldah, Jael, Anna, Priscilla. They never tired of pointing to the example of Jesus' attitude toward women. They knew that the King James translators had done all women a disservice by calling Phoebe a "servant" in Romans 16:1, when Paul called her a "deacon" or "minister." They were quick to point out all of the women whom Paul designates as his coworkers in spreading the gospel. They also had ready arguments against traditional interpretations of Paul's dictum: "Let your women keep silence in the churches," which was used against women speaking in all public forums. Their usual line of reasoning followed that developed by Brown in her Oberlin term paper. She noted that traditionalists had never taken the prohibition literally as they claimed but let women sing in church, pray at family altars, and teach Sabbath schools. She argued that the passages in question commanded women only to cease chattering or gabbling in the public meetings but did not prohibit edifying discourse such as prayers, prophesying, preaching, lecturing, etc. Concerning 1 Timothy 2:11-12 Brown pointed out that the crucial word was *usurp*, which meant to "dictate" or to take to oneself authority that belonged to another. Thus a woman could be duly ordained or licensed to preach, given her own authority. In her speeches Brown argued that in the Garden of Eden God did not say that the husband "shall" rule over the wife, but that he "will." God would not command anyone to commit an intrinsically evil act, said Brown, reflecting the New Divinity's efforts to avoid any theology that would make God the author of sin.[60]

The women also developed several new arguments. One was based simply on the Golden Rule. Angela Grimké used it in regard to slavery in 1829 when she asked a friend in Charleston if she would wish to be a slave. When the woman answered no, Angelina suggested that she should not own slaves, then.[61] Antoinette appealed to the same source in Cleveland in 1853: "I claim that this movement is pre-eminently a great christian movement. It is founded in the christian doctrine 'Thou shalt love the Lord thy God supremely, and thy neighbor as thyself;' and the Golden Rule of the new gospel."[62]

Another argument highly developed in this era was the pentecostal argument. The title of Phoebe Palmer's book referred to it: *The Promise of the Father; or, a Neglected Speciality of the Last Days*. She also wrote a tract titled *The Tongue of Fire on the Daughters of the Lord*. Text for the argument, used by many women and men in the nineteenth century, is found in Peter's speech at the founding of the church in Jerusalem on Pentecost. In Acts 2:17-18 he quoted the prophecy of Joel:

> And it shall come to pass in the last days, saith God, I will pour out of my Spirit upon all flesh: and your sons and your daughters shall prophesy, and your young men shall see visions, and your old men shall dream dreams:
>
> And on my servants and on my handmaidens I will pour out in those days of my Spirit; and they shall prophesy.

With sarcasm Palmer asked rhetorically if anyone seriously thought that when the twelve apostles saw the tongues of fire fall on their sisters, they called a "session" or "vestry" meeting to vote on whether or not their sisters should be allowed to speak. Time and time again the women quoted Acts 2:4, always with the same emphasis: "They were *all* filled with the Holy Ghost, and began to speak." Women admitted that women had been denied their rights in the past but argued that the age of change had arrived. As early as 1856 Palmer was drafting parts of her book and she wrote in her diary:

> The dispensation of the Spirit is now entered upon,—the last dispensation previous to the last glorious appearing of our Lord and Saviour Jesus Christ . . . . Male and female are now one in Christ Jesus. The Spirit now descended alike on all. And they were *all* filled with the Holy Ghost, and began to speak as the Spirit gave utterance.[63]

In her book she exclaimed:

> What a resurrection of power we shall witness in the church, when, in a sense answerable to the original design of God, women shall come forth, a very great army, engaging in all holy activities; when, in the true scriptural sense, and answerable to the design of the God of the Bible, women shall become the "help meet" to man's spiritual nature![64]

This argument embodied the Finneyite understanding of conversion and perfection as more than legal justification. It affirmed that Christians were not only justified before God but also regenerate, reborn, made new, capable of being restored to the Edenic state. For women it made possible the sweeping away of centuries of patriarchal, misogynist culture in the instant of conversion. The argument that "this is the way we've always done it" holds no power for someone for whom "all things have been made new."

### *"There Is No Need for Any Written Authority"*

The reinterpretation of the Bible in regard to woman's rights was carried on with fervor throughout the nineteenth century and into our present one. But it is an enterprise that has not been analyzed at length. The early volumes of the *History of Woman Suffrage* contain ample information concerning the debates, but the movement then very consciously turned away from them. The turning point came at the conventions in Syracuse in 1852 and Cleveland in 1853. Brown had put heart and soul into the struggle to answer the movement's clerical critics. She proposed a resolution to the delegates in Syracuse: "*Resolved*, That the Bible recognizes the rights, duties and privileges of Woman as a public teacher as every way equal with those of man; that it enjoins upon her no subjection that is not enjoined upon him; and that it truly and practically recognizes neither male nor female in Christ Jesus." She defended the resolution in a lengthy, closely argued speech. But other, older leaders in the movement were tired of the seemingly endless discussions of the same old issues. After two days of acrimonious debate fueled by harangues from visiting clergymen, Ernestine Rose, a Polish Jew, declared:

> For my part, I see no need to appeal to any written authority, particularly when it is so obscure and indefinite as to admit of different interpretations. When the inhabitants of Boston converted their harbor into a teapot rather than submit to unjust taxes, they did not go to the Bible for their authority; for if they had, they would have been told from the same authority to "give unto Caesar what belonged to Caesar." Had the people, when they rose in the might of their right to throw off the British yoke, appealed to the Bible for authority, it would have answered them, "Submit to the powers that be, for they are from God." No! on Human Rights and Freedom, on a subject that is as self-evident as that two and two make four, there is no need for any written authority.[65]

In an effort to make peace, Quaker elder Lucretia Mott abandoned her chair as president and spoke in opposition to Brown's resolution. She recalled her experiences in trying to refute proslavery arguments based on the Bible. She said that abolitionists had seen the futility of trying to match biblical arguments with the proslavery clergy and finally learned "to adhere to their own great work—that of declaring the inherent right of man to himself and his earnings—and that self-evident truth needed no argument or outward authority."[66] She moved that the resolution therefore be tabled, which it was.

A very similar debate ensued the next year, 1853, in Cleveland. Again Antoinette Brown put forth her position on Scripture in a careful exegesis ranging from Genesis through Jesus to Paul and Peter. Though conceding perhaps wifely submission, Asa Mahan defended the Bible and his former student. But again Rose stood to rebuke Brown:

> "There is a time and a season for everything," and this is no time to discuss the Bible. I appeal to the universal experience of men, to sustain me, in asking whether the introduction of Theological quibbles, has not been a fire-brand wherever they have been thrown? We have a political question under discussion; let us take that question and argue it with reference to right and wrong, and let us argue it in the same way that your fathers and mothers did, when they wanted to throw off the British yoke.[67]

Stephen Foster, Abby Kelley's husband, jumped into the discussion as well:

> There is not a religious society, having an organized body of ministers, which admits woman's equality in the Gospel. . . . If the Bible is against woman's equality, what are you to do with it? One of two things: either you must sit down and fold up your hands, or you must discard the divine authority of the Bible. Must you not? You must acknowledge the correctness of your position, or deny the authority of the Bible. . . . Now, either the Bible is against the Church and clergy, or else they have misinterpreted it for two hundred years, yes for six thousand years. You must then either discard the Bible or the priesthood, or give up Woman's Rights.[68]

Before Brown's speech Mott had said of her,

> She is familiar enough with these passages to present some of them to you; for it is important when the Bible is thus appealed to, and thus perverted, that it should be read with another pair of spectacles. We have been so long pinning our faith on other people's sleeves that we ought to begin examining these things daily, ourselves, to see whether they *are* so; and we should find on comparing text with text, that a very different construction might be put upon them.

But after Brown's speech and a great deal of heated debate, Mott said:

> I am not troubled with the difficulties about the Bible. My education has been such, that I look to that Source whence all the inspiration of the Bible comes. I love the truths of the Bible. I love the Bible because it contains so many truths; but I never was educated to love the errors of the Bible; therefore it does not startle me to hear Joseph Barker point to some of those errors. And I can listen to the ingenious interpretations of the Bible, given by Antoinette Brown, and am glad to hear those who are so skilled in the outward, when I perceive that they are beginning to turn the Bible to so good an account. . . . It is a far less dangerous assertion to say, that God is unchangeable, than that man is infallible.[69]

And so the discussion ended and the movement moved in a more secular direction, concentrating on more strictly political goals and principles.

One wonders what might have happened if the feminists had instead followed the example of the abolitionists, who built their movement on the conviction that slaveholding was not only a violation of a person's political rights but morally sinful. What would have happened if nineteenth-century feminists had called sexism sin in an age that still believed in the concept?

Their reinterpretations of the Bible gave them a base from which to confront antifeminism, but they chose to abandon it.

FIVE

# New Measures

The role of women in public life first became an issue of concern as one of Charles Finney's New Measures in the revivals of 1826. Scholars have debated the significance of the New Measures but all have agreed that the question of women praying in mixed public assemblies was by far the most controversial.

The New England revivalists—Timothy Dwight, Lyman Beecher, Asahel Nettleton—believed that revivals should be conducted with decorum and respect for social order. Revivals were conducted only by the pastor in charge of a congregation or by a man whom he invited to assist him. The minister solemnly and without passion presented the gospel message and those who found it persuasive accepted it. Since these revivalists' theology still included a belief in election, they felt it useless to try and compel sinners to respond. The elect would do so in time and the damned were without hope. Nettleton's basic message was "repent and be solemn, be still."[1] Remembering the excesses of James Davenport in the First Great Awakening, Nettleton feared any emotional excitement in his meetings. At the first sign of such a disturbance, he would dismiss an audience and urge them to return to their homes in silence. He taught converts to be "meek, humble, docile, and confiding."[2] Eric Newberg argues that the basic thrust of New England revivalism was community regulation, social control. He cogently demonstrates that Beecher and Nettleton encouraged inquirers to be submissive, passive, and obedient members of church and society—whether this was cause or result of the fact that two-thirds of the members of the churches were women, one can only speculate.

Finney's concern was quite the opposite: "Religion is a thing to do!" His cry was, "Decide now! Come forward!" He deliberately adopted techniques "not to defend the status quo," says Newberg, "but to stimulate change and create a new order," an order in which religion did not control the people but the people controlled religion.[3]

The new measures may have been born partly out of the frontier spirit of western New York. Its residents had moved there to break free of the confinements—geographical, social, emotional, religious—of the East Coast. Innovation was essential to life on the frontier. At about the time of his conversion, Finney was impressed by the revival techniques of Jedediah Burchard, a pupil of Gale who, with his wife, held revival meetings in Adams in late September 1821. But Finney learned the revival art from neither the Burchards nor his theological mentor George Gale. He seems to have just adapted and improvised as he went along, adopting as a regular feature of his meetings whatever seemed to work successfully. Garth Rosell has termed them "strategic rather than dogmatic."[4] Richard Carwardine suggests that many of his ideas came from the Methodists, who were at that time multiplying faster than any other denomination in the country, and especially in western New York.[5] Finney took the Methodist measures, introduced them into an even wider segment of society, and made them palatable to a somewhat more respectable class of people.

The debate about Finney's measures was a long time in the brewing. Finney styled his revivals as he went along. In 1825 he had no theology, but he did have a method. His legal training initially shaped his sermonizing more in the form of a lawyer's summation for the jury. Thus his language was colloquial, his illustrations pungent, his argument pointed. In his *Lectures on Revivals* Finney advised, "A minister must preach just as he would talk, if he wishes to be fully understood. . . . The minister ought to do as the lawyer does when he wants to make a jury understand him perfectly. He uses a style perfectly colloquial." Ministers should use the "language of common life," and "all preaching should be *practical*." In fact, said Finney, "the proper end of all doctrine is practice. Any thing brought forward as doctrine, which cannot be made use of as practical, is not preaching the gospel." He condemned most preaching as "*doctrinal*, as opposed to *practical*" and declared that the "very idea of making this distinction" is a "device of the devil."[6]

Finney's earliest experience was as a missionary for a female missionary society. He was not a regularly settled pastor but worked a territory where churches were often without pastors. The ongoing power resided with the leading laity of the church, who could call in revivalists and arrange protracted meetings as they felt led. Finney adopted the practice of holding protracted meetings at Western in 1825, preaching every evening and three times on Sunday. Spontaneity was the order of the day. In 1824 Finney was asked to preach in a small settlement near Antwerp. He had not chosen a text beforehand but simply mounted the pulpit and began to preach on the text, "Up, get you out of this place; for the Lord will destroy this city." He could not even remember where it came from, but it seemed appropriate to illustrate it with the story of Lot's rescue from Sodom. "An awful solemnity seemed to settle down upon" the people and then they began to fall from their seats begging for mercy. Afterward Finney learned that the name of the settlement was Sodom and Lot the man who brought him there to preach!

One of his earliest associates was Father Daniel Nash, who joined him in Evans Mills in late spring of 1824. Nash was a great believer in and practitioner of agonized public prayer. Contemporary witnesses reported that one could hear him praying for miles around. And he was not afraid to be explicit about which sinners needed the Lord's touch. It was Nash who organized circles of women in Finney's meetings to pray for their unconverted husbands. He also organized the "holy bands" of laypeople who visited from house to house, inviting people to the meetings, inquiring about the state of souls. Women seem to have come to a more prominent role in the Utica revival of 1826. Also at Utica Finney adopted the practice of holding "anxious" meetings for those concerned about the state of their souls, an extension of the "inquirers' meetings" begun in Rome in January of that year, The "anxious bench" does not seem to have been a regular part of Finney's meetings until 1830 in Rochester. Until he took the church in New York City, Finney was never a settled pastor. He was an evangelist for the Oneida Evangelical Association, which he founded with his colleagues in December 1826.

### *"Civil War in Zion"*

Finney's first criticism came from the Universalists of Utica, led by Dolphus Skinner, who declared that the efforts of Finney's "holy band," swelled by fervid student assistants, reminded some of the seven sons of Sceva who undertook to imitate Paul. Skinner and Samuel Aiken, Finney's host pastor in Utica, engaged in a running battle by letter in the columns of the *Utica Evangelical Magazine*, the Universalist publication, throughout the spring of 1826. Skinner tried to exacerbate tensions already apparent between theological parties within the Oneida Congregationalist Association, which had recently been reorganized by arch conservative William Weeks. Finney was also attacked by a Unitarian evangelist named Henry Ware, Jr., who wrote under the pseudonym Ephraim Perkins, supposedly a farmer from Trenton, a village near Utica. His vituperative pamphlet was titled *A "Bunker Hill Contest," A.D.*

*1826. Between the "Holy Alliance" For the Establishment of Hierarchy, and Ecclesiastical Domination Over the Human Mind, on the one side; And the Asserters of Free Inquiry, Bible Religion, Christian Freedom and Civil Liberty on the Other. The Rev. Charles Finney, "Home Missionary," And High Priest of the Expeditions of the Alliance in the Interior of New York; Headquarters, County of Oneida*. Among other charges, Ware implied that Finney's anxious meetings, held in darkened, crowded rooms at night, pressured converts into capitulation.

In the fall of 1826 Finney's friends issued an official *Narrative of the Revival of Religion in the County of Oneida; particularly in the bounds of the Presbytery of Oneida in the year 1826 to combat Ware's "Trenton Sham Fight," A.D. 1826, Between Unitarians, Writers of Anonymous Letters, and Opposers of Bible, Tract and Missionary Societies, and Revivals of Religion; in support of "The Prince of Power of the Air," On the One Side; and Bugbears, Sprites, Fairies, Ghosts, and Hobgoblins, of their Own Conjuration, on the other, Mr. Ephraim Perkins, Deacon of the Unitarian Church, and Commander in Chief of the Allied Forces in the Interior of New York: Headquartered, Oldenbarnevelt, near Trenton Falls*. Finney's friends listed thirteen "Means Which Appear to Have Been Blessed in Promoting These Revivals."

More significant than local opposition, however, was the growing hostility from the East. Weeks, pastor in nearby Paris Hill, began to feed copies of local criticism and his own jaundiced reports on the Oneida County revival to Old School revivalist Asahel Nettleton. Outraged, Nettleton began a letter war to undermine Finney's efforts in Troy. Finding his own influence insufficient, he enlisted Lyman Beecher's help to restore decency, order, and respectability to revivalism. Beecher wrote several of Finney's friends, labeling certain of their alleged practices as "a violation of civilized decorum and christian courtesy." He warned that society was "on the confines of universal misrule and moral desolation."[7] A letter from Nathaniel Taylor was even circulated, calling the popular western revivalists "mostly liars and impostors." Finney replied with a sermon from Aiken's pulpit: "Can Two Walk Together Except They Be Agreed?" It was a ringing attack on "cold ministers" who oppose revivals and a defense of religious excitements that raise "lukewarm Christians and sinners" either to criticism or conversion. Fuel was added to the fire by publication of William R. Weeks's *Pastoral Letter of the Ministers of the Oneida Association to the Churches Under Their Care on the Subject of Revivals of Religion* in May 1827. Among the twenty-nine "Evils to Be Guarded Against" were "allowing anybody and everybody to speak and pray in promiscuous meetings of whatever age, sex, or qualification."[8]

Finally the two sides in the "civil war in Zion" agreed to meet in New Lebanon, on 18 July 1827. The points of real contention were six: protracted meetings, the denunciation of pastors who opposed revivals, colloquial preaching and prayer, use of the anxious meeting and bench, the hasty admission of converts to church membership, and, most of all, allowing women to pray in mixed assemblies.

The New Lebanon meeting,[9] which included Finney, Nettleton, Beecher, and an even distribution of pastors from East and West, began with a day of prayer and devotion. On the morning of Thursday 19 July the group began consideration of resolutions concerning the nature of revivals. They unanimously agreed with little debate on the first seven, concerning the appropriateness and ends of revivalism. Then late in the day Justin Edwards of Andover introduced a motion that "in social meetings of men and women, for religious worship, females are not to pray." Discussion was inconclusive so they adjourned. Friday the discussion went on from 8:00 A.M. to 1:00 P.M. According to Finney,

> Dr. Beecher brought up that objection, and argued it at length, insisting upon it, that the practice was unscriptural and inadmissible. To this Dr. Beman replied in a very short address, showing conclusively, that this practice was familiar to the apostles; and that in the eleventh chapter of Corinthians, the apostle called the attention of the church to the fact that Christian women had given a shock to Eastern ideas, by their practice of taking part, and praying in their religious meetings, without their veils. He showed clearly that the apostle did not complain of their taking part in the meeting, but of the fact that they did so, laying aside their veils; which had given a shock to the prevalent sentiment, and occasion of reproach to heathen opposers. The apostle did not reprove the practice of their praying, but simply admonished them to wear their veils when they did so. To this reply of Dr. Beman, no answer was made or attempted. It was manifestly too conclusive to admit of any refutation.[10]

After a lunch break and prayer at 2:30 P.M. Aiken moved and Finney seconded a motion that "Further consideration of the proposition be postponed, till we shall have gone into an inquiry into matters of fact." Finney wanted to find out the sources of information on which the eastern men were making their charges. But after an unfruitful discussion and more prayer this motion was withdrawn and a vote taken on Edwards's motion. Nine voted for it, led by Beecher, Nettleton, and Weeks. Nine declined to vote, including

Finney, Gale, Aiken, and Beman. John Frost of Whitesborough then moved and Finney seconded a request to answer the following question: "Is it right for a woman in any case to pray in the presence of a man?" Edwards tried to postpone consideration of this question but did not succeed. Instead Dirck Lansing of Auburn tabled it in favor of a substitute motion seconded by Frost: "There may be circumstances in which it may be proper for a female to pray in the presence of men." This got eight favorable votes, including those of Finney, Gale, Aiken, et al., while ten declined to vote, including Beecher, Nettleton, Weeks, and friends, thus ending discussions for that day. After adopting eight more propositions on which they agreed without too much discussion, Beman again, several days later, raised the issue of women praying in public, but the Beecher-Nettleton forces refused to discuss it further.[11]

### *Women in Promiscuous Assemblies*

Finney did not "invent" the custom of allowing women to pray in mixed assemblies. John Wesley had allowed women to be class leaders and lay preachers in the early days of British Methodism. Barbara Heck is often credited with establishing the first Methodist class meetings and churches in the United States and in Canada.[12] Of course, Anne Hutchinson was banished from Puritan Massachusetts Bay for, among other things, advancing her own theological ideas in a group of laypeople. During the First Great Awakening, women formed prayer groups, and in the early nineteenth century women's groups sprang up to prosecute a variety of reforms. Among the Free Will Baptists many women preachers appeared in the late eighteenth century.[13] Mrs. Burchard had organized women into prayer circles and Daniel Nash organized them during Finney's crusades.

At the time of Finney's Utica meetings, it was not particularly unusual for women to pray aloud or to testify in prayer circles (both women's and mixed groups) and in revival meetings. But during those meetings the practice received a boost from Theodore Weld. In a later letter to the Grimké sisters, he claimed that

> the very week that I was converted to Christ in the city of Utica during a powerful revival of religion under brother Finney—and the first time I ever spoke in a religious meeting—I urged females both to pray and speak if they felt deeply enough to do it, and not to be restrained from it by the fact that they were *females*. I made these remarks at a meeting when not less than two

> hundred persons were present of both sexes, and *five* ministers of the gospel at least, and I think more. The result was that seven females, a number of them the most influential female christians in the city, confessed their sin in being restrained by their sex, and prayed publickly in succession at that very meeting. It made a great deal of talk and discussion, and the subject of female praying and female speaking in public was discussed throughout western New York. As I was extensively acquainted west of Utica I had opportunity to feel the pulse of the ministry and church generally, and I did not find one in ten who *believed* it was unscriptural, fully. They grieved and said perhaps, and they didn't know, and they *were opposed to it*, and that it [was] not best; but yet the practice of female praying in promiscuous meetings grew every day and now all over that region nothing is more common in revivals of religion. I found wherever the *practice* commenced *first* it always held its own and gained over crowds; but where it was *first* laid down as a *doctrine* and pushed, it always went hard and generally forestalled the practice and *shut it out*.[14]

Finney apparently thought it the custom of the place and did nothing to stop it.

> It was true . . . that in a few instances women,—and some very prominent women, who were strongly pressed in spirit,—would lead in prayer, in the social meetings which we held daily from house to house. No opposition, that I know of, was manifested to this either at Utica or at Rome. I had no agency, in introducing the practice among the people, and do not know whether it had existed there before or not. Indeed it was not a subject of much conversation or thought, so far as I know, in the neighborhood where it occurred.[15]

Finney does not seem to have encouraged women to pray or speak spontaneously in his main services, but he did ask them to testify publicly to their conversion experiences.

Neither the Universalist Dolphus Skinner nor Unitarian Henry Ware, Jr., appears to have been particularly perturbed by the practice. From Weld's and Finney's reports it seems that the majority of people in western New York were not overly concerned, perhaps reflecting the freedom and flexibility of frontier life. But the Connecticut Congregational revivalists became emotional about the issue and charged that it undermined the very foundation of the revival system. Nettleton labeled it as the cause of a split in Beman's church in Troy[16] and declared:

> Whoever introduces the practice of females praying in promiscuous assemblies,—let the practice once become general,—will ere long find to his sorrow, that he has made an inlet to other denominations, and entailed an

> everlasting quarrel in those churches generally. If settled pastors choose to do it on their own responsibility, so be it. For one, I dare not assume so great responsibility. In this way churches were once laid waste. And it is by keeping out and carefully avoiding every thing of this kind, that some of them have again been built, and others kept orderly, and the character of revivals, for thirty years past has been guarded. If the evil be not soon counteracted, a generation will arise, inheriting all the obliquities of their leaders, not knowing that a revival ever did, or can exist without all these evils.[17]

Beecher was also especially shocked at the idea of "female prayer in promiscuous assemblies."[18] In a January 1827 letter to Beman, he declared it the greatest "evil to be apprehended." He feared that

> the softness and delicacy so natural to the sex is exchanged for masculine boldness, and those fine sensibilities, that tenderness and gentleness for which we so much admire them is set aside.
>
> There is *generally*, and *should be* always, in female character, a softness and delicacy of feelings which shrinks from the notoriety of public performance. It is the guard of female virtue; and invaluable in its soothing, civilizing influence on man; and a greater evil, next to the loss of conscience and chastity, could not befall the female sex, or the community at large, than to disrobe the female mind of those ornaments of sensibility, and clothe it with the rough texture of masculine fibre.[19]

Even Finney's friends found the practice controversial. George Gale reported to Finney that in March 1827 the Oneida presbytery had issued a formal statement: "With respect to Females praying in the presence of men and praying for individuals by name except when requested, Presbytery gave it as their opinion that they should ordinarily be confined to social circles which you know with few exceptions they have been with us."[20] When Timothy Dwight eventually invited Finney to address the students at Yale in 1831, he warned him, "For fear there may be some misapprehension of the subject of *measures* to be adopted, I would state, that no objection will be made to calling the anxious forward to be prayed for; but I do suppose, if females were called upon to pray in promiscuous assemblies, it would be objected to" because the custom was "entirely contrary to our habits and feeling."[21]

Despite the criticism, Finney continued to champion the right of women to pray and speak, and encouraged them to do so. In his 1835 *Lectures on Revivals of Religion*, he said it was most desirable in prayer meetings to "give the meeting to the Spirit of God," to let anyone pray who felt led to do so rather than to call on specific people. He said there should be numerous prayer meetings so "as to exercise the gifts of every individual member of the church—male and female."[22] In an 1845 issue of the *Oberlin Evangelist* he replied to a question from a Miss A. E. of Vermont, who asked how she should react when she felt an impulse to speak in a public meeting or was requested to do so. He acknowledged that "some have supposed that the Scriptures plainly prohibit the speaking or praying of women in promiscuous assemblies," but said, "I do not so understand the teachings of the Bible." He warned her to be sure to check her impulses to certify that they came from the Spirit and not Satan, and suggested she be guided by circumstances. But "if benevolence manifestly requires you to speak or pray anywhere, at any time, your duty is plain. . . . If you feel constrained by the love of Christ to pray or speak, and if the circumstances are such that by doing so you would not offend God's little ones, you may no doubt do so with propriety." He even conceded her right to do so in the face of objections.[23]

The subject of woman's right to speak in public was a controversial one at Oberlin, and Finney's position in the faculty discussions is unclear. In 1838 the principal of the Ladies' Department, Mrs. Alice Welch Cowles, wrote in her diary: "God will not lead me to *speak* or instruct assemblies because, if I mistake not, he has told me with other females, not to do so."[24] Yet the second Mrs. Cowles presided at an 1853 temperance convention in Columbus. Her husband was still saying in the 1859 *Oberlin Evangelist* that women could not speak to large assemblies "without violating the natural sense of propriety which God has given us, or the real sense of scripture."[25] In the 1840s President Mahan and Professor James Thome supported women's right to participate in coeducational rhetoric classes and even began one in 1839 but the women petitioned to be excused, more shy than the women who succeeded them. Stone and Brown begged Thome to let them debate, which he did once, but this brought down the wrath of the Ladies' Board, and that was the end of that. Stone, Brown, Tracy, and several other women organized their own debating society. Brown and Stone began to lecture in neighboring towns. On 1 August 1846 Stone gave a speech at a black celebration of the anniversary of the emancipation of West Indian slaves. Called on the carpet by the Ladies' Board, she was asked by Mary Mahan if she were not "embarrassed and frightened" to be exposed on a platform with all those men. Stone replied that "those men" were President Mahan and her professors and she was not a bit afraid of them.[26] Mahan worked to obtain for Stone the privilege of reading her graduation paper, but could not persuade the faculty to allow her in 1847 nor his own daughter Anna in 1848 to read a paper.[27] Stone, therefore, refused to write one even though she had been chosen by her classmates to do so.

The term Brown began her theological studies Finney led a meeting one evening in which all new theological students were asked one by one to testify to their religious experience and their call to the ministry. When someone suggested it was alphabetically Brown's turn, he looked surprised and remarked, "Oh, the women, we don't ask them to speak now." She left the room in tears, and then someone explained to Finney that she was not just a visitor but a student. He apologized and said, "Oh, of course, then, she must tell us why she wishes to become a minister." Brown reported that "he called upon me on the next similar occasion and from that time on no one could have been more helpful or more considerate in making my position both easy and satisfactory than Professor Finney." She explained that he had been away when the faculty had debated her admission.[28] At first Finney would not call on Brown for class devotions as he did male students, perhaps assuming that she as a woman would not wish to participate. Again another student informed him she was hurt, so one day when he met her on the street he exclaimed: "Antoinette, you may pray! You *shall* pray! I did not know you wanted to pray!"[29] She participated regularly after that. Finney had a practice in another class of drawing students' names out of a hat and asking them to discourse extemporaneously on whatever topic was at hand. Brown's name came up so often that other students complained that Finney was playing favorites![30] Finney's first wife Lydia reportedly discouraged Brown from her aspirations to become a minister, but "the second Mrs. Finney was very liberal and said—'Antoinette, always follow your own convictions.' "[31]

The second Mrs. Finney, Elizabeth Ford Atkinson, began to attend and take part in women's meetings during their wedding trip to England. One day she was asked to attend a "tea-meeting of poor women, without education and without religion." She consented, "having no thought that gentlemen would remain in the meeting, while she made her address." But stay they did. After apologizing for her behavior, "she spoke three-quarters of an hour and with good results": the women were "greatly moved and interested" and the men expressed their satisfaction. While they had initially been prejudiced against women speaking in public, they said, "they saw that it was manifestly calculated to do great good."[32] Finney admitted that he feared her speaking would do more harm than good, but he did not forbid her and said that after more consideration he encouraged her. She continued her ministry when they returned home and led many meetings at Oberlin during revivals there.

*"The Right Use of Means"*

Finney believed that "a revival is the result of the *right* use of the appropriate means." This is how God works: "God has found it necessary to take advantage of the excitability there is in mankind, to produce powerful excitements among them, before he can lead them to obey." Finney defined "measures" as "what things should be done to get the attention of the people, and bring them to listen to the truth." He explained: "As sure as the effect of a measure becomes stereotyped, it ceases to gain attention, and then you must try something new. You need not make innovations in every thing. But whenever the state of things is such that any thing *more* is needed, it must be something *new*, otherwise it will fail." Since "the Bible has laid down no specific course of measures to promote revivals," ministers are free "to adopt such as are wisely calculated to secure the end." In the Old Testament worship forms were carefully prescribed, but in the New, Jesus simply said preach, disciple, baptize. He did not say how, just: "Do it—the best way you can—ask wisdom from God—use the faculties he has given you—seek the direction of the Holy Ghost—go forward and do it."[33]

Finney was much less worried about social disorder than were his critics. "In an intelligent, educated community, great freedom may be given in the use of means, without danger of disorder," he said. His faith in his fellow human beings was evident in his next statement:

> Indeed wrong ideas of what constitutes disorder, are very prevalent. Most churches call anything disorder to which they have not been accustomed. Their stereotyped ways are God's order in their view, and whatever differs from these is disorder and shocks their ideas of propriety. But in fact nothing is disorder that simply meets the necessities of the people. In religion as in every thing else, good sense and a sound discretion will, from time to time, judiciously adapt means to ends. The measures needed will be naturally suggested to those who witness the state of things, and if prayerfully and cautiously used, let great freedom be given to the influences of the Holy Spirit in all hearts.[34]

Finney clearly was not an innovator for the sake of innovation, but adopted those practices that seemed efficient and effective means of producing revivals. His method did not grow from any philosophical or theological base, but from simple pragmatism, Yankee ingenuity. The sanction was not biblical stipulation[35] or ecclesiastical precedent, but success. In his *Lectures on Revivals* he declared:

> A measure may be introduced *for effect* to produce excitement, and be such that when it is looked back upon afterwards, it will look nonsensical, and appear to have been a mere trick. In that case, it will re-act, and its introduction will do more hurt than good. . . .
>
> But when the blessing evidently follows the introduction of the *measure itself*, the proof is unanswerable, that the measure is wise. . . . If [God] blesses the *measure itself*, it is rebuking God to pronounce it unwise.

The test of any measure is simple: "The success of any measure . . . demonstrates its wisdom."[36] As William McLelland has commented, "The success of the 'Measures' became the measure of success."[37]

Although Dwight, Beecher, and Nettleton had managed to weather the church's disestablishment in Connecticut, they had not yet fully grasped the significance of the voluntary principle. Finney, having no experience with an established church, knew intuitively that if the church was to give birth to converts and adopt them as new members, it was going to have to rely on revivals—as the Methodists were doing so successfully. If the church wanted to survive, it had to use techniques that foster growth: adapt or die.

### *Silence or Service*

For women, the decision to speak within a religious context was often the prelude to public service. As Palmer noted in *Promise of the Father*, a woman often hesitated to speak

> not so much from an unwillingness on her own part to open her lips in the proclamation of the gospel as from the known restraints she would meet with from others. . . . If it was from an enemy that she was to meet these anticipated repulses, it were comparatively a light matter; but brethren belonging to the same household of faith with herself, she too well knew, would be unwilling that she should enter the same field with themselves, and would contest the point of her right so to do.

Palmer wrote the book after hearing a woman in a testimony meeting, perhaps the Tuesday Meeting, agonize over whether to follow the prohibitions of her church elders or the promptings of the Spirit.[38] When women found encouragement from pastors, revivalists, and other women, they were liberated indeed, but when they did not, they were still often liberated by the force of their religious experience. For example, Lydia Sexton, who became a licensed evangelist in the United Brethren Church in Ohio in 1851, reported that it was only "alarm at my unpardonable neglect of Christian duty" that overcame her prejudices against women's public participation:

> I would not pray in prayer-meeting nor speak in class. Oh, no, indeed! that was not woman's place—so I tried to make myself believe. I would say, when called on, or rather when the brethren and sisters would urge me to duty, "Let your women keep silence in the church," I considered that unanswerable, and sufficient to silence all importunity. . . . Why, the old Baptist Church never thought of letting their women pray or exhort. . . . I was so fixed in my ideas and conceptions of my duties and sphere of action by my early training, that my prejudices yielded very stubbornly to my convictions.[39]

When a presiding elder at a quarterly meeting rebuked sisters who would address themselves to political questions but not say a word in prayer or class meetings, Sexton felt guilty, convicted, "humbled in the dust," and so "formed a resolution, God being my helper, that I would never neglect a known duty again."

Another woman, Sadie J. Hart, in her testimony in the *Guide to Holiness*, reported that for two years following her conversion, she refused to pray at prayer meetings: "I told them it was a matter of *principle* with me; that I was reared a Presbyterian of the *straitest sect* of the Presbyterians, and that I considered it neither right nor proper for ladies to pray in public." When an irreligious friend, however, told her jokingly that she should seek sanctification, that it would overcome her fears and she might even pray in public, she immediately realized that "that was the one step between me and the kingdom. But oh, it was an insurmountable barrier. I could not act in opposition to a fixed principle." At the next quarterly meeting she arose in the presence of half a dozen Methodist ministers and asked whether women should keep silence or speak in the church. The presiding elder J. L. Clark gave her a "talking to." When he finished, she said, "He convinced me it was a *prejudice* and not a *principle*" so she went to the altar and received sanctification.[40]

Osie M. Fitzgerald had a similar experience. Born in 1813 in Bernardsville, New Jersey, she was converted at fifteen during a revival at the local Presbyterian church. When James Caughey, noted holiness revivalist, visited the Methodist Episcopal church in Newark in December 1856, Fitzgerald sought entire sanctification. The Spirit of God first asked if she would give her children to the Lord, then her husband, and then all her property. To each request she acceded, but she did not experience sanctification. Finally the Spirit said, "If I give you a clean heart, and sanctify you wholly will you speak before this people and tell them what I have done for you?" "Having been brought up a Presbyterian," she explained,

> I was very much opposed to women speaking in the church. I thought no one but a bold Methodist woman would speak in church. Consequently I said, "No; it is not the place for a female to speak." Again the question was repeated. I then said, "I will do it if the Lord requires it, but He does not, for there are plenty of men to speak." My agony of soul increased.

Finally she surrendered: "Yes, Lord, though it be before a thousand people." And immediately, she received witness of the experience of sanctification. Soon she felt led to pray at a meeting but hesitated until it was too late. Chided the Spirit: "What but a man-fearing or a man-pleasing spirit prevented you?" She subsequently preached as well as prayed in public.[41]

The Spirit's words to Fitzgerald are reminiscent of a prayer Sexton frequently uttered whenever she met a sister who felt called to the ministry or whom Sexton felt to be called: "May God give her the victory over the man-fearing or man-pleasing spirit."[42]

### *A Right to Be Defended*

The right of women to speak in church required vigilant defense. The practice came and went in Methodist churches at various times in its history. Theodore Weld advised the Grimké sisters that if they said nothing to defend their rights but simply kept on speaking they would be allowed that privilege. Had they been lecturing on anything less controversial, the advice might have been sounder. They would probably have been tolerated, as Fanny Wright had been, as a curiosity, a sideshow. But they assessed their situation differently. They did not wish to be freakish exceptions to the rules; they contended not for their own rights but the rights of all women. They feared, with good reason, that ministers would "*close every church to us*, if we give the community no reasons to counteract the sophistry of priests and levites." Without a defense of their rights they would be vulnerable to opponents who declared, "Silence is *our* province, submission *our* duty." In fact, "if then we 'give *no reason* for the hope that is in us,' that we have *equal rights* with our brethren, how can we expect to be permitted *much longer to exercise those rights*?" Cried Angelina to Theodore Weld and John Greenleaf Whittier:

> We *must* meet it, and meet it *now* and meet it like *women* in the fear of the Lord. . . . They utterly deny *our right* to interfere with this or any other moral reform except in the particular way *they* choose to mark out for us to walk in. If we dare to stand upright and do our duty according to the dictates of *our own* consciences, why then are we compared to Fanny Wright and so on. Why, my dear brothers can you not see the deep laid scheme of the clergy against us as lecturers? They know full well that if they can persuade the people it is a *shame* for us to speak in public, and that every time we open our mouths for the dumb we are breaking a divine command, that even if we spoke with the tongues of *men* or of angels, we should have *no hearers*. They are springing a deep mine beneath our feet, and we shall *very* soon be compelled to retreat for we shall have *no* ground to stand on. If we surrender the right to *speak* to the public this year, we must surrender the right to petition next year and the right to *write* the year after and so on. What *then* can *woman* do for the slave when she is herself under the feet of man and shamed into *silence*?[43]

Neither the Grimkés nor any of the other women of the nineteenth century ever surrendered or ceased to defend the freedom to speak granted them initially by Finney's New Measures revivalism. They spoke first of their own religious experiences, then of the need of others for salvation, and finally for the reformation of the world.

SIX

# Soul-Winners

As a new method, the New Measures were significant. They systematized, professionalized revivals. They provided "machinery" for "working up" religious excitement. They were also a democratizing force in the church and community—all, including women, were invited to participate. Particularly affected was the definition of ministry and thus the status of the parish minister.

In colonial times when the church was established in many areas, the pastor occupied a position of respect, status, and power. The Congregational Church was still the established church in Massachusetts until 1833. When it was disestablished in Connecticut in 1818, Lyman Beecher predicted "impending revolution and downfall of the standing order."[1]

Beecher himself in Boston felt embattled with those Congregationalists who were becoming Unitarian. Other settled ministers felt the results within their denominations of the theological splits generated by the First Great Awakening. In many areas of the country ministers of the "respectable" churches felt threatened by the rapid growth of such groups as the Methodists and Baptists. Some pastors saw revivals as a way to build their churches and enhance their own positions. Others saw revivals as a threat to their authority. Asahel Nettleton spoke for the right of the local pastor to control his own congregation when he said:

> Settled pastors [should] occupy nearly the whole field of operation. They have, and ought to have, the entire management of their own congregations. Each one has a right to pursue his own measures, within his own limits; and no itinerant has any business to interfere or dictate. It will ever be regarded as intermeddling with other men's matters. If they do not choose to invite me into their field, my business is meekly and silently to retire. I have no right to complain. But many young men are continually violating the rules of ministerial order, and christian propriety, in these respects. . . . They are now pulling down, in many places, the very things which I have been helping ministers to build up; and for which I have often received their warmest thanks.[2]

Nettleton, a Yale graduate and a member of the eastern establishment, held revival meetings only at the invitation of a local minister. His friend Lyman Beecher, also a Yale graduate and a settled pastor in Litchfield, Connecticut, then Boston, viewed revivals from that perspective and was appalled at the Finneyites' disrespect.

The easterners represented and regarded the ministry as one of the learned professions, the foremost, in fact. Like many other professions in the same period, it was undergoing professionalization. Both Puritans and Presbyterians had always expected their clergy to be educated. Now in addition to Harvard, Yale, and Princeton colleges, there were Andover, Princeton, and Hartford seminaries to train ministers.

Finney became a minister as he had become a lawyer, by apprenticeship. In his *Memoirs* Finney said that the St. Lawrence presbytery urged him to apply to study theology at Princeton in 1822, but that he declined, first on the grounds of poverty[3] and, when they offered him a scholarship, on the grounds that he did not want to put himself "under such an influence as they had been under" theologically.[4] George Gale, in his autobiography, told a somewhat different story. He revealed that he unsuccessfully attempted to get a scholarship for Finney at Princeton, Andover, and Auburn.[5] Whatever the case, Finney was not a product of the increasing professionalization of the Presbygational ministry. Nor did he serve any extended time as a settled pastor, except later in life when he pastored the First Congregational Church in Oberlin during his presidency. He was a revivalist, an itinerant. He came into churches, often at the invitation or pressure of laypeople, and stirred up excitement where the local minister had been unable to or capitalized on a revival that the pastor had started. People from nearby churches often flocked to the meetings, deserting their own congregations. Pastors who opposed revivals were soundly castigated, as at least "lukewarm" if not "cold," as "formalists" if not "old hypocrites," "old apostates," or "dumb dogs" by Finney's young "holy band."

Among the propositions offered by the New England revivalists against the Finneyites at New Lebanon was one that stated: "Speaking against ministers of the Lord Jesus Christ, in regular standing, as cold, stupid, or dead, as unconverted, or enemies to revivals, is improper."[6] For the easterners this smacked too much of the ranting of Gilbert Tennant in 1740 concerning "The Dangers of an Unconverted Ministry," which they felt led directly to the excesses of James Davenport. Nettleton seems especially offended that women were involved in these attacks on resident ministers:

> A host of imitators have risen and run out from these places in all directions, thinking to teach ministers and churches how to have revivals, and the great secret is, to get females to pray in school houses and circles where men, and *ministers especially* are present to see and *hear* them pray for them and others by name.[7]

Finney told story after story of laypeople who initiated revivals, and often of women who did so. He told of one young woman from "a very wicked family" who, after her conversion, expressed concern about older church members' theology, which seemed to question God's readiness to act. At first her pastor tried to reason with her theologically, but then he read his Bible, learned she was correct, preached the new truth, and awakened instant revival. Another woman in New Jersey was positive her church was ready for a revival but the minister would not hold any meetings, so she hired a carpenter, had seats made, and invited people to her house. Again instant revival ensued. Examples could be multiplied. Finney said quite candidly:

> I would not wake up any wrong feeling towards ministers, but it is time it should be known, that Christians do often get spiritual views of things, and their souls are kindled up, and then they find that their minister does not enter into their feelings, that he is far below the standard of what he ought to be, and in spirituality far below some of the members of his church.[8]

With Finney making statements like these, pastors unsympathetic to revival techniques were bound to feel threatened. Their positions as theological authorities, ecclesiastical leaders, and church administrators were clearly being challenged by revivalists and by the laity they encouraged. The challenge was indeed an integral part of their principles. Said Charles Hodge: "Let these principles be carried out, and there is an end to all social subordination." Although the topic of his article was ostensibly slavery, the example he used to substantiate that assertion had to do with women:

> If our women are to be emancipated from subjection to the law which God has imposed upon them, if they are to quit the retirement of domestic life, where they preside in stillness over the character and destiny of society; if they are to come forth in the liberty of men, to be our agents, our public lecturers, our committeemen, our rulers; if, in studied insult to the authority of God, we are to renounce, in the marriage contract, all claim to obedience, we shall soon have a country over which the genius of Mary Wolstoncraft would delight to preside, but from which all order and all virtue would speedily be banished.

Hodge saw such "anarchical opinions" as a threat to all "human governments, civil and ecclesiastical."[9]

### *A Learned Clergy*

As an essentially self-educated person, Finney had little respect for the "learned clergy." In fact he told the St. Lawrence presbytery in 1822 that he was "confident they had been wrongly educated, and were not ministers that met my ideal of what a minister of Christ should be." In his *Memoirs* he said that he was conscious that he "lacked those qualifications that would make me acceptable, especially to ministers" since he "had not enjoyed the advantages of the higher schools of learning." He had no higher ambition than to preach on the frontier and was surprised when even the "most educated classes" found his preaching edifying and acceptable. Finally he said,

> The more experience I had, the more I saw the results of my method of preaching, the more I conversed with all classes, high and low, educated and uneducated, the more I was confirmed in the fact that God had led me, had taught me, had given me the right conceptions in regard to the best manner of winning souls. . . .
>
> . . . the schools are to a great extent spoiling the ministers. Ministers in these days have great facilities for obtaining information on all theological questions; and are vastly more learned, so far as theological, historical, and Biblical learning is concerned. . . . Yet with all their learning, they do not know how to use it. . . . A man can never learn to preach except by preaching.[10]

It was clear to Finney that "a minister may be *very learned and not wise*." In fact,

> Some plain men, that have been brought up to business, and acquainted with human nature, are ten times better qualified to win souls than those who are educated on the present principle, and are in fact ten times as well acquainted with the proper business of the ministry. These are called "uneducated men." This is a grand mistake. They are not learned in science, but they are learned in the very things which they need to know *as ministers*. They are not ignorant ministers, for they know exactly how to reach the mind with truth. They understand the minds of men, and how to adapt the gospel to their case. They are better furnished *for their work*, than if they had all the machinery of the schools.[11]

Describing a Chicago "mission band" of evangelists, a writer of similar persuasion commented: "They learned some important lessons in the school of practical work for Christ that they never could have learned from books or the schools. No man can be a success in the work of God till he attends and goes through the school of experience."[12]

Beecher charged that this "popular prejudice against learning, and a learned ministry" was comparable to the invasion of the Roman Empire by the barbarian hordes and future historians would brand the times "the dark age of our republic." He was sure it would "throw revivals back at least fifty years" and "roll back the wheels of time to semi-barbarism."[13] Professor James Fairchild at Oberlin shared Beecher's aristocratic view of the ministry and argued that women were not suited to this "learned profession." But C. C. Foote objected in an article in the *Oberlin Quarterly*. He pointed out that none of the apostles was "learned" in terms of formal education nor had two-thirds of his own contemporary clergy been to college. Scripture speaks of a minister, said Foote, as simply one who is "apt to teach." He then added precision to his intent: "These words were not directed toward 'learning' but toward the exclusiveness of a 'learned' ministerial aristocracy or cast[e]."[14]

Finney declared flatly that "the end of the ministry, is the salvation of the soul." Commenting on the text, "He that winneth souls is wise," Finney said that "the amount of wisdom [of a minister] is to be decided, 'other things being equal,' by the *number* of cases in which he is successful in converting sinners."[15] He commended the Methodists for their use of very effective, if untrained preachers on the frontier and noted that Presbyterians had been left behind because of their insistence on educated ministers.

This goodwill and admiration of another denomination was characteristic of the ecumenicity of revivalism. Finney usually held his meetings in Presbygational churches, but he often commented about people of other denominations who attended. The Tuesday Meeting was very broadly ecumenical, as was the holiness movement in general. Although the concept of Christian perfection was initially Methodist, the Tuesday Meeting drew Baptists, Congregationalists, Dutch Reformed, German Reformed, Episcopalians, and Quakers. Another example often cited by nineteenth-century writers was Antoinette Brown's ordination. She was ordained to the Congregational ministry in a Baptist church with a Wesleyan Methodist (Luther Lee) giving the sermon and a Presbyterian (Gerrit Smith) the charge. Unitarians would have been in attendance except that they feared their presence would taint the service with heterodoxy. All were her friends, a part of the ecumenical network that revivalism fostered.

With the ministry divorced from positions of social control, intellectual leadership, sacramental power, and ecclesiastical discipline, with the job description pared down to simply soul-winning, the field was wide open to women—who had been culturally defined as the keepers of religion anyway. Finney's opponents saw it coming. Said one, "Set women to praying? Why, the next thing, I suppose, will be to set them to preaching!" Finney concluded his lecture, "A Wise Minister Will Be Successful" with the call: "Men—women—you are bound to be wise in winning souls."[16] In another sermon, "Converting Sinners a Christian Duty," he declared, "Each one, male or female, of every age, and in any position in life whatsoever, should make it a business to save souls."[17]

Women saw the implications clearly. Lucy Stone asked repeatedly why,

> when Antoinette Brown felt that she was commanded to preach, and to arrest the progress of thousands that were on the road to hell; why, when she applied for ordination they acted as though they had rather the whole world should go to hell, than that Antoinette Brown should be allowed to tell them how to keep out of it?[18]

When the Massachusetts General Association of Congregational Ministers attempted to outline the limits of woman's ministry to the Grimké sisters in their *Pastoral Letter*, Sarah replied heatedly in terms spawned a decade before in Oneida County:

> But woman may be permitted to lead religious inquirers to the PASTORS for instruction. Now this is assuming that all pastors are better qualified to give instruction than woman. This I utterly deny. I have suffered too keenly from the teaching of man, to lead any one to him for instruction. The Lord Jesus says,—"Come unto me and learn of me." He points his followers to no man; and when woman is made the favored instrument of rousing a sinner to his lost and helpless condition, she has no right to substitute any teacher for Christ; all she has to do is, to turn the contrite inquirer to the "Lamb of God which taketh away the sins of the world." More souls have probably been lost by going down to Egypt for help, and by trusting in man in the early stages of religious experience, than by any other error. . . . That woman can have but a poor conception of the privilege of being taught of God, what he alone can teach, who would turn the "religious inquirer aside" from the fountain of living waters, where he might slake his thirst for spiritual instruction, to those broken cisterns which can hold no water, and therefore cannot satisfy the panting spirit. The

> business of men and women, who are ORDAINED OF GOD to preach the unsearchable riches of Christ to a lost and perishing world, is to lead souls to Christ, and not to Pastors for instruction.[19]

### *"The Unction Makes the Preacher"*[20]

The bedrock of a set-apart ministry for the revivalists and for women was simply a "call." Antoinette Brown reported that "when President Finney heard me give my reasons for wanting to become a minister he said that some women had been called to preach and I might be of that number."[21] Indeed, it was this sense of "call" that gave women the courage to step into new ministerial roles. As Sarah Grimké wrote, concerning the ministry of women:

> It is truly marvellous that any woman can rise above the pressure of circumstances which combine to crush her. Nothing can strengthen her to do this in the character of a preacher of righteousness, but a call from Jehovah himself. And when the voice of God penetrates the deep recesses of her heart, and commands her to go and cry in the ears of the people, she is ready to exclaim, "Ah, Lord God, behold I cannot speak, for I am a woman." I have known women in different religious societies, who have felt like the prophet. "His word was in my heart as a burning fire shut up in my bones, and I was weary with forbearing." But they have not dared to open their lips, and have endured all the intensity of suffering, produced by disobedience to God, rather than encounter heartless ridicule and injurious suspicions. I rejoice that we have been the oppressed, rather than the oppressors.[22]

Sarah spoke from experience, for she herself had felt called to the public ministry and had been continually discouraged by Quaker elders.[23]

Methodist women were inspired by a litany of foremothers. In *Promise*, Phoebe Palmer reminded her readers that John Wesley, as an Anglican priest, did not favor lay preachers until his mother rebuked him: "I charge you before God, take care what you do, for that man is as truly called of God to preach the gospel as ever you were." And he had to recognize the same call in a woman's life. Palmer quoted a letter from Wesley to Mary Bosanquet Fletcher in which he wrote, "My dear sister, I think the strength of the cause rests here—in *your* having an extraordinary call; so I am persuaded, has *every* one of our lay preachers; otherwise I could not countenance their preaching at all." Palmer quoted another Methodist leader as counseling another woman "on whose head the tongue of fire had fallen": "Your call is of God; I would have you go in at every open door, but do not wait till the door is thrown open wide; go in if it be on the jar."[24]

Palmer was confident of her own call:

> That God has called me to stand before the people, and proclaim His truth, has long been beyond question. So fully has God made my commission known to my own soul, and so truly has He set His seal upon it, before the upper and lower world, in the conversion of thousands of precious souls, and the sanctification of a multitude of believers, that even Satan does not seem to question that my call is divine. It has been many years since I remember to have had a temptation to doubt. Well do I, as a daughter of the Lord Almighty, remember the baptism of fire that fell upon me, over thirty years since. Not more assuringly, perhaps, did the tongues of fire, fall in energizing, hallowing influences on the sons and daughters of the Almighty, when they ALL spake as the Spirit gave utterance, on the day of Pentecost, than I felt its consuming, hallowing, energizing influences fall on me, empowering me for holy activities and burning utterances.[25]

Or as she said elsewhere:

> Had Gabriel been commissioned to come and assure me, that the Lord would have me open my lips and speak of the power of his saving grace, . . . I could not be more certain of a divine call. The hundreds whom we have yearly witnessed brought over to the ranks of the saved during the past twenty years, . . . puts doubt to flight, and makes the opinions of men seem lighter than vanity, where these opinions would seem to contradict the order of God.[26]

Her conception of the minister's task coincided with Finney's:

> Preach we do not; that is not in a *technical* sense. We would do it, if called; but we have never felt it our duty to sermonize in any way by dividing and subdividing with metaphysical hair-splittings in theology.
>
> We have nothing to do more than Mary, when, by the command of the Head of the Church, she proclaimed a risen Jesus to her brethren. . . . We occupy the desk, platform, or pulpit, as best suited to the people, in order that all may hear and see; believing that, in thus acting according to the dictates of reason, we act most manifestly in God's order.[27]

She never applied for nor was given any kind of a preaching license by the Methodist Episcopal Church. But as one eulogist commented:

> Her license came from no subordinate source. She was accredited from on high. Her authority and credentials were conferred by the Holy Ghost. She was set

> apart and gifted as a gentle leader. . . . She was vested with a remarkable power to produce immediate results. Nor were these fruits evanescent. They were life-long and permanent.[28]

That was the type of "ordination" she urged on other women:

> And now, my dear sister, do not be startled, when I tell you that you have been *ordained* for a great work. Not by the imposition of mortal hands, or a call from man. No, Christ, the great Head of the church, hath chosen you, "and ordained you, that ye should go and bring forth fruit." O my sister, yours is indeed a high and holy calling. Alas for you, if you are not found faithful to the trust committed.[29]

To resist such a call was to risk damnation. Palmer's biographer put it clearly: "It is always right to obey the Holy Spirit's command, and if that is laid upon a woman, to preach the Gospel, then it is right for her to do so; it is a duty that she cannot neglect without falling into condemnation."[30] An article in the *Oberlin Quarterly* on the ministry of women made a similar point. The author contended that if a woman is qualified and there is a need, she would be sinful to withhold her gifts: "She is a traitor to human necessity, and no woman."[31] The literature abounds with stories of women who resisted the call and suffered dire consequences. Palmer tells the story of Sarah Mallet Boyce, a friend of John Wesley's. For some years she felt called to preach but resisted. Then one day she fell into a "fit" in which she thought herself to be in another town preaching. Over a period of a year or so, she had eighteen such spells until she yielded to the Spirit and began preaching in reality. She was never troubled by "fits" again. Wesley allegedly gave her a letter from the conference at Manchester in 1787 stating: "We give the right hand of fellowship to Sarah Mallet, and have no objection to her being a preacher in our connection, so long as she preaches the Methodist doctrine, and attends to our discipline."[32]

A small pamphlet published in this period by a woman in Oneida County told of a similar struggle. When Deborah Peirce first experienced conversion, she felt constrained to tell others, but hesitated, "knowing I had spoken much against those females that attempted to speak in public." Eventually she found the courage to speak, only to be rebuked by church leaders. So she desisted, thinking that perhaps she had not been "impressed by the Spirit of God," since she believed that "the Spirit would not lead contrary to the scriptures." But this led to backsliding and loss of spiritual power, so she concluded that it was the church leaders who were contrary to Scripture, and not her call. After two years of agony, she returned to the place where she had first felt the Spirit's urgings, began to exhort sinners to repentance, and immediately felt her soul at peace. But again there was so much opposition that she refrained. This time she felt as though she had committed the unpardonable sin. Neither sacraments, prayer, nor counsel could restore a sense of communion with God. She studied Scripture on the issue, and "when I found it was practiced and approved of in the old and new testament, and declared it should be in the latter days, I saw I was without excuse; but I could not get rid of the fear of man, but wandered in disobedience, till I lost all hope of happiness." Her conscience accused her of "the murdering of souls" and such horror filled her soul that she was even tempted to suicide. Eventually she found peace again when she gave her "soul up wholly to do and suffer the will of God."[33]

Is it any wonder then that the women of Seneca Falls in 1848 in their list of grievances complained of their "exclusion from the ministry" and declared that man "has usurped the prerogative of Jehovah himself, claiming it as his right to assign for her a sphere of action, when that belongs to her conscience and to her God"?[34]

### *The Question of Ordination*

With this new understanding of the ministry, many women proceeded to join the ranks of the profession. Scriptural defenses of woman's right to preach the gospel proliferated throughout the century.[35] And for the first time in modern history, women asked for and received full ordination. Usually honored as the first is Antoinette Louisa Brown, ordained 15 September 1853 by the First Congregational Church of Butler and Savannah, Wayne County, New York. I have not been able to uncover any record of another ordination until that of Olympia Brown (no relation) to the Universalist ministry in June 1863 in Malone, New York. Both Browns were active workers for woman's rights throughout their lives. Their example led to a number of ordinations within the Universalist and Unitarian denominations, but only a very limited number in other groups. I have found no record of another woman being ordained as a minister by the Congregationalists or Presbyterians, though Matilda Gage mentions the ordination of five women to the deaconate in August 1869 by the First Presbyterian Church of Philadelphia.[36] Women may have been ordained among the Wesleyan Methodists as early as the 1860s.[37] In 1880 Anna Oliver and Anna Howard Shaw requested full ordination from the Methodist Episcopal Church and were denied—and the licenses to preach that had been extended to other women were revoked! Anna Shaw, who later became president of the National American Woman Suffrage Association, was then ordained by the Methodist Protestants. Among the Disciples a controversy arose in 1883 over the ordination of three missionary wives along with their husbands. Apparently the first woman ordained for the home ministry was Clara Celestia Hale in 1888.[38] The revivalist Scandinavian groups that eventually became the Evangelical Free Church in America ordained women in the 1890s,[39] as did many of the holiness groups formed when the movement splintered into denominations.[40]

Ordination was then, as today, a key issue concerning women's place within ecclesiastical power structures, though few of the women saw it. One who did was Sarah Grimké. In her reply to Theodore Weld, who bragged that he had allowed women to pray in revivals, she cut through to the heart of the issue. He had argued that "the feeling of opposition to female praying, speaking, etc., which *men* generally have is from a stereotyped notion or persuasion that they are not competent for it. It arises from habitually regarding them as inferior beings." He advised the sisters simply to keep speaking but not to push the idea of woman's rights.[41] Sarah saw the issue differently:

> I do not think women being *permitted* to pray and tell their experience in revivals is any proof that Christians do not think it wrong for women to preach. This is the touchstone, to presume to teach the brethren. Let a woman who has prayed in a revival claim to be the appointed minister of Jesus and to exercise that office by teaching regularly on the sabbath, and she will at once be regarded as a fanatic, or a fool. I know the opposition "arises (in part) from habitually regarding women as inferior beings" but chiefly, I believe, from a desire to keep them in unholy subjection to man, and one way of doing this is to deprive us of the means of becoming their equals by forbidding us the privileges of education to fit us for the performance of duty.[42]

In her *Letters on the Equality of the Sexes*, she raised the question of why women were permitted to teach in Sabbath schools, sing in choirs, and work in the benevolent societies and yet were prohibited from officially preaching. Why? Said Sarah:

> Simply, as I believe, because in the one case we subserve *their* views and their interests, and act in *subordination to them*; whilst in the other, we come in contact with their interests, and claim to be on an equality with them in the highest and most important trust ever committed to man, namely, the ministry

> of the word. It is manifest that if women were permitted to be ministers of the gospel, as they unquestionably were in the primitive ages of the Christian church, it would interfere materially with the present organized system of spiritual power and ecclesiastical authority, which is now vested solely in the hands of men. It would show that all the paraphernalia of theological seminaries, &c. &c. to prepare men to become evangelists, is wholly unnecessary, or it would create a necessity for similar institutions in order to prepare women for the same office; and this would be an encroachment on that learning, which our kind brethren have so ungenerously monopolized.[43]

Sarah saw clearly that the issue was one of social status and power: "I believe the secret of the exclusion of women from the ministerial office is, that that office has been converted into one of emolument, of honor, and of power."[44] Angelina shared her evaluation of the clerical opposition to their speaking: "The fact is it involves the interests of every minister in our land and therefore they will stand almost in a solid phalanx against woman's rights."[45]

One has only to read the cries of their clerical critics to know the Grimkés had struck a tender spot. Wailed one reverend gentleman: "The question is not in regard to *ability*, but to *decency*, to order, to Christian propriety." Bemoaned another: "What a sad wreck of female loveliness is she then! She can hardly conceive how ridiculous she appears in the eyes of all sober, discreet, judicious Christian men, or how great the reproach she brings upon her sex."[46]

Finneyites modified the issues in two ways: they shifted the definitions of "ordination" and of "church." As we have seen, for Finney, a minister was not a person who had graduated from seminary or one who had been approved by a denominational hierarchy, but a winner of souls. The crucial factor was one's call from God. Luther Lee articulated this view of ordination most clearly in the conclusion of his sermon for Antoinette Brown:

> There are in the world, and there may be among us, false views of the nature and object of ordination. I do not believe that any special or specific form of ordination is necessary to constitute a gospel minister. We are not here to make a minister. It is not to confer on this, our sister, a right to preach the gospel. If she has not that right already, we have not power to communicate it to her. Nor have we met to qualify her for the work of the ministry. If God and mental and moral culture have not already qualified her, we cannot by anything we may do by way of ordaining or setting her apart. Nor can we, by imposition of our hands, confer on her any special grace for the work of the ministry, nor will our hands if imposed upon her head, serve as a special medium for the communication of the Holy Ghost, as conductors serve to convey electricity;

> such ideas belong not to our theory, but are related to other systems and darker ages. All we are here to do, and all we expect to do, is, in due form, and by a solemn and impressive service, to subscribe our testimony to the fact, that in our belief, our sister in Christ, Antoinette L. Brown, is one of the ministers of the New Covenant, authorized, qualified, and called of God to preach the gospel of his Son Jesus Christ.[47]

The Finneyites saw the church as a voluntary association of believers bound together by their experience of conversion. They rejected the traditional conceptions of the church based on covenant, establishment, or sacrament. Their concept of the church was much less churchly than that of the New England leaders, and basically anti-institutional. This led Finneyites to establish "free" churches and "abolition" churches. The First Free Presbyterian Church was officially established 27 June 1830 when Finneyite Joel Parker moved from Rochester to New York City to become its pastor. Finney's first real pastorate was Chatham Chapel, the Second Free Presbyterian Church. From there in 1836 he moved to the Sixth Free Church, Broadway Tabernacle. The free churches were an attempt to make the church a classless society by moving into the poorer neighborhoods and rejecting the traditional Presbygational financial structure based on pew fees (Methodist and Baptist churches, except those trying to compete socially with the Presbygational churches, were usually free). The egalitarian thrust of this arrangement is clear in a comment from Lewis Tappan, the leading organizer: "Free seats attract the poor, and those who are unable or unwilling to purchase or hire pews; sitting promiscuously in the house of God abates the pride of the rich; and it is well that men should feel humble before each other, at least in the sanctuary of the Almighty."[48] The movement continued with phenomenal growth until about 1840, with eleven churches in all established in the New York City area. Another goal of the movement was to free the churches of interference from the regular Presbyterian hierarchy so that they could agitate for "immediate conversion" and "immediate reform." Finneyites formed their own "Third Presbytery" so that they could refuse membership to those who would not sign temperance pledges or support immediate abolition.

Women saw this as a model to be imitated, though their efforts never really materialized. Antoinette Brown sought to use part of a bequest in 1858 to found a free church where she could "preach woman's rights with the gospel."[49] Among Susan B. Anthony's "many schemes for regenerating the world" was one to sponsor such a church in Rochester. In 1859 she hired Corinthian Hall for Sunday evenings. Brown was one of a series of speakers who each preached for a month that year.[50] Frances Willard toyed with the idea off and on for many years.[51]

### *"Many Women Carried the News"*

The lack of ordination or of churches sympathetic to woman's rights did not deter women from ministry. Eric Newberg has commented that "what truly is significant about Finney's emphasis on personal feeling is not the free expression and emotionalism that it entailed, as much as the new class of indigenous religious leaders that appeared as its heralds."[52] Finney himself began the trend with the founding in December 1826 of the Oneida Evangelical Association. Finney was the first person to be commissioned as one of its itinerant evangelists. The association supported, among others, his role model Jedediah Burchard, his prayer partner Father Daniel Nash, Daniel Nash, Jr., Herman Norton, Luther Myrick, and Augustus Littlejohn (the last two were eventually suspended from the Presbyterian ministry and joined the Methodist Church).

Although women were seldom ordained, they were more frequently licensed to preach as evangelists. Just as Sarah Grimké predicted, they were rarely accepted as settled pastors, but they increasingly had an itinerant, revival-preaching, church-founding ministry. For evangelists Phoebe Palmer and Maggie Newton Van Cott, that right to preach was enough. A eulogist commented concerning Palmer: "she wanted no higher right than this, the grandest right ever given to man or woman—the right to commend the Lord Jesus Christ to a dying world." As her biographer pointed out,

> No license, no ordination, no pastoral charge, no ecclesiastical power, did this true wife and mother request of the church, though she knew that Wesley and the Methodist Church had licensed women, and that the deaconesses of primitive times were ordained by imposition of episcopal hands. She only asked and received the liberty to speak for Christ, "to edification, and exhortation, and comfort."[53]

Her converts numbered more than twenty-five thousand. A report on Van Cott's meetings in Fond du Lac, Wisconsin, noted:

> It presents woman in its true sphere—vying with men not in political strife, but on the platform, as in the "Woman's Foreign Missionary Society," and in the

pulpit winning souls for Christ, with the eloquence unknown since Pentecost, and moving the whole Church as it never was moved before. She has demonstrated the right of woman to call sinners to repentance, feels that she has her rights, and seeks no other.[54]

A convert of the lay revival of 1857-58 herself, Van Cott was, however, licensed officially by the Methodist Episcopal Church. With the issuance of an "exhorter's license" by A. C. Morehouse, Windham Center, New York, in September 1868 and a "local preacher's license" on 6 March 1869 by the quarterly conference of Stone Ridge, Ellenville, New York, she became the first woman licensed to preach in the American Methodist Episcopal Church. By the time of her retirement in 1902, an estimated seventy-five thousand people had experienced conversion under her ministry and half of them had joined the Methodist Church. Yet in 1880, after a lengthy and heated debate, the Methodist Church revoked all licenses to women, including Van Cott's, and women were not allowed to be ordained as elders in the church until 1956.

Although Van Cott was not active in the woman's movement,[55] another early Methodist evangelist was. Amanda Way was born in Winchester, Indiana, a birthright Quaker. An active member of the Methodist Church for twenty years, she was licensed to preach by them in 1871, but when they rescinded her license in 1880, she went back to being a Quaker and eventually pastored a church in Whittier, California. An ardent abolitionist, she called the first woman's rights convention in Indiana at an antislavery meeting.[56]

Formed in that crucible of reform, New York's Genesee County in 1860, the Free Methodists debated the issue of woman's ministry at their second conference in 1861. In response to the question, "Do we, as a Church, approve of female labors?" the delegates replied, "*Most heartily*. It is the duty of Christian women to exercise in social and public meetings, by way of prayers, personal testimony, or exhortation, according as their abilities may warrant or the occasion may offer." But to the question, "Do we approve of female preaching?" they replied, "We do not." Their reasons included lack of authorization by either Old or New Testament, the fact that "it clashes with the ordinary duties and relations of the female sex," it "tends to awaken prejudice and produce confusion in carrying on the work of God," and it is contrary to church custom. Yet the same conference began to license women as local preachers in 1873 and B. T. Roberts, one of the denomination's founders, was a staunch advocate of woman's rights.[57]

Another Methodist-derived body, the Wesleyan Methodists, at their 1864 general conference in Adrian, Michigan (where Asa Mahan was president of the denomination's college), debated the motion of a minister from Rochester to disapprove the licensing and ordaining of women. But the motion failed to pass and the general conference left annual conferences free to act on their own—which presumably they were doing. The question came up again in 1879 and it was then decided that "it would be the policy of the connection to license them to preach, but not to ordain women as elders." This rule was repealed in 1891. Advocates of women's ordination were unable to get a positive rule passed and so the subject was left as if no legislation at all existed on the subject. The ministry of women at all levels that church continued to be common until the Second World War.[58]

Lydia Sexton was first licensed as "an approved preacher" in 1851 by the Ohio quarterly conference of the United Brethren Church, a German Methodist body. That license was renewed for seven years, but when the local body recommended her to the annual conference in 1859, she was told that the 1858 delegates had resolved that no woman should be licensed in the church. They did "recommend" her as a preacher for life, a "Christian lady of useful gifts as a pulpit speaker," and "a useful helper in the work of Christ." In her autobiography she mentioned numerous women who either felt called to the ministry or whom she felt were gifted for it. One resisted the call with a perceptive comment: "Aristocracy! The Methodist Episcopal Church is too aristocratic these days, to let a woman preach, though they used to do so."[59] Although Sexton appears not to have been active in any woman's rights organizations, she certainly displayed a feminist spirit.

Women preachers were active in several other small groups, though they were neither licensed nor ordained. A group of women preachers existed among the "Free Will" (as opposed to the Calvinist) Baptists in New Hampshire and Vermont in the late eighteenth century. They held revival meetings all over New England. One also finds references to women preachers among the "Christians," who appear to be a New England offshoot of Congregationalism rather than relatives of the Campbellites. Sarah Righter Major was converted in 1826 under the ministry of Whittier's "Pilgrim Stranger," Harriet Livermore. She petitioned the Church of the Brethren yearly meeting in 1834 for license or ordination but they denied it to her. She continued to preach anyway in New England and then Ohio.[60]

Women were active in a variety of ministries from the ordained and licensed preaching ministry to local exhorters, class leaders, Bible teachers, and benevolent society "visitors." A number expressed their religious ideas, particularly defenses of the ministry, in print. Many were honored by the publication of autobiographies and biographies, which gave them the opportunity to become role models for other women. Despite the anticlerical stance of the organized woman's suffrage movement, women ministers were always highly honored by these groups and given prominence on platforms, committees, and executive slates. Meetings were opened with prayers by women ministers and by clergymen sympathetic to the cause.

## *The Gospel of Reform*

Revivalism also spawned another form of ministry. Some might call it a secularized form, but in the minds of Finneyites it was more a corollary of evangelism: the reform lecturer. Theodore Weld was probably the archetypal example. After his conversion in Finney's 1826 revival in Utica, he became part of Finney's "holy band" of revivalists. Then Arthur Tappan hired him to lecture on temperance and the desirability of manual training in literary institutions. He became involved in abolition activity and within two years converted the majority of people in the Ohio Valley to immediate abolition. When his own voice failed, he and Henry Stanton (Elizabeth's future husband) trained the Seventy, including the Grimké sisters. They were the first woman's rights lecturers, though they were soon joined by many others. Somewhat against its will, Oberlin trained Lucy Stone, Antoinette Brown, and Sallie Holley. Others such as Elizabeth Cady Stanton, Susan B. Anthony, Abby Kelley, and Mary Livermore came by other routes.

But the messages were similar: selfishness, slavery, drunkenness, discrimination against women were all sinful. Those who continued such practices were damned, excluded from the society of the just, forbidden to enter the coming millennium. Those who wished to repent of their sins and be converted should step forward and sign—church membership rolls, temperance pledges, antislavery or suffrage petitions. Converts were counted and became among the elect, admitted to the community of fellow believers, and eligible to attend Anniversary Week meetings each May at Chatham Chapel in New York City.

As a result, at least in part, of Finney's revivals, women in nineteenth-century America began to fill new roles as pastors, preachers, evangelists, exhorters, and lecturers. Their goal was to win souls, to usher in the millennium, to institute the Kingdom of God on earth. Their critics said that allowing women to assume these new roles would change the structure of society. They were right.

SEVEN

# On Being Useful

"No period has existed since the creation of the world when it was so easy to do good," according to the *Panoplist and Missionary Magazine* in 1814.[1] The nineteenth century was indeed an age of doing good, of extensive and intensive reform. While the Benevolence Empire was largely a creation of the first quarter of the century, Finney's understanding of salvation as a turning from selfishness to benevolence, expressed in the doing of good works, released a dynamic spirit among his converts that transformed benevolence from philanthropy to reform.

Finney believed that every Christian must be "useful," active in doing good. He declared in *Lectures on Revivals*, "If filled with the Spirit, you will be useful. You cannot help being useful."[2] The spirit of the Christian is "necessarily that of the reformer," said Finney. "To the reformation of the world they stand committed."[3] He advised converts to

> set out with a determination to *aim at being useful in the highest degree possible*. They should not rest satisfied with merely being useful, or remaining in a situation where they can do *some* good. But if they see an opportunity where they can do more good, they must embrace it, whatever may be the sacrifice to themselves. No matter what it may cost them, no matter what danger or what suffering, no matter what change in their outward circumstances, or habits, or employments it may lead to.[4]

If taken seriously, those are revolutionary words. In a set of "Letters on Revivals" published in the *Oberlin Evangelist*, Finney decried "The Pernicious Attitude of the Church on the Reforms of the Age." He asserted that "the great business of the church is to reform the world—to put away every kind of sin. The church of Christ was originally organized to be a body of reformers." Its job was "the universal reformation of the world" and it should be aggressive in its attempts "to reform individuals, communities, and governments, and never rest until . . . every form of iniquity shall be driven from the earth." He vehemently denounced the ministry for "neglecting or refusing to speak out and act promptly and efficiently on these great questions of reform." Such action, said Finney, grieves and quenches the Spirit, making revivals impossible to promote.[5]

In order to promote revivals, Finney declared, "the church must take right ground in regard to politics" and on slavery, temperance, and moral reform. Finney repeatedly labeled slavery a sin: "The fact is that slavery is, pre-eminently, the *sin of the church*." Revivals would be hindered if there was resistance to temperance reform (which Finney first included in his Rochester meetings in 1830) or reforms regarding "any question involving human rights." Although Finney never actually listed woman's rights specifically, it was not difficult for his students at Oberlin and for others to make the application.[6]

Revivalists have often been charged with offering personalistic answers to social questions, claiming that personal conversion alone would solve the world's ills. Finney could be charged with this fault. In 1836 he cautioned Weld, "If abolition can be made an appendage of a general revival of religion all is well. . . . We can now, with you and my theological class, bring enough laborers into the field to, under God, move the whole land in 2 years." This was based on the assumption that "the subject is now before the publick mind. It is upon the conscience of every man, so that now every new convert will be an abolitionist of course." But "some of them are reckless" (he named Henry Stanton) and Finney feared what did indeed happen twenty-five years later, "a civil war, . . . one common infernal squabble that will roll a wave of blood over the land."[7] Finney's own personal calling was primarily to convert sinners, but he did not believe in Garrisonian nonresistance. He did not eschew the necessity of political action. By 1848 he was saying, "Moral Government is surely a system of moral suasion, but moral suasion includes whatever is designed and adapted to influence the will of a moral agent." While "a great many people mean by moral suasion nothing more than flattery and palaver," for Finney it also included "law, rewards, and punishments." He rebuked those who "when efforts are made to secure legislation that shall put these abominations away," are "afraid to employ government lest it would be a departure from the system of moral suasion."[8] It was the Finneyite wing of the American Anti-Slavery Society that favored political action and eventually participated in the formation of the Liberty and Republican parties.[9]

### *The Duty of Woman*

For Finney's converts, benevolence and reform were a matter of duty, not choice. "Holiness, happiness and usefulness are inseparable" according to a column filler in the *Guide to Holiness*.[10] Women felt themselves to be no exception to these rules. As Sarah Grimké proclaimed:

> WHATSOEVER IT IS MORALLY RIGHT FOR A MAN TO DO, IT IS MORALLY RIGHT FOR A WOMAN TO DO; . . . confusion must exist in the moral world, until woman takes her stand on the same platform with man, and feels that she is clothed by her Maker with the *same rights*, and, of course, that upon her devolve the *same duties*.[11]

Speaking somewhat tongue-in-cheek, Grimké declared that "as woman is charged with all the sin that exists in the world, it is her solemn duty to labor for its extinction." Religious exercises were not enough: "the woman who prays in sincerity for the regeneration of this guilty world, will accompany her prayers by her labors." Women must regard themselves, "as they really are, FREE AGENTS" and therefore must "assert their privileges, and . . . perform their duties as moral beings."[12] Sarah's sister Angelina felt this compulsion to be useful from the moment of her conversion. She felt called to some great mission, though she did not recognize the causes to which she was to devote her life until much later. She was driven by "the need to use her powers and to have them be of use."[13] In a series of letters to Sarah in 1836 she wrestled with that need. On 3 July she wrote: "The door of usefulness in our Society seems as if it was bar'd and double lock'd to me. I feel no openness among Friends; my spirit is oppressed and heavy laden and shut up in prison." Yet the next day she wrote, "The door of usefulness among *others* seems to have been thrown open in a most unexpected and wonderful manner." The following day she mused, "What have we done with the talents committed to us. I sometimes feel frightened to think of how long I was standing idle in the marketplace."[14] The call to become an antislavery lecturer was just becoming clear to her. Within six months she was writing to her friend Jane Smith:

> How little! how *very little* I supposed, when I used so often to say "I wish I was a man that I might go out to lecture"—that *I* ever would do such a thing—the idea never crossed my mind that *as a woman* such work could possibly be assigned to me, but the Lord is "wonderful in counsel, excellent in working"—making a way for his people where there seems to be *no* way—Dear Jane, I love the work, I count myself greatly favored in being called to it, and

> I often feel as if the only earthly blessing I have to ask for, is to be made the unworthy instrument of rousing the slumbering energy and dormant sympathy of my northern sisters on this deeply painful and interesting subject.[15]

In reply to a question from George S. Chase, Angelina wrote:

> I believe Woman is bound to labor in all Moral Reformations. Because she is a moral, intellectual, and responsible being, standing on the *same* platform of human rights and human responsibilities with man, created like him only a little lower than the Angels and crowned with honor and glory, and not as our brethren supposed, created a little *lower than man*. . . .
>
> Under the Jewish Dispensation women were called to fill the highest offices in Church and State. See Miriam, Deborah and Huldah. They were coworkers in the reformation of their day with their brethren. . . .
>
> Those who are engaged in the moral reformation of the day are the true prophets of this age.[16]

Other women felt the same need to be useful. Lucy Stone, in a July 1853 love letter to Henry Blackwell, wrote: "The privations I have learned to endure, and the isolation, I scarcely regret; while the certainty that I am *living usefully* brings a deep and *abiding* happiness."[17] Abby Price expressed the same conviction in a speech at the first national woman's rights convention in Worcester in 1850: "Human beings cannot attain true dignity or happiness except by true usefulness. This is true of women as of men. It is their duty, privilege, honor, and bliss to be useful. Therefore give them the opportunity and encouragement."[18] The determination to be useful was one of the original resolutions at Seneca Falls: "*Resolved, therefore*, That, being invested by the Creator with the same capabilities, and the same consciousness of responsibility for their exercise, it is demonstrably the right and duty of woman, equally with man, to promote every righteous cause by every righteous means."[19]

The duty to be useful empowered women to go beyond traditional roles. Phoebe Palmer, one of the more socially conservative women I have been following, expresses this most clearly: "The Spirit of truth will never lead us into any unscriptural or unintelligible modes of usefulness. It will not lead us to unseemly or untimely utterances, or to any course which will not betoken soundness of mind. But it may lead us to a course which may occasionally be extraordinary."[20] The call of God often drew these women beyond woman's sphere as prescribed by society, and gave them courage to answer their opposition. Lydia Sexton was away on a preaching trip when her son Thomas died. When she packed to leave again soon after his funeral, a neighbor said,

"Well, if one of my children died when I was away from home I would never forgive myself." To which Lydia answered,

> Well, . . . perhaps you would be governed by circumstances. If you had no motive or object in leaving home other than to visit or to pass time, and your visit was not likely to amount to anything but a little prodigality of time and money, you would not be justifiable, and, of course, would not be so ready to forgive yourself. But if you were working for God, in a work that would tell to your advantage and the advantage of hundreds of others of the human family in time and eternity, or if thereby you were an instrument in the hands of God in waking them up to see their dangerous condition by nature and practice and what they must be by grace divine, or be an instrument in turning many from darkness to light and from the power of Satan to God,—if your motive-force was to promote the glory of God and the salvation of never-dying souls, you would then feel as I do. . . . My children belong to God. He gave them to me; and when it is his best time, he will take them. Oh, I only want grace to say, "Thy will be done."[21]

Sexton went on to comment that her neighbor was a "kind-hearted and noble lady, with all the warm emotions of a mother's love but without the pressing call of the Spirit to the ministry." As for Lydia herself, she thanked God that she "now had light to pursue a different course."

Yet even society's definition of woman's sphere strengthened some to go beyond it. In October 1835 a riot ensued in Boston when the women of the Boston Female Anti-Slavery Society attempted to hold a meeting with William Lloyd Garrison and English abolitionist George Thompson. In their annual report they replied, to someone who asked if they regretted their actions, that they stood their ground for several reasons:

> It was not for the slave and his master only that we did it;—the right of association, the right of freely speaking, the right of occupying our own buildings, and walking our own streets,—were denied to ourselves. . . . It was for our CHILDREN we did it; and we need not now turn conscience-stricken from their trusting gaze: for we have done what lies with us, to preserve them "an inheritance pure and undefiled, and that fadeth not away."[22]

These women believed, as good Finneyites, that social reform was an integral part of their faith. As Antoinette Brown said, "Christianity is the heart and soul of them all, and those reforms which seek to elevate mankind and better their condition, cling round our Christianity, and are a part of it. They are like the cluster of grapes, all clinging about the central stem."[23]

*The Benevolence Empire*

Middle-class women were in the midst of a transition. In the colonial and revolutionary periods they were an important part of the community, equally valued with men as workers, skilled craftspersons, small shopkeepers. On the frontier and in a struggling new nation all hands were needed; society was flexible and innovative. The early national period saw a stratification of women's roles, a codification of the cult of true womanhood, and a drastic limitation of the options open to women, at precisely the same time as the Industrial Revolution and the rise of the business classes gave certain women leisure beyond child-rearing and housekeeping. And almost every person mentioned in this study had domestic servants.

Thus the Benevolence Empire then (as to a certain extent today) was based on the voluntary work and fund-raising of middle-class women. Since the cult of true womanhood decreed that religion was part of woman's natural sphere, it was also natural that in the name of religion women should extend their maternal and domestic expertise to those of the community less able to care for themselves. One of the first benevolent societies in America founded in 1797 by a Scots Presbyterian widow, Isabella Graham, was the Society for the Relief of Poor Widows with Small Children, which eventually became the New York Orphan Asylum. Graham and her daughter Joanna Bethune were also largely responsible for the growth of the Sunday school movement. Baptist and Congregational women in Boston in 1800 formed a Female Society for Missionary Purposes to raise money and to organize a "concert of prayer" for home missionaries to the Indians and the "heathen" on the churchless frontier. After the founding of the all-male American Board of Commissioners for Foreign Missions in 1810, women supported the foreign missionaries. Women gave money to help the American Education Society to train ministers, the American Home Missionary Society to send pastors to frontier churches, the American Bible Society to print Scriptures, and the American Tract Society to pass out pious literature.

As Charles Foster, John R. Bodo, Clifford Griffin, and Joseph R. Gusfield all contend, the thrust of the original Benevolence Empire was socially conservative. "Christianity was a social palliative, a soothing unguent for social sores," said Foster. "The Evangelicals wanted no changes in the social machinery; they would grease the gears."[24] Society names tell the story: the New York Association for the Relief of Respectable, Aged, Indigent Females; the Philadelphia Society for the Encouragement of Faithful Domestics; the

Connecticut Society for the Suppression of Vice and the Promotion of Good Morals; the Society for the Suppression of Intemperance. While the participants were motivated by genuine Christian concern, their goals were not to eliminate poverty or social inequity, but to teach the poor their proper place, train them in domesticity and religion, sober them up, and make them honest, docile domestics or laborers. Isabella Graham, in speaking of her own children, wrote: "I am equally indifferent what station of life they may occupy, whether they swim in affluence or earn their daily bread, if they only act their part properly, and obtain the approbation of their God in that station wherein he in his infinite wisdom sees fit to place them." One of her role models in benevolence was one of her own early patrons, Lady Glenarchy in Edinburgh, of whom Graham said: "She never encouraged idleness or pride, and often remarked that it was better to assist people to do well in the sphere which Providence had assigned them, then to attempt to raise them beyond it."[25] Nurtured by older forms of Calvinism, these women assumed that social classes were part of God's providence.

Visitors from the benevolence societies worked mostly among their country people returned from the frontier or among Anglo-Saxon immigrants, sometimes among free blacks, but seldom among "foreigners" and/or Roman Catholics. The Rev. Ward Stafford, in his 1817 address to the Female Missionary Society for the Poor of the City of New-York and its Vicinity, noted that "a respectable Female Association for the relief of the sick and afflicted, some time ago, resolved not to aid those who lived on certain streets, supposing that no person of decent character would live in such places, and that it would be unsafe for females to visit them."[26]

The early benevolence societies were not only attempts to socially control the poor, but they were instruments for social control of men over women. Most societies were under the control of the local pastor who opened each meeting with religious exercises and gave the annual lecture to be reprinted with the society's annual report. The clergy often used the occasion to reinforce the cult of true womanhood. As late as the 1860s a minister admitted to Sarah Platt Haines Doremus, founder of the Woman's Union Missionary Society of America for Heathen Lands, the first women's sending agency, that he always went to the meetings of any woman's society in his church because one could never be sure for what women might be praying.

Yet most ministers encouraged women to work in benevolence. As one asked in 1817, "Who will say, they ought not be engaged in performing that service for Christ, which is suited to their sex and station? Who will not delight in the sweet and heavenly work of honouring the weaker vessels, and of endeavoring to make them ornamental and useful in the house of God?" Quite the contrary:

> The pious parent, guardian, husband—and especially, the enlightened and feeling minister of the Gospel, who wishes to imitate Jesus and his apostles, must esteem it one of his most noble and happy employments to cheer and animate the female part of the Church in performing their appropriate duties. As they are circumscribed in their means; and as their sense of modesty and subordination is in proportion to their piety, so it is very easy for parents, husbands, or ministers of the Gospel to check them in their attempts to serve their Lord. Wise and good men will, therefore, be very cautious how they condemn those female projects which have in view the glory of God. . . . They will *carefully* examine whether they are consistent with the female character or not: what is wrong, they will tenderly and affectionately correct; what is good, they will cordially approve; and, rather than be instrumental in checking a good work, they will even bear with *inexpediences*, provided they be *lawful*.

Turning to the female members of his audience, the good pastor advised:

> While the pious female, therefore, does not aspire after things too great for her, she discovers that there is a wide field opened for the exercise of all her active powers, in which she may do much for the honour of God and the good of men; and in which she can gratify all her benevolent wishes. Knowing that her true dignity and usefulness consist in filling that station marked out for her by the God of nature and grace, she is satisfied in being an *assistant* of man.[27]

At times the male clergy were patronizing. When Mrs. Ann Rhees asked her Baptist pastor in Philadelphia if she could start a Sabbath school, he replied: "Well, my sister, you can but try it; blossoms are sweet and beautiful, even if they produce no fruit."[28] The elders in Medway, Massachusetts, seemed more aware of the real implications: "These women will be in the pulpit next."[29]

For the first quarter of the nineteenth century the Benevolence Empire was in many ways an extension of the Presbyterian-Congregational Plan of Union. Methodists were so convinced that the Great Eight were under the control of the Presbygationalists that they formed their own societies. The interlocking directorates were full of Presbygational clergy who believed in a clerically dominated social order. They held a federalist political philosophy that considered society best controlled by the educated, the well born, and the wealthy. They thought of themselves as "moral stewards," "trustees" of society. Lyman Beecher once wrote to Asahel Hooker: "I am persuaded that the time has come when it becomes every friend of this state [Connecticut] to wake up and exert his whole influence to save it from innovation and democracy."[30]

*From Philanthropy to Reform*

In the late 1820s, however, the Benevolence Empire, captured by the Finneyite revivalists, began going through some radical changes. To the older philanthropists' ideas of moral ability and accountability they added "immediatism": immediate radical conversion and immediate reformation of the whole world. Not only were people capable of reforming themselves, but they were also capable of reforming the world. As Beecher noted in shock, the Finneyites treated all sinners alike, "without respect to age or station in society."[31] They welcomed the poor and blacks into their churches, women and blacks into their societies. Against the Boston-Yale Presbygational axis was formed the New York Association of Gentlemen and the Third (Free) Presbytery. A battle for control of the Benevolence Empire ensued. As the Tappans' biographer suggests, the issues were many: lay versus clerical control, Yorker versus Yankee, yeomen versus urban sophisticates, rural pietists versus timid keepers of the Ark. The Tappans teamed up immediately with the Finneyites. They invited Finney to New York City for a short revival in the summer of 1828 and lured him back in 1832 to accept the pastorate of the Second Free Presbyterian Church. They founded the *New York Evangelist*, a magazine to publicize both revivals and their own benevolent enterprises.

Finney did not ask converts to submit to the standing moral order but exhorted them to build a new moral order. He did not call people to order but to excitement and zeal, enthusiasm and participation in a new popular movement emerging in both religion and society. He counseled Christians to form societies outside the church if necessary reforms could not find support among "doctors of divinity, ecclesiastical bodies, colleges and seminaries."[32] And he counseled "immediatism."

The antislavery movement became the battleground. Gradualism had been the nation's answer to the issue in the early national period. The Constitution had decreed that the slave trade would end in 1808. Northern states passed laws gradually ending slavery within their boundaries. None of this ended slavery in the South, however. There it flourished. And so those concerned with the issue formed the American Colonization Society. Beecher and members of the New England establishment were prominent members.

Garrison and the New York Tappans became convinced that the British were right in calling for "immediate" abolition.[33] Garrison began publication of *The Liberator* on 1 January 1831 and founded the New England Anti-Slavery Society on 13 November 1831. Amid a riot, the "Friends of Immediate Abolition"—Finney, the Tappans, et al.—formed the New York City Anti-Slavery Society in a lecture room at Chatham Street Chapel on 2 October 1833 and began to publish the *Emancipator*. They formed the core of the American Anti-Slavery Society founded 4 December 1833, with Arthur Tappan as president.

Immediate abolition was not, however, a popular idea. In February 1834 the issue came up for debate at Lane Seminary in Cincinnati, to which the Tappans had contributed, of which Beecher was president, and at which Theodore Weld had been quietly proselytizing for abolition for several months. For nine nights the students considered the question: "Ought the people of the slaveholding states to abolish slavery immediately?" At first Beecher consented to participate, but after counsel with advisers he declined to attend, sending his daughters Catharine and Harriet instead. After hearing southern students and freed slaves testify to the cruelties of slavery, and to Weld and Henry Stanton expound the moral issues, the students voted unanimously for immediate abolition. For another nine evenings they discussed whether the American Colonization Society's goals were such as to "entitle it to the patronage of the Christian community." The answer was negative, despite Catharine Beecher's presentation of her father's "plan of assimilation," which would somehow have found a canopy broad enough to encompass both colonizationists and abolitionists. Many of the trustees, New England theocrats, were upset, Beecher was equivocal, and eventually the students were expelled. They, Mahan, and the Tappans' money transferred to Oberlin. Immediate abolition became the platform for the Yorkers of the city, of upstate New York, and of the Western Reserve.

Interestingly, the debate was replayed three years later when Catharine Beecher published *An Essay on Slavery and Abolitionism, with Reference to the Duty of American Females* and Angelina Grimké replied with *Letters to Catherine E. Beecher, in Reply to An Essay on Slavery and Abolitionism*. Catharine argued that it was unfeminine and unchristian for women to join abolition societies or to sign petitions, or even to concern themselves with such issues of national policy. Angelina replied that women had every right, and responsibility, to think, speak, and act on all the great moral questions of the day. Woman's right to do so could not be given or taken away by men because "her *rights* are an integral part of her moral being," created by and responsible to God alone.[34]

Woman's participation in philanthropy and women advocating abolition were viewed quite differently. For example, the *Christian Register* commented:

> Their charitable associations of humble pretensions, we admire. . . . Their charity should be set forth in public by devotional exercises and expositions of their benevolent designs. But when we come to the grave subjects of political reform, embracing complicated national interests, it might be wiser in the gentler sex to seek information at home, and lend their influence in a more private way.

When women had distributed notices of their benevolent society meetings to pastors to be announced on Sunday, they were lauded as "woman, stepping gracefully to the relief of infancy and suffering age," but when they sent notices of antislavery meetings, the notices were destroyed, the ministers refused to make any announcements, and they were accused of seeking "undue publicity" and told they "had better stay at home."[35]

### *Moral Reform*

A similar, though much less analyzed change was taking place in a reform closer to women's hearts. In the spring of 1830, just after Finney's first New York City revival, a young Princeton divinity student, John R. McDowall, arrived in the big city as a summer missionary for the American Tract Society. With women converts from Finney's crusade, he held Sunday school classes in prisons and almshouses of the notorious Five Points area. He also began working with the prostitutes of the area. Arthur Tappan, who had visited the Magdalen Asylum in London, wanted to duplicate the British efforts. So with McDowall as superintendent, he and the Association of Gentlemen founded the Magdalen Society of New York and persuaded it to open an "Asylum for Females who have Deviated from the Paths of Virtue."

McDowall was dedicated to his work and had the instincts of a social worker. Within a year he had collected the facts and published them graphically in *The Magdalen Report*, which he had persuaded Tappan and two physicians to sign. All were unprepared for the shock and outrage that greeted their report. First, city fathers at Tammany Hall were chagrined at McDowall's statistics claiming that "every tenth female in our cities is a prostitute," ten thousand in all with a working-life expectancy of only five years; and second, they were infuriated that instead of blaming prostitution on the moral weakness of the women, McDowall pointed the finger at the men of wealth and status who patronized them. Tappan stood by McDowall when he was tried by the presbytery on charges of being an irresponsible scandal-monger and an obscene seeker of notoriety, but he quietly closed the Magdalen "House of Refuge." McDowall did not back down. In 1832 he enlarged his charges in a second report, *Magdalen Facts*, and he began to publish the monthly *McDowall's Journal*. The breach between McDowall and the Association of Gentlemen became increasingly acrimonious, with charges of financial irresponsibility being traded. Tappan formed a successor, the Society for Promoting the Observance of the Seventh Commandment. He declared it would have no asylums:

> An asylum . . . is not the Gospel mode of converting sinners. Did Jesus Christ say "Go ye into all the world and build *asylums* for every sinner?" Never! . . . The word of God is the "sword of the spirit," and if properly wielded by Christians would subjugate more sinners . . . in three months than all the asylums on earth would ever rescue from damnation.[36]

He had given up on the reform of prostitutes but he would still denounce prostitution by preaching morality.

The Finneyite women were not so easily discouraged. On 12 May 1834 they rallied to form the Female Moral Reform Society. Lydia Andrews Finney was its first "directress." Finney addressed the society at a December 1834 meeting in Chatham Chapel and encouraged their work.[37] In the final issue of *McDowall's Journal*, dated 28 January 1835, McDowall published the full text of the accusations made against him and his own point-by-point rebuttal. And then in what might be called a literary "will," titled "To My Friends," he made a final bequest:

> To the New York Female Moral Reform Society, I give the *Journal* and all the donations placed at my disposal to promote the cause. . . .
>
> These ladies defended my character through evil report, and through good report. They stood by me in dark hours, when sorrows of oppression weighed heavily on my soul, and brought my partner nigh unto death.[38]

The women retitled the *Journal* the *Advocate of Moral Reform*. By 1837 they had sixteen thousand subscribers, the majority of them in the burned-over district. Their first goal was to convert the nation to moral purity; converting and reforming the lost women of the city was a secondary concern. They attacked the problem at its source by publishing the initials and hometowns of men known to frequent the brothels. Exhibiting an unspoken feminism in their institutional history, by 1836 they had hired two women to edit the *Advocate* and two other women as agents to tour New England and New York State, explaining the work, organizing auxiliaries, soliciting subscriptions. By 1839 the society had 445 branches and had become a national organization. The House of Refuge that Tappan had abandoned was changed from a place for the conversion of prostitutes to an employment agency for women (most of those women who became prostitutes did so out of economic need) and hired two female missionaries. The women of the executive committee constituted themselves "visitors" and began canvassing assigned districts. By 1837 they were spending so much time visiting that they voted to pay themselves salaries. At first they visited middle- and lower-class homes, fearful of the rich, but by 1838 they began reaching out tentatively to the poor and finally concentrated their efforts there, seeking to get at the root causes behind prostitution. After the Panic of 1837 they became experts concerning slum conditions. In 1841 they hired a woman bookkeeper, in 1843 women typesetters and assemblers, until the organization was staffed entirely by women, a very unusual phenomenon for the age. They were actually doing very much the same kind of thing Jane Addams became famous for pulling together at Hull House half a century later.

In 1847 they founded a Home for the Friendless and a House of Industry, giving shelter to indigent women, offering education, an employment agency, job training, piecework, sewing machine rental, union organizing, an industrial school for children, etc. They published in-depth analyses of public health conditions, housing, milk inspection, and prisons. They forced the city to hire female wardens for female prisoners, and they lobbied for an antiseduction law in 1848 to curb "white slavery." In the 1850s they increasingly defined reform in environmental terms and began to work more directly with children. In 1860 they were renamed the American Female Guardian Society.[39]

An allied effort was the Five Points House of Industry, founded in 1854, mainly through efforts of members of the Ladies Home Missionary Society of the Methodist Episcopal Church. Palmer was a prime mover in this effort. Their initial motivation was the conversion of the poor. Members had been holding Bible classes, Sunday schools, and prayer meetings in the Five Points area since 1843. They wanted to provide a permanent chapel and a resident minister. In May 1850 they hired Louis M. Pease. Together they saw the causes of poverty as intemperance and unemployment, but gradually they came to see drunkenness not as a lack of moral fortitude to be remedied by signing pledges and reading tracts, but as a response to the want and despair of slum life. Pease immediately arranged with a local textile manufacturer to get piecework, and converted his evening prayer meeting room into a sewing shop by day. Like the Female Moral Reform Society, the women of the Five Points Mission also began to concentrate on saving the children, educating them, offering day care, and even adoption. Yet they did not forget the adults. By the 1860s they were providing four thousand hot meals a week to adults.

Carroll Smith-Rosenberg and Keith Melder have both pointed to the feminism inherent in this movement. Says Smith-Rosenberg,

> With such close ties to Finney and his new theology—and the commitment it implied to Christian action—the ladies of the Moral Reform Society occupied an extreme wing in the evangelical movement. They were not content to remain at home, satisfied with educating their children in the ways of piety and with praying for the millennium. Finney's preaching had convinced them that silence in the face of sin amounted to complicity. Like the New York abolitionists—many, of course, Finneyites, . . . they felt themselves unable any longer to compromise with the devil; sin must be assailed wherever and in whatever form it existed.[40]

The Moral Reform movement gave pious, middle-class women permission, and in fact motivation, to move outside the home. It provided them with a journal, written and managed by women, devoted to discussions of immediate interest to them. It offered more than twenty thousand women a significant work to do in ushering in the millennium. Most significantly, however, it functioned somewhat as modern consciousness-raising groups do, to attune women to the injustice oppressing them and to allow them avenues to give vent to the anger that such consciousness engenders. As leadership in the movement passed into female hands, its emphasis moved from the protection of young men, which was Tappan's ideal, to a bold defense of women. The society's war on the double standard and its exposure of men's lechery gave respectable, family-oriented women a means to control men's behavior and an outlet for their hostility toward men. Smith-Rosenberg quotes a letter to the *Advocate* from a rural subscriber, typical of the rage expressed: "They are so passingly mean, so utterly contemptible, as basely and treacherously to contrive . . . the destruction of happiness, peace, morality, and all that is endearing in social life. . . . O let them not be trusted." Even the *Advocate*'s editors sometimes vented their anger: "It makes us indignant that our sex should any longer be imposed upon by men, who pass as gentlemen and yet are guilty of loathsome and disgusting conduct. It is a justice which we owe to each other, to expose their names."[41] Members of the Boston society resolved not to "turn aside to contend with obstacles or opposition. . . . The cause of moral reform involves principles which, if fully and perseveringly applied, will elevate woman to her proper standing in society." In order to do so, sisterhood was essential: "Resolved, that in maintaining the *rights* of women, we will not neglect her appropriate duties, one of the principal of which duties is to guard our daughters, sisters, and female acquaintances from the delusive arts of corrupt and unprincipled men."[42]

The *Advocate of Moral Reform* was one of the few journals Lucy Stone remembered reading as a girl. Undoubtedly other advocates of woman's rights were among its subscribers. At Oberlin Lucy was secretary-treasurer of the Female Moral Reform Society and its leading spirit.[43] Antoinette Brown served on its executive committee.[44] Both Phoebe Palmer and Maggie Van Cott were very much involved in the Five Points Mission. When Brown graduated from Oberlin, she went to New York to work at the mission and was introduced to it by Palmer. They joined in conducting Sunday services there. However, Brown's feminism was too pronounced for the pious Methodist ladies, and she soon severed her connections with the mission, though she eventually spent a year working in the city's slums.[45]

## *On Being Useful*

The women eventually involved in the woman's rights movement were previously active in abolition and temperance. Most were members of other benevolent enterprises as well. They taught Sunday school and regular school. During the Civil War some worked with the Sanitary Commission. All felt the call to be "useful." In the Benevolence Empire they found nourishment for what later blossomed in the woman's movement.

These women were genuinely concerned about conditions that oppressed their fellow human beings. Finneyite revivalism stressed Christians' duty to help others, to reform society. They were motivated by a faith and a fervor that sustained them in the face of difficulty and oppression. The Grimké sisters, for example, fought for their own rights primarily because they felt so deeply compelled to continue their battle against slavery.

Reform work was a permissible way to get out of the house, to invest energies in something other than husband and children, to find meaningful, purposeful work. Not that they were trying to escape family responsibilities, for their devotion to their families was clear, but the Finneyite emphasis on usefulness and reform taught women that their call to serve God extended beyond their doorsteps.

The Benevolence Empire was an invaluable training ground for women. They founded organizations, kept the books, presided at meetings, spoke in public, wrote for journals, engineered petition campaigns, and celebrated substantial victories. The leaders of the woman's movement "served apprenticeship in the reforms which flourished in Western New York. . . . Delayed though it was, this later crusade owed a great deal to the Burned-over District's moral reformation," declares Whitney Cross.[46]

Their consciences were honed by exposure to very real injustice and oppression in a nonthreatening way, since initially they were looking at the oppression of those of another race by those of another region, not their own oppression by their closest relatives.

They found outlets for their own rage and hostility in attacking the problems of society. I have shown how clear this was in the Moral Reform movement. It is equally clear in the rhetoric of Sarah Grimké's *Letters on the Equality of the Sexes* and in the reports of the Boston Female Anti-Slavery Society, to cite only two more examples.

The women mastered sophisticated arguments against social, legal, religious, moral, and political injustice. Schooled in the arguments concerning abolition and temperance, they found it easier to develop cogent defenses of woman's rights.

Finally, the Benevolence Empire provided an arena for confrontation between men and women over issues that were clearly matters of moral consequence, and not simply matters of self-interest. I have detailed the confrontation within the Moral Reform movement. There were innumerable confrontations in the temperance movement—Luther Lee opened his church in Syracuse to a meeting called by Susan B. Anthony and Amelia Bloomer after they were ousted from the men's temperance group. Antoinette Brown, supported by Caroline Severance and Wendell Phillips, created a cause célèbre in 1853 after she was denied the opportunity to thank delegates to the Whole World's Temperance Convention for accepting her credentials from two local societies in Rochester and South Butler. The election of Abby Kelley Foster to a post in the American Anti-Slavery Society was one of the precipitating factors in the split of abolition forces between the New England Garrisonians, who accepted women into full membership and participation, and the New Yorkers, primarily the Tappans, who did not. Of course, the history of the woman's rights movement per se is usually dated from the meeting of Lucretia Mott and Elizabeth Cady Stanton in London in 1840 when Mott and several other woman were denied seats at the World's Anti-Slavery Convention.

In comparison to the confrontations in which many of these women had participated in the male-dominated Benevolence Empire, the confrontations of the early woman's rights conventions were friendly discussions. The women of the Boston Female Anti-Slavery Society had marched through a mob of their rioting townsmen. Angelina Grimké had spoken in Philadelphia with a mob destroying the building around her. Stone and Anthony had everything from fruit to rocks hurled at them. How could mere words hurt? Women who had endured such abuse in other causes could no longer be intimidated. They could stand on their own platforms and return verbal attacks with reasoned arguments.

EIGHT

# "To Touch It Was Contamination"

Angelina Grimké considered woman's rights the root of all other injustices, lying deeper than even the issues of chattel slavery. "The slave may be freed and woman be where she is, but woman cannot be freed and the slave remain where he is," she told Weld.[1] Few, however, realized the radical truth of that assertion and even fewer seemed ready to act on it. Thus the phenomena I have been discussing languished, went underground, turned brackish, and have been overlooked by most historians. The reasons for this are manifold.

## *Life Moves On*

A basic fact of most women's lives has been that they get married, submerge their identities and aspirations behind those of their husbands, have children and concentrate on their rearing, set aside careers outside the home at least until their children are semigrown. None of the early woman's rights leaders except Susan B. Anthony deviated widely from this pattern. Angelina Grimké and Theodore Weld were married on 14 May 1838. Their three children were born in 1839, 1841, and 1844. Angelina suffered at least one miscarriage as well. She was incapacitated, fatigued, and frustrated by childbearing and nursing. By choice or default, most of the child care fell to Sarah. Although some of their ideas about diet simplified cooking, the sisters had full care of the children, the house, the farm, and the meager family finances, particularly while Weld was away in Washington for several congressional sessions. Even their move to the Raritan Bay community did not free the women to work on their favorite causes. For much of their lives both had to teach in various schools to help the family make ends meet. The hiatus between Elizabeth Cady Stanton's resolve to do something about woman's rights at the 1840 World's

Anti-Slavery Convention in London and her call for the 1848 meeting in Seneca Falls may in part be attributed to the birth of three of her five sons and two daughters. Lucy Stone married Henry Blackwell in 1855 and their daughter Alice Stone Blackwell was born in 1857. A second child died shortly after his birth in 1859. Alarmed by a nursemaid's negligent care for Alice, Lucy gave up outside engagements for nearly a decade. Antoinette Brown married another Blackwell brother, Samuel, in 1856, eventually mothering seven children. Despite supportive husbands and domestic help, all of these women had to curtail their public activities to some extent. Susan Anthony protested, reprimanded, and threatened, but her sisters in the movement continued to get married and to have babies. Life moved on.

The Finneys had completed their family of six children by the early 1840s. Lydia Root Andrews died in December 1847. In 1848 Finney married Elizabeth Ford Atkinson, a widow from Rochester, who appears to have been a feminist in her own way. But the Finneys' impact on the Oberlin and New York scenes may have been lessened by the fact that they went off for evangelistic tours of the British Isles from 1849 to 1851 and again from 1858 to 1860. Asa Mahan left Oberlin in 1850. Finney was president from 1850 to 1865, but he was followed by James Fairchild, who was less sympathetic to woman's rights. The Palmers also spent four years in the Old World, 1859 to 1863, during which time the holiness movement in this country took a different direction, becoming more institutionalized and clerical, thus limiting women's participation.

## *The Civil War*

A second factor one cannot overlook is the Civil War's impact, which was profound and complex. Feminists ceased holding national conventions, feeling that demands for woman's rights were inappropriate during this time of national crisis. Many of the women turned their attention and their energies to the war effort, organizing the Women's Loyal National League, and working in the Sanitary Commission. Women in Western society have been schooled since the writing of Genesis that they are to be helpers of men. Millennia of enculturation have made it difficult for women to champion their own rights. The momentum of the abolition movement had acted as an icebreaker ship, propelling women into demanding their own rights in order to help the slaves. As that impetus diminished during and after the war, the woman's movement stalled for a time. Women were told to step back and wait: "This is the Negro's hour." So the Women's Rights Association became the American Equal Rights Association, campaigning for passage of the new constitutional amendments dealing with emancipation.

Women assumed that if they devoted themselves to the war effort they would be rewarded with suffrage as well as other civil rights. When the Fourteenth Amendment containing the word *male* was introduced before Congress in 1866, women began to see how mistaken that assumption was. Whereas before the war women had worked at the state level to seek more rights, they realized that if the Fourteenth Amendment passed, only another constitutional amendment could undo its work in excluding women black and white. Passage of the amendment granting only black men the right to vote also served to focus the subsequent woman's movement on political issues. The country had finally arrived at a purely political solution to the issue of slavery, leaving unresolved economic, social, and even deeper emotional issues. Some women realized this immediately, and Oberlin women like Sallie Holley and Caroline Putnam devoted the rest of their lives to educating freed blacks. But women in general, and particularly those leading the organized women's associations, focused their efforts on a similar political solution to their own quest, one that did little to challenge the underlying patriarchalism of Western culture. This tendency to move in the direction of simplified and superficial solutions robbed the woman's movement, as it had abolitionism, of a certain rigor, energy, and moral power.

It also fragmented the movement through quarrels over ends and means. In many ways the Civil War and the 1860s represented the culmination of a splintering that had been taking place among the Finneyites for several decades. When the river hit the rapids, the rocks channeled it into several divergent streams. Finney had naively believed that Christians should support all reform efforts, and between all that were good and right there would be no conflict of loyalties. Early Finneyites, men like Wheaton College president Jonathan Blanchard and women like Hannah Tracy Cutler, were members of both peace and abolition societies, but eventually the two commitments came into conflict. Finneyites thought they could accomplish abolition through moral persuasion, but some became convinced it would require political action. The division of the abolition movement in 1839 was caused in part by that issue, in larger part by the question of whether or not woman's rights should be included along with the slave's. After the war, the Fourteenth Amendment again forced abolitionists to decide whether they would fight only for the black man's rights or if they would try to include woman's rights. Most opted for the former. The issue eventually split the women's ranks as well. Stanton and Anthony in a semisecret meeting in New York City in 1869 organized their own National Woman Suffrage Association against the American Equal Rights Association. Their group took a stand against passage of the amendment, excluded men from membership, and eventually favored a national constitutional amendment to obtain suffrage. Excluded from the National, such women as Lucy Stone, Julia Ward Howe, and Mary Livermore, along with such men as Henry Blackwell and Methodist editor Gilbert Haven, formed the American Woman Suffrage Association at a convention in Cleveland later that year. The American favored ratification of the Fourteenth Amendment and the Fifteenth, which guaranteed black men the right to vote. Organized on a delegate basis, rather than welcoming all comers at their conventions, they admitted men to membership and even leadership (Haven was president at the 1875 convention). They worked to gain woman's rights at the state level.

### *"Too Much Ridicule and Scorn"*

Ironically, a third factor in the eclipse of the woman's movement centered in certain of Stanton's and Anthony's involvements, which led the cause into scandal and alienated many women. During a tour of Kansas in 1867 in a futile attempt to have woman's suffrage included in the state's constitution, Stanton and Anthony teamed up with the eccentric George Francis Train. In the course of their return trip to New York City, Train proposed putting up the money to publish a journal for them. Since they had harbored such a dream for many years, they jumped at the opportunity. In 1869 Anthony launched *Revolution*. Before a year had elapsed, Train was in a British prison, money for the paper had dried up, and Train's articles on Fenianism and currency questions had given it a reputation that Stanton's views on divorce and Anthony's on labor unions did not help.

The two women were also unwise in embracing the flamboyant Victoria Woodhull and her sister Tennessee Claflin. In January 1871 Woodhull claimed a constitutional right to vote in a masterful speech before a congressional committee. Impressed with her logic and captivated by her forceful personality, Stanton and Anthony invited her to speak to the National Association, meeting in Washington at the time. Although Anthony headed off Woodhull's efforts to take over the organization the next year, it was already stigmatized by her antics, including her bid for the presidency and her views on "free love."

In November 1872 Woodhull opened still another controversy by revealing in *Woodhull & Claflin's Weekly* that a friend of the feminists, Henry Ward Beecher, son of Lyman, noted preacher in his own right and former president of the American Association, had conducted a longtime affair with Elizabeth Tilton, wife of editor, reformer, and politician Theodore Tilton. Both suffrage associations defended Mrs. Tilton, but the American was less tainted by the scandal because it said little about it in the *Woman's Journal*, while Stanton and Anthony lost no occasion to show how the case revealed the law's inequities in regard to women.

As a result, the woman's rights movement became suspect among respectable, middle-class, church-going women. When Frances Willard felt compelled by a religious experience in 1876 to support woman's rights, it was considered "too advanced and radical a thing, connected in those days with too much ridicule and scorn, a thing unwomanly and unscriptural, and to touch it was contamination."[2] When she addressed the issue at the National Woman's Christian Temperance Union convention in Newark, some of her friends wept "at the thought of the ostracism which, from that day to this, has been its sequel."[3] At the close of her speech, the WCTU president, Annie Wittenmyer, a leading Methodist laywoman, whispered, "You might have been a leader, but now you'll be only a scout."[4] Three years later Willard challenged her for the presidency and won, holding the office for the next eighteen years.

Following Willard's speech, Hannah Whitall Smith, Palmer's successor as one of the leaders of the holiness movement and author of the classic *The Christian's Secret of a Happy Life*, found an older woman sobbing. Trying to comfort her, Smith asked the cause of her tears. "Frances Willard just convinced me that I ought to want to vote, and *I don't want to*!" came the reply. Another woman, who may well have been Smith herself, is quoted as saying that she had held aloof from the suffragists for years because of fears for their orthodoxy, but she too now felt duty-bound to join the cause, and so,

> I asked God to gather up my prejudices as a bundle and lay them aside. They remained tangible and tough, but I laid them aside. . . . It came after nights of waking and weeping, for I felt the dear Lord was preparing me for something, and He did not want me to be burdened with that bundle. Now, in Methodist parlance, "my way grows brighter and brighter."[5]

Willard worked diligently to formulate a new line of argumentation supporting woman's rights and gaining the union's endorsement, but it was an uphill fight because of the reputation of the major suffrage associations.

*Shifting Alliances*

A fourth cause of the submerging of the themes I've discussed was the natural institutionalism that seems inevitably to overtake creative, innovative social movements. Finney did not hold any more revivals on the scale of the 1830-31 Rochester campaign after writing his *Lectures on Revivals of Religion* in 1835, the book that became the manual for all subsequent revivalists. The art became stereotyped and ritualized. Evangelists became as professionalized as the settled clergy. The holiness movement also changed from local prayer meetings organized by laypeople to national camp meetings run by professional clergymen and holiness evangelists. The spirit-oriented spontaneity of testimonies gave way to doctrinal polemics.[6] The suffrage movement itself evolved from spontaneous local and national conventions to two competing national organizations with entrenched leaders and conflicting programs.

A fifth factor concerned the changing theological climate within evangelicalism. In the Presbyterian church, the New School was losing vigor and drifting back into reunion with the Old School. Princeton theology was gaining ascendancy, growing ever more "fundamentalistic," dogmatically literal in its interpretation of Scripture, culminating in Charles Hodge's and B. B. Warfield's 1881 affirmation of the Bible's inerrancy "in the original autographs." Revivalists increasingly stressed the personal nature of salvation, omitting the correlate of social reform the Finneyites had stressed. This trend may have also been accelerated by the rise of a pessimistic premillenarianism as opposed to the utopian postmillenarianism of the Finneyites. Finney extolled the efficacy of God's grace to remake the world and exhorted followers to form a perfect society that would become Christ's millennial kingdom. D. L. Moody and many other evangelical Christians in the second half of the nineteenth century, influenced by the "dispensational" speculations of Britisher John Nelson Darby, stressed the sinfulness of the world and looked for instant rescue from it. They expected the world to get worse, not better, and believed that working for improved social conditions might actually delay Christ's coming. Their social efforts tended to be individualistic—rescue missions, homes for unwed mothers, etc. Some of the energy that had formerly gone into revivals was channeled into Bible prophecy conferences that sprang up in the 1880s.

Events themselves may also have tempered the optimism of the postmillennial vision. The world was not converted to abolition and the bloodbath that Finney predicted as the alternative came. Men and even some women were not immediately impressed with the justice of woman's rights, did not experience conversion to the cause, or hasten to implement the situation in which there is neither male nor female in Christ. And even the advances that were made did not solve underlying problems. Despite emancipation and political rights, blacks still needed education and economic aid, among other things. The millennium, a "Christian America" (read "Protestant"), just did not appear, despite the hard work of the Finneyites. Christ might have to come and set up the kingdom himself. Perhaps symbolic of this point is the fact that after winning the vote for women in England, suffragist Cristabel Pankhurst became a lecturer and writer in that country and this on premillennial topics.

## *The River Flows On*

Though one may speak of the woman's movement as submerging for a time, particularly among evangelical church people, the assertion is actually misleading because the movement toward greater freedom and opportunity for women progressed steadily in certain areas of the church even though after the 1850s it diverged somewhat from the public and more well-documented woman's *suffrage* movement. Donald W. Dayton and Lucille Sider Dayton have pointed to this fact.

Those groups most strongly rooted in the revivalist and abolitionist tradition maintained a feminist stance, as did those in the holiness movement. The Wesleyan Methodists have always ordained women. Although the Free Methodists did not fully ordain women until 1974, their founder B. T. Roberts wrote one of the most radically egalitarian defenses of woman's rights in 1891, *Ordaining Women*. Another of the church's bishops raised the same issues in an 1894 volume titled *Why Not? A Plea for the Ordination of Those Women Whom God Has Called to Preach the Gospel* (published by the denominational publishing house). Baptist A. J. Gordon, founder of what has become Gordon College and Gordon-Conwell Theological Seminary in Massachusetts, was "bred in the strictest sect of the abolitionists." He advocated women's "complete enfranchisement and their entrance into every political and social privilege enjoyed by men."[7] Abolitionist and Methodist editor-bishop Gilbert Haven continued to be an outspoken proponent of woman's rights until his death. Bishop Matthew Simpson and many other Methodist ministers also support the woman's cause.[8]

As the holiness movement became institutionalized into denominations, they allowed women more freedom than any other branch of the church. When the Church of God (Anderson, Indiana) emerged in the 1880s, as many as 25 percent of its ministers were women. "Forty years before the time of the woman's suffrage on a national level," said church historian John Smith, "a great company of women were preaching, singing, writing, and helping to determine the policies in this religious reform movement." In fact, he wagered "that no other movement, either religious or secular, in this period of American history, except the suffrage movement itself, had such a high percentage of women leaders whose contribution was so outstanding."[9] The first constitution of the Church of the Nazarene in 1894 specifically provided for the right of women to preach. In fact, one whole conference in west Tennessee had only women ministers for a time. In 1905 the church published *Women Preachers*, which contained the testimonies of a dozen such women. The Pilgrim Holiness Church had as many as 30 percent women ministers in its early days. The small Pillar of Fire denomination was founded by a woman, Alma White, the wife of a Methodist Episcopal minister. Consecrated bishop by her denomination, she claimed to be the first woman to hold that office in Christian history. Ardently feminist, she titled her periodical *Woman's Chains*. Among other things it published biting cartoons depicting woman's plight. Of course, the Salvation Army never totally departed from the feminist stance of its mother Catherine Booth. Her daughter Evangeline became general of the international organization in 1934.

The clearest channel for the continuation of the confluence of Finneyite, Arminian, evangelical revivalism, and feminism is found in the life of Frances Willard. Descended from two presidents of Harvard, she was born 28 September 1839 in Churchville, near Rochester. Her father longed to be a minister and in the autumn of 1841 the family migrated to Oberlin. Both parents enrolled in the college and the family joined the Congregational church that Finney pastored. Like the young women students at Oberlin during that decade, one of Frances's most vivid memories was of the frightfully thundering sermons of Finney, warning sinners of their fate. But she also remembered Lucy Stone, and perhaps the women students' debate class in the woods. In 1846 the family was compelled by father Josiah's health to move on to Wisconsin. Through the influence of a Methodist circuit rider, the family changed denominational loyalties and Frances eventually enrolled in the church's North Western Female College in Evanston, Illinois. During a revival meeting held by "Dr. and Mrs. Phoebe Palmer" in 1866, she experienced assurance of sanctification.[10] After a career of teaching (she became the first American woman college president of her alma mater for one year, and was the first dean of women at Northwestern University), church fund-raiser, and evangelist with D. L. Moody, she became the leader of the WCTU. In 1880 she secured its endorsement of her Home Protection Ballot, in 1882 she inaugurated a Franchise Department, and in 1883 the Union endorsed an equal suffrage plank. Throughout the decade, Willard and the Union worked to secure woman's suffrage on local and state levels, first on the issue of liquor laws, then on educational matters. She also worked to get the major political parties to endorse suffrage and to build new parties, primarily the Prohibitionists and the Populists, which would fight for woman's suffrage as one of their major goals. She all the while maintained a running battle with the Methodist Church, becoming in 1888 one of the first women elected as a delegate to its General Conference. The women were denied the right to take their seats.

Biographer Mary Earhart suggests that Willard successfully rallied grass roots women to the suffrage cause while the national suffrage associations were in a period of complete disarray because of her "astute analysis of human nature and public opinion. . . . Mrs. Stanton based her futile arguments on reason, Miss Willard based her appeals on emotion." She knew that "the vast majority of women were interested in just two things—their homes and their church. Of all the women-leaders of that period, she alone had the imagination to see that any reform movement which would enlist the women must be associated with these two special institutions."[11] In the Finney tradition, Willard convinced women that fighting for suffrage was not a selfish "right," but a matter of Christian duty. "Not rights, but duties; not her need alone, but that of her children and her country; not the 'woman,' but the 'human' question is stirring women's hearts and breaking down their prejudices today."[12] She quoted a granddaughter of Jonathan Edwards, "a woman with no toleration toward the Suffrage Movement," as saying: "If, with the ballot in our hands, we can, as I firmly believe, put down this awful traffic, I am ready to lead the women of my town to the polls, as I have often led them to the rum shops." Women believed, said Willard, that "as God led us into this work by way of the saloon, He will lead us out by way of the ballot. We have never prayed more earnestly over the one than we will over the other. One was the Wilderness, the other is the Promised Land."[13] The language echoes the postmillennial optimism of the Finneyites. Willard firmly believed that "man and woman have been steadily traveling back to Eden."

> Under the curse, man has mapped out the state as his largest sphere, and the home as woman's largest; under the blessing, men and women shall map out home as the one true state, and she who, during centuries of training, has learned how to govern there, shall help man make the great, cold, heartless state a warm, kind and protecting home. The White Ribbon women are tired of this unnatural two worlds in one, where men and women dwell apart; they would invade the solitude of the masculine intellect, break in upon the stereotyped routine of the masculine hierarchy in church and state; and ring out in clear but gentle voices the oft-repeated declaration of the Master whom they serve: "Behold, I make all things new."[14]

Willard not only formulated the arguments that eventually proved successful in motivating the mass of women, but she also trained the leaders. She was a master of strategy and a charismatic leader who knew how to delegate authority. Superintendents of the Franchise Department included Mary Livermore, Anna Howard Shaw, and Alice Stone Blackwell. It was Alice who brought the divided woman's suffrage movement together again in 1889-90, and it was Anna Howard Shaw, Methodist Protestant minister and medical doctor, who served as superintendent of the Franchise Department from 1888-92, vice president of the National American Woman Suffrage Association under Anthony from 1892-1904, and as its president from 1904-15.

The more theological side of the struggle was continued in this century by another Willard lieutenant, Katharine C. Bushnell. One might call her the successor to Antoinette Brown. Bushnell, an Illinois native, was a member of the first medical class of Northwestern University in 1879. She became a Methodist missionary to China for several years, founding an infants' hospital. Upon her return she became a friend of Willard, an evangelist for the WCTU, and eventually a carrier of its Polyglot Petition against alcohol and narcotics to England. While investigating vice and narcotics traffic in the Empire, she still found time to translate into English one of the oldest known Latin Bibles, for which she was decorated by the British government. She also began writing a series of Bible studies on "problem passages" concerning women, which she eventually published as ***God's Word to Women: One Hundred Bible Studies on Woman's Place in the Divine Economy***. A. J. Gordon's daughter, who lives on Cape Cod, still reads from a Bible laced with "interleaves," which

Bushnell put out to help evangelical women and men understand Scripture in a less sexist way than it has been traditionally interpreted.

Thus the river of feminism that sprang from Finneyite revivalism has never disappeared into the sands of some secular desert, though it has for the most part meandered far from the political groups that most people have identified as the "woman's movement." The two streams parted toward the end of the 1860s, then reunited for a time under Frances Willard and Anna Howard Shaw in the 1880s and 1900s. Once women achieved the right to vote in 1920, the woman's movement on all levels seemed to languish, though women made further progress in many areas of society.

The movement became visible again when what are now called "mainline denominations," the nineteenth century's "evangelical empire," began granting full ordination to women in the 1950s: the United Presbyterian Church and the Methodist Church in 1956. Journalists invariably perpetuate the myth that this was a great breakthrough for women, unparalleled in history, when in fact holiness denominations continue to ordain women as they have always done. Despite a sharp decline in the number of women ministers ordained in these groups in the 1940s and 1950s, they still have a higher percentage of women ministers than any of the more "liberal" denominations (6 percent among the Nazarenes as compared to 1 percent among United Methodists).

The "women's liberation movement" began to get headlines only after it emerged from the black civil rights struggles in the early 1960s and the publication of Betty Friedan's *The Feminine Mystique* in 1963. Today's conservative evangelical women are slowly coming to realize that the stream is theirs too, with the Daytons' work, the publication of *All We're Meant to Be*, which I coauthored with Letha Scanzoni, and the formation of the Evangelical Women's Caucus.

The river flows steadily onward.

# Notes

## INTRODUCTION

1. Harriet H. Robinson, *Massachusetts in the Woman Suffrage Movement* (Boston: Roberts Brothers, 1881), p. 17.
2. Alice Rossi, *The Feminist Papers* (New York: Bantam Books, 1973), pp. 250-52. For a detailed discussion of the shift in women's roles see Elizabeth Anthony Dexter, *Career Women of America 1776-1840* (Francestown, N.H.: Marshall Jones Company, 1950).
3. James H. Fairchild, *Moral Philosophy or, The Science of Obligation* (New York: Sheldon & Company, 1869), p. 252.
4. Catharine E. Beecher, *An Essay on Slavery and Abolitionism, with Reference to the Duty of American Females* (Philadelphia: Henry Perkins, 1837; reprint ed., Freeport, N.Y.: Books for Libraries Press, 1970), p. 99.
5. Justin Dewey Fulton, *Woman as God Made Her; the True Woman* (Boston: Lee and Shepard, 1869), p. 51.
6. Barbara Welter, "The Cult of True Womanhood: 1820-1860," *American Quarterly* 18 (Summer 1966):152.
7. Barbara Welter, "The Feminization of American Religion: 1800-1860," in William L. O'Neill, ed., *Insights and Parallels: Problems and Issues of American Social History* (Minneapolis: Burgess Publishing Company, 1973), pp. 305-32. Also reprinted in Mary Hartman and Lois W. Banner, eds., *Clio's Consciousness Raised* (New York: Harper & Row, 1974), pp. 137-57.
8. Beecher, *Essay on Slavery*, pp. 101-2.
9. Fulton, *Woman as God Made Her*, p. 6. R. W. Hogeland, "'The Female Appendage': Feminine Life-Styles in America, 1820-1860," *Civil War History* 17 (June 1971):101-14, offers a more detailed categorization of men's definitions of woman's sphere: (1) "Ornamental Womanhood," the most restrictive and conservative, held by such Old School stalwarts as Charles Hodge, which relegated women to peripheral ornaments supporting men's achievements; (2) "Romanticized Womanhood," or Barbara Welter's "Cult of True Womanhood," touted by the Beechers and the ladies' magazines, which made women the keepers of the sanctuary; (3) "Evangelical Womanhood," "derivative of the reform impulse associated with such figures as Charles Finney, Theodore Weld," which encouraged women to struggle for moral justice but denied them any positions of authority; and (4) "Radical Womanhood," held mostly by Unitarian

clergy such as Samuel J. May and Thomas Wentworth Higginson, which gave women more equality in leadership because woman's role was the "moral refinement of the race," i.e., the betterment of man's lot.

10. John L. Hammond, "Revival Religion and Antislavery Politics," *American Sociological Review* 39 (April 1974):175-86.
11. Rossi, *Feminist Papers*, pp. 6, 249.
12. Beverly Harrison, "The Early Feminists and the Clergy: A Case Study in the Dynamics of Secularization," *Review and Expositor* 72 (Winter 1975):45, 46.
13. Donald W. Dayton, *Discovering an Evangelical Heritage* (New York: Harper & Row, Publishers, 1976), pp. 85-86. This represents an expansion of Donald W. Dayton and Lucille Sider Dayton, "Recovering a Heritage: Part II. Evangelical Feminism," *Post-American*, August-September 1974, pp. 7-9.
14. Robinson, *Massachusetts*, p. 27.

## CHAPTER ONE

1. Richard Hofstadter, *Anti-Intellectualism in American Life* (New York: Alfred A. Knopf, 1966), p. 92.
2. Charles G. Finney, *Memoirs of Rev. Charles G. Finney* (New York: A.S. Barnes & Company, 1876); George Frederick Wright, *Charles Grandison Finney* (Boston: Houghton, Mifflin and Company, 1893); James E. Johnson, "The Life of Charles Grandison Finney" (Ph.D. dissertation, Syracuse University, 1959), hereafter designated Johnson dissertation; James E. Johnson, "The Life of Charles Grandison Finney" (manuscript, 1975) hereafter designated Johnson book.
3. Finney, *Memoirs*, pp. 18, 12, 18.
4. Ibid., p. 7.
5. Benjamin P. Thomas, *Theodore Weld: Crusader for Freedom* (New Brunswick, N.J.: Rutgers University Press, 1950); Gilbert H. Barnes and Dwight L. Dumond., eds., *Letters of Theodore Dwight Weld, Angelina Grimké Weld and Sarah Grimké, 1822-44* (New York: Appleton-Century-Crofts, 1934; reprint ed., Gloucester, Mass.: Peter Smith, 1965); Gilbert Hobbs Barnes, *The Anti-Slavery Impulse 1830-1844* (1933; reprint ed., New York: Harcourt, Brace & World, Inc., 1964).
6. D. Dayton, *Discovering*, p. 27.
7. Weld to A. and S. Grimké, New York, 26 August 1837, Barnes and Dumond, *Letters*, 1:432-33.
8. Ella Giles Ruddy, ed., *The Mother of Clubs* (Los Angeles: Baumgardt Publishing Co., 1906), p. 55.
9. Ibid.
10. Ibid.
11. Elizabeth Cady Stanton, *Eighty Years and More* (New York: European Publishing Company, 1898; reprint ed., New York: Schocken Books, 1971;

Theodore Stanton and Harriot Stanton Blatch, eds., *Elizabeth Cady Stanton as Revealed in Her Letters, Diary, and Reminiscences* (New York: Harper Brothers, Publishers, 1922; reprint ed., New York; Arno Press, 1969); Alma Lutz, *Created Equal: a Biography of Elizabeth Cady Stanton, 1815-1902* (New York: J. Day, 1940).

12. Stanton, *Eighty Years*, p. 21.
13. Ibid., pp. 41, 43.
14. Finney, *Memoirs*, pp. 214, 220.
15. Lewis Tappan, *The Life of Arthur Tappan* (New York: Hurd and Houghton, 1870); Bertram Wyatt-Brown, *Lewis Tappan and the Evangelical War Against Slavery* (Cleveland: The Press of Case Western Reserve University, 1969).
16. Finney, *Memoirs*, pp. 280-81.
17. Ibid., pp. 300-301.
18. Henry Brewster Stanton, *Random Recollections* (New York, 1882).
19. Mrs. Claude Gilson, "Antoinette Brown Blackwell: The First Woman Minister," Blackwell Family Papers, Radcliffe College, Schlesinger Library, Cambridge, Mass. (This typewritten manuscript was made from notes on conversations with Antoinette Brown Blackwell in 1909; it compares so closely with Brown's own notes for an autobiography, contained in the same collection, that it can be regarded as autobiographical); Laura Kerr, *Lady in the Pulpit* (New York: Woman's Press, 1951); Elinor Rice Hays, *Those Extraordinary Blackwells* (New York: Harcourt, Brace & World, Inc., 1967).
20. Information on her life can be found in Edward T. James, ed., *Notable American Women 1607-1950*, 3 vols. (Cambridge, Mass.: The Belknap Press of Harvard University Press, 1971); Elizabeth Cady Stanton, et al., *History of Woman Suffrage*, 6 vols. (New York: Fowler & Wells, 1881), 1:283-89, hereafter cited as *HWS*.
21. *Notable American Woman*, s.v. "Davis, Paulina Kellogg Wright," by Alice Felt Tyler.
22. Finney, *Memoirs*, p. 315.
23. Barnes and Dumond, *Letters*; Catherine H. Birney, *The Grimké Sisters* (Boston: Lee and Shepard, 1885; reprint ed., Westport, Conn.: Greenwood Press, 1970); Gerda Lerner, *The Grimké Sisters from South Carolina: Rebels Against Slavery* (Boston: Houghton Mifflin, 1967; reprint ed., New York: Schocken Books, 1967); Katharine DuPre Lumpkin, *The Emancipation of Angelina Grimké* (Chapel Hill: The University of North Carolina Press, 1974); Weld Family Papers, William L. Clements Library, University of Michigan, Ann Arbor, Mich.
24. Lerner, *Grimké Sisters*, p. 40; Sarah Grimké, "Religious Feelings," 3 June 1827, pp. 2-5, Weld Family Papers.
25. A. Grimké to Jane Smith, New York, 10 August 1837, Weld Family Papers.
26. Asa Mahan, *Autobiography: Intellectual, Moral and Spiritual* (London: T. Woolmer, 1882); Barbara Brown Zikmund, "Asa Mahan and Oberlin Perfectionism," (Ph.D. dissertation, Duke University, 1969).
27. Mahan, *Autobiography*, pp. 2, 5.

28. Finney, *Memoirs*, p. 340.
29. Richard Wheatley, *The Life and Letters of Mrs. Phoebe Palmer* (New York: W.C. Palmer, Jr., Publisher, 1876); John A. Roche, *The Life of Mrs. Sarah A. Lankford Palmer* (New York: George Hughes & Co., 1898); George Hughes, *Fragrant Memories of the Tuesday Meeting and "The Guide to Holiness," and Their Fifty Years' Work for Jesus* (New York; Palmer & Hughes, 1886); George Hughes, *The Beloved Physician, Walter C. Palmer, M.D.* (New York: Palmer & Hughes, 1884); Melvin Easterday Dieter, "Revivalism and Holiness," (Ph.D. dissertation, Temple University, 1972).
30. Phoebe Palmer, ed., "Gracious Revivings," *Guide to Holiness* 33 (January 1858):10.
31. Mary Mahan to Weld, Oberlin, 21 February 1836, Weld Family Papers.
32. Finney, *Memoirs*, p. 375.
33. Ibid., p. 169.
34. Gilson, "Antoinette Brown Blackwell," pp. 52, 88.
35. Oberlin finally awarded Brown an honorary A.M. in 1878 and a D.D. in 1908.
36. Alice Stone Blackwell, *Lucy Stone: Pioneer of Woman's Rights* (Boston: Alice Stone Blackwell Committee, 1930); Elinor Rice Hays, *Morning Star: A Biography of Lucy Stone, 1818-1893* (New York: Harcourt, Brace & World, Inc., 1961).
37. Hays, *Morning Star*, p. 33.
38. John White Chadwick, *A Life for Liberty: Anti-Slavery and Other Letters of Sallie Holley* (New York, 1899).
39. Hannah Maria Conant Tracy Cutler, "Autobiography," *Woman's Journal*, 19 September to 17 October 1896.
40. *HWS*, 1:110.
41. Finney, *Memoirs*, pp. 401, 412-13.
42. Ibid., p. 421.
43. Luther Lee, *Autobiography* (New York: Phillips & Hunt, 1882); Luther Lee, *Five Sermons and A Tract by Luther Lee*, Donald W. Dayton, ed. (Chicago: Holrad House, 1975); "Rev. Luther Lee, D.D.," *The Ladies Repository* 30 (September 1870):209-12.
44. Ida Husted Harper, *The Life and Work of Susan B. Anthony*, 3 vols. (Indianapolis: The Bowen-Merrill Company, 1899, 1898, 1908); Rheta Childe Dorr, *Susan B. Anthony: The Woman Who Changed the Mind of a Nation* (New York: Stokes, 1928; reprint ed., AMS Press, 1970); Katharine Susan Anthony, *Susan B. Anthony: Her Personal History and Her Era* (New York: Doubleday, 1954); Alma Lutz, *Susan B. Anthony: Rebel, Crusader, Humanitarian* (Boston: Beacon Press, 1959).
45. Dexter C. Bloomer, *Life and Writings of Amelia Bloomer* (Boston: Arena Publishing Co., 1895; reprint ed., New York: Schocken Books, 1975).
46. Samuel Joseph May, *Memoir* (Boston: Roberts Brothers, 1873).
47. Samuel Joseph May, *Some Recollections of the Antislavery Conflict* (Boston: Fields, Osgood & Co., 1869), pp. 234-35, as quoted in Lerner, *Grimké Sisters*, p. 197.

48. Finney, *Memoirs*, p. 443.
49. Ibid., p. 444.
50. Catherine Booth, *Female Ministry* (London: Morgan & Chase, n.d.; reprint ed., New York: The Salvation Army Supplies Printing and Publishing Department, 1975). "All the controversial portions have been expunged," according to the London edition, which all copies in this country appear to follow.
51. The Palmers' friends included editor and Bishop Gilbert Haven and Bishop Matthew Simpson in the Methodist Epsicopal Church, and B. T. Roberts, one of the founders of the Free Methodist denomination, all outspoken supporters of woman's rights.
52. Wheatly, *Palmer*, p. 442, 446; *Guide to Holiness*, 3 September 1867, pp. 87-88.
53. *HWS*, 2:756-60.

## CHAPTER TWO

1. Lucy Aiken to William Ellery Channing, 26 December 1828 in Anna Letitia Le Breton, ed., *Correspondence of William Ellery Channing. D.D., and Lucy Aiken from 1826-1842* (Boston, 1874), as quoted in Wyatt-Brown, *Lewis Tappan*, p.60.
2. Gerald O. McCulloh, ed., *Man's Faith and Freedom: The Theological Influence of Jacobus Arminius* (New York: Abingdon Press, 1962), p. 28.
3. See Owen Chadwick, *The Reformation* (Harmondsworth, England: Penguin Books, 1964), pp. 211-47.
4. Sydney E. Ahlstrom, *A Religious History of the American People* (New Haven: Yale University Press, 1972), p. 388.
5. Ingvar Haddal, *John Wesley* (New York: Abingdon Press, 1961), p. 11.
6. Hildrie Shelton Smith, *Changing Conceptions of Original Sin* (New York: Charles Scribner's Sons, 1955), p. 18. My discussion of the theological shift in nineteenth-century Calvinism is indebted to Smith.
7. Antoinette Brown's church in South Butler illustrated the point. She reported that it had formerly belonged to the presbytery, but "leading members had become liberalized so much that they withdrew and became congregational," Gilson, "Antoinette Brown Blackwell," p. 167. The "liberalizing" was usually both in theological terms and in independence. Brown's congregation was heavily abolitionist.
8. Charles Hodge, *Semi-Centennial Commemoration of the Professorship of Rev. Charles Hodge . . .* (New York, 1872), p. 52, as cited in Ronald W. Hogeland, "Charles Hodge, The Association of Gentlemen and Ornamental Womanhood: 1825-1855," *Journal of Presbyterian History* 53 (Fall 1975): 241.
9. In 1837 the Presbyterian General Assembly, controlled by the Old School conservatives, read out of the denomination on charges of heresy four synods predominately in upstate New York and the Western Reserve, which eventually included 533 churches and more than 100,000 members. They also dismantled the Benevolence Empire by decreeing that henceforth Presbyterians would work

only within their own denominational agencies. See Melvin L. Vulgamore, "Social Reform in the Theology of Charles Grandison Finney" (Ph.D. dissertation, Boston University, 1963), p. 36.

10. Garth Mervin Rosell, "Charles Grandison Finney and the Rise of the Benevolence Empire" (Ph.D. dissertation, University of Minnesota, 1971), p. 95.
11. Finney, *Memoirs*, p. 241.
12. Sydney Ahlstrom, *Theology in America* (New York: The Bobbs-Merrill Company, Inc., 1967), p. 43.
13. H.S. Smith, *Changing Conceptions*, p. 106.
14. James E. Johnson, "Charles G. Finney and a Theology of Revivalism," *Church History* 38 (September 1969): 341.
15. Charles G. Finney, *Lectures on Revivals of Religion*, ed. William G. McLoughlin (Cambridge, Mass.: The Belknap Press of Harvard University Press, 1960), p.15, defines a revival as "the return of the church from her backslidings, and in the conversion of sinners."
16. Bernard Weisberger, *They Gathered at the River* (Boston: Little, Brown and Company, 1958), p. 83.
17. Charles G. Finney, *Lectures on Systematic Theology, Embracing Lectures on Moral Government* (Oberlin: James M. Fitch; Boston: Crocker & Brewster; New York: Saxton & Miles, 1846), includes thirty lectures on "Moral Government" out of a total of forty-four.
18. Johnson, "Theology of Revivalism," p. 340, notes that Finney may have spent a night at Taylor's home, but no one has proved a direct theological influence of Taylor on Finney.
19. Finney, *Memoirs*, p. 7.
20. John Mattson, "Charles Grandison Finney and the Emerging Tradition of 'New Measures' Revivalism" (Ph.D. dissertation, University of North Carolina, 1970), argues for the influence of his legal studies on Finney's theology.
21. Finney, *Lectures on Revivals*, pp. 178, 188.
22. Rosell, "Benevolence Empire," p. 103; Eric Nelson Newberg, "The Civil War in Zion: Charles Grandison Finney and the Popularization of American Protestantism during the Second Great Awakening, 1795-1835" (draft of Master's thesis, Pacific School of Religion, 1974), p. 61.
23. Newberg, "Civil War," p. 63; Mattson, "Emerging Tradition," p. 166.
24. Finney, *Lectures on Revivals*, p. 207.
25. Ibid., pp. 108, 316, 318.
26. Charles G. Finney, *Lectures on Systematic Theology* (Grand Rapids: William B. Eerdmans, Publishing, 1951), p. 247, as quoted in Vulgamore, "Social Reform," p. 86.
27. Finney, *Lectures on Revivals*, p.40.
28. Ibid., pp. 207-9, 107-8, 372, 374.
29. Charles G. Finney, *A Sermon Preached in the Presbyterian Church at Troy, March 4, 1827* (Troy: Tuttle and Richards, 1827), pp. 14-15, as quoted in Rosell, "Benevolence Empire," p. 112.

30. Wright, *Charles Grandison Finney*, p. 318.
31. Asa Mahan, *Scripture Doctrine of Christian Perfection* (Boston: D. S. King, 1839), p. 188, as quoted in Donald W. Dayton, "Asa Mahan and the Development of American Holiness Theology," October 1973, p. 3, (mimeographed). See also Mahan, *Christian Perfection*, p. 232, and Donald W. Dayton, "Asa Mahan and the Development of American Holiness Theology," *Wesleyan Theological Journal* 9 (Spring 1974):60-69.
32. Zikmund, "Asa Mahan," pp. 113-14; Mahan, *Autobiography*, pp. 322-24.
33. Zikmund, "Asa Mahan," p. 118.
34. Asa Mahan, *Out of Darkness into Light* (New York: Willard Tract Repository, 1876), p. 135, quoted in Zikmund, "Asa Mahan," p. 122.
35. Finney, *Memoirs*, pp. 347, 373-78; Wright, *Finney*, pp. 203, 207; Johnson book, pp. 216-17. In his final striving to attain perfection, Finney, like so many others, struggled to commit his spouse to God. Lydia was sick at the time and Finney could not give her over to God's will. But finally he was able to do so and attained peace. Finney's language in describing his struggle is remarkably similar to Palmer's. He speaks of "laying" his wife "upon the altar of God," *Memoirs*, p. 375.
36. The first issue of the *Guide to Christian Perfection* was issued in Boston in July 1839 with Timothy Merritt as editor. In 1843 it was retitled *Guide to Holiness*. In 1853 the *Beauty of Holiness* appeared in Delaware, Ohio. In 1864 the Palmers bought the two periodicals and merged them.
37. Mahan's *Scripture Doctrine of Christian Perfection* was published by D. S. King, publishing partner of Timothy Merritt, who quoted from the book in the first issue of the *Guide to Christian Perfection*.
38. Zikmund, "Asa Mahan," p. 142.
39. Charles G. Finney, *Lectures to Professing Christians* (New York: Fleming H. Revell Company, 1878), pp. 340-41.
40. Zikmund, "Asa Mahan," p. iv.
41. Several conferences were held to try and reconcile opposing camps. Significantly, the first was held in July 1841 in Rochester and the next year two were held in Buffalo and LeRoy, New York. See Ibid., p. 168.
42. The Oberlin Perfectionists drew philosophically on Scottish Common Sense Realism.
43. *Methodist Quarterly Review* 23 (April 1841): 307-8, as quoted in Dayton, "Asa Mahan" (mimeographed), p. 4.
44. Wheatley, *Palmer*, p. 251.
45. Ibid., p. 509.
46. Phoebe Palmer, *The Way of Holiness* (New York: Foster & Palmer, Jr., 1867), p. 63. This is the fiftieth American edition and contains endorsements to the second edition from Asa Mahan, as printed in the *Oberlin Evangelist*, on p. 8.
47. Roche, *Sarah Lankford Palmer*, p. 261.
48. Palmer, *Way of Holiness*, p. 34.

49. Dr. and Mrs. Palmer, *Four Years in the Old World* (New York: Walter C. Palmer, Jr., Publisher, 1870), pp. 56-57.
50. Angelina Grimké, Diary, 30 October 1827, Weld Family Papers.
51. Ibid.
52. A. Grimké, Diary, 23 February 1828, Weld Family Papers.
53. A. Grimké to Jane Smith, 8 August 1840, Weld Family Papers. Her language here showed that she preferred Finney's formulation of the doctrine to that of Wesley.
54. A. Grimké to Jane Smith, 15 March 1843, Weld Family Papers.
55. Lucy Stone to Bowman Stone, 28 June 1840, as quoted in Blackwell, *Lucy Stone*, p. 39.
56. Wheatley, *Palmer*, p. 67.
57. Ibid., p. 205.
58. Weisberger, *They Gathered*, p. 69.
59. *Oberlin Evangelist* 1 (1 November 1838):8, as quoted in Zikmund, "Asa Mahan," p. 130, n.
60. *Beauty of Holiness* 8 (December 1857):365, as quoted in Dieter, "Revivalism and Holiness," p. 47.
61. Charles G. Finney, "Letters to Ministers of the Gospel of All Denominations," *Guide to Holiness* 28 (December 1855):167.
62. Angelina Grimké, "Marriage," pp. 21-22, Weld Family Papers.
63. Robinson, *Massachusetts*, pp. 209-10.
64. A. Grimké to Jane Smith, 10 August 1837, Weld Family Papers, as quoted in Lumpkin, *Emancipation*, p. 120.
65. Palmer, *Promise*, pp. 52, 271, 328.
66. "Woman in the Church," *Guide to Holiness* 8 (June 1869):191, reprinted from the *Pittsburgh Christian Advocate*.
67. Eunice Cobb, "Letter from Marengo," *Guide to Christian Perfection* 44 (November 1863):142. See Mary Weems Chapman, *Mother Cobb, or Sixty Years' Walk with God* (Chicago: T. B. Arnold, Publisher, 1896). Mother Cobb (1793-1877) was born Eunice Parsons on 13 February 1793 in Litchfield, Connecticut. Her father was a merchant-tailor of no religious persuasion and her mother a Universalist. When she was fourteen, her father died and the family moved to Cazenovia, New York, where at age twenty-four she joined the Presbyterian church. At twenty-five she married a prosperous businessman, Whitman Cobb. When the Methodists began holding meetings in Cazenovia she became interested and finally joined their church. At age thirty she was sanctified and felt called to wear only blue calico, which disturbed her fellow Methodists who were by now very prosperous, to the point of even renting a few pews. In protest the Cobbs migrated first to Laporte County, Indiana, and then to Marengo, Illinois, where Mother Cobb became well known as an itinerant exhorter. Although she was in sympathy with the Free Methodist Church and is regarded as one of their patron saints, she remained a Methodist. She died in Marengo on 3 January 1877.

# CHAPTER THREE

1. Stanton, *Eighty Years*, pp. 41-42.
2. Ruddy, *Mother of Clubs*, pp. 55-56.
3. Gilson, "Antoinette Brown Blackwell," p. 49.
4. Phoebe Palmer, "The New Year," editorial, *Guide to Holiness* 47 (January 1865):14.
5. William McLoughlin, *Modern Revivalism* (New York: The Ronald Press Company, 1959), p. 36; Finney, *Lectures on Revivals*, pp. xix-xx.
6. Hogeland, "Charles Hodge," pp. 245-46.
7. Finney, *Memoirs*, p. 7.
8. *Report of the Boston Female Anti-Slavery Society* (Boston: Published by the Society, Isaac Knapp, Printer, 1836), p. 75.
9. Sarah M. Grimké, *Letters on the Equality of the Sexes and the Condition of Woman* (1838; reprint ed., New York: Burt Franklin, 1970), p. 8.
10. Ibid., p. 9.
11. Ibid., p. 117.
12. Angelina E. Grimké, *Letters to Catherine E. Beecher, in Reply to an Essay on Slavery and Abolitionism* (Boston: Isaac Knapp, 1838), pp. 114-15, 118. See also Grimké to Jane Smith, 10 August 1837, Weld Family Papers.
13. Finney, *Lectures on Revivals*, p. 287.
14. *Proceedings of the National Woman's Rights Convention, held at Cleveland, Ohio, on . . . October 5th, 6th, & 7th, 1853* (Cleveland: Gray, Beardsley, Spear, & Co., 1854), pp. 123-24.
15. *Report, Boston Female*, pp. 50, 52.
16. Mary A. Livermore, *The Story of My Life or The Sunshine and Shadow of Seventy Years* (Hartford, Conn.: A. D. Worthington & Co., Publishers, 1897), pp. 130-42. The Rice family attended the First Baptist Church of Boston, staunchly Calvinist. Livermore comments:

> Undoubtedly, I often received impressions that my religious instructors did not intend to give. But in some way, I had come to regard God as only a judge, who tried human beings, condemned or acquitted them, and sent them to reward or punishment. But Jesus Christ, the beloved Son of God, loved the world so much that he died to save it, and he would save everybody if he could. To this forgiving, loving, all-befriending Saviour would I pray; and I ceased addressing my prayers night and morning to God, and instead of beginning my petitions, "Our Father who art in heaven," I addressed them to "Our Jesus who art in heaven." My father became aware of this and sought to change my custom. But he only succeeded when I was required to pray aloud in his presence. In his absence I continued to address my prayers to Jesus. My mother never condemned me for it. Once

she said, "God the Father is good and to be loved as well as Jesus Christ. He doesn't want any one to be lost." p. 60

17. *Notable American Women*, s.v. "Paulina Kellogg Wright Davis," by Alice Felt Tyler.
18. Stanton, *Eighty Years*, p. 43. In reading Stanton's remarks, as well as those of many of the other women I discuss, one must remember that usually they represent the perspective of at least half a century after the events. One must also remember that few of the women other than Antoinette Brown were really aware of the theological shifts taking place. Nor do people always recognize the factors that brought them to where they now are.
19. Ibid., pp. 24-25.
20. Gilson, "Antoinette Brown Blackwell," p. 66.
21. Blackwell, *Lucy Stone*, p. 59. Stone was also disillusioned by the proslavery attitudes of much of the church.
22. Hays, *Morning Star*, p. 51. Stone was disturbed by some of the Oberlin faculty's concession that "war is sometimes right." She and most women at Oberlin leaned toward William Lloyd Garrison's views of nonresistance. See p. 52.
23. Gilson, "Antoinette Brown Blackwell," p. 48.
24. *Proceedings, Cleveland*, p. 100.
25. Antoinette Brown Blackwell to Weld, Boston, June, 1879, Weld Family Papers.
26. Wheatley, *Palmer*, p. 314.
27. Chapman, *Mother Cobb*, p. 62.
28. *HWS*, 1:466.
29. Ibid., 1:284.
30. Phoebe Palmer, "Model Revival," editorial, *Guide to Holiness* 46 (September 1864):61.
31. Gilson, "Antoinette Brown Blackwell," pp. 72-73.
32. Wheatley, *Palmer*, p. 67. Martha Inskip was the partner of John Inskip, founder of the National Campmeeting Association for the Promotion of Holiness.
33. Palmer, *Four Years*, p. 635.
34. Wheatley, *Palmer*, p. 317.
35. Ibid., p. 283.
36. F. de L. Booth-Tucker, *The Life of Catherine Booth: The Mother of the Salvation Army*, 2 vols. (London: The Salvation Army Printing Works, 1892), 1:253-57.
37. Finney, *Lectures on Revivals*, p. 115.
38. Bloomers were actually first worn publicly in upstate New York by Elizabeth Smith, daughter of Gerrit Smith, and cousin of Elizabeth Cady Stanton, but Mrs. Bloomer popularized the costume through the *Lily*. The Smiths at one time were "strict Presbyterians, they believed in all the doctrines of Calvin! Then, an indefinite gloom pervaded their home. Their consciences were diseased," according to Stanton. She reported that members of the household in Peterboro, New York, "passed through every stage of theological experience," including three kinds of baptism. But "the position of the Church in the anti-slavery conflict, opening as it did all questions of ecclesiastical authority, Bible interpretation, and church discipline, awakened them to new thought and

broader views on religious subjects." See Stanton, *Eighty Years*, p. 53. Gerrit Smith (1797-1874) was a financial backer of many reforms; active in temperance, abolition, and woman's rights himself; a politician, and a leader in the "union church" movement. See Ralph Volney Harlow, *Gerrit Smith, Philanthropist and Reformer* (New York: Henry Holt, 1939).

39. Ibid., p. 142. Mrs. M.R. Lemert, "The Religious Use of Woman's Tongue Divinely Required," *Christian Standard* 12 (January 1884):9, argued that

> woman is not only permitted to use her tongue in the church assembled but is required to make the same use of it that is required of the man; in speaking the word of the Lord, in prayer, praise, thanksgiving, exhortation, etc. In so saying, let it not be understood that any service belonging to the elders, by virtue of their office, is intended.

Mrs. Lemert, a member of the Disciples denomination, was trying to widen woman's role, but still find a middle ground. Alexander Campbell, "Woman's Rights," *Millennial Harbinger*, April 1854, pp. 203, took the position that woman is not equal. Speaking of Adam and Eve (in contrast to Finney's language), Campbell declared: "His lordship was earthwide, her queenship is naturally and rightfully only housewide."

40. Mrs. P.L.U. [Phoebe L. Upham], "Woman's Freedom in Worship," *Guide to Holiness* 43 (April-May 1863):114-15.
41. S. Olin Garrison, ed., *Forty Witnesses* (1888; reprint ed., Freeport, Pa.: The Fountain Press, 1955), pp. 69-77.
42. Dieter, "Revivalism and Holiness," p. 50.
43. Wheatley, *Palmer*, pp. 558-59.
44. Phoebe Palmer, "Fragments from My Portfolio," *Guide to Holiness* 26 (1845):10.
45. M. Annesley, "Speaking in Meeting," *Guide to Holiness* n.s. 7 (May 1868):145.
46. *Guide to Christian Perfection* 1 (July 1839):24.
47. Lerner, *Grimké Sisters*, pp. 358-66.
48. Amanda Smith, *An Autobiography, The Story of the Lord's Dealings with Mrs. Amanda Smith* (1893; reprint ed., Noblesville, Ind.: Newby Book Room, 1972), p. 80. Mrs. Smith found sanctification under the ministry of John Inskip.
49. Ibid., p. 226.
50. Wheatley, *Palmer*, pp. 198-99.
51. A. Grimké to Weld, Groton, Mass., 12 August 1837, Barnes and Dumond, *Letters*, 1:416.

## CHAPTER FOUR

1. Finney, *Memoirs*, p. 42.
2. Ibid., p. 60.

3. Antoinette Brown Blackwell, "Life Work," Blackwell Family Papers, Radcliffe College, Schlesinger Library, Cambridge, Mass., p. 11 (typewritten).
4. For a discussion of the Princeton position see Ernest R. Sandeen, *Roots of Fundamentalism 1800-1930* (Chicago: University of Chicago Press, 1970).
5. C.C. Foote, "Woman's Rights and Duties," *Oberlin Quarterly Review* 3 (October 1349):406. This prowoman article followed those by Brown and Fairchild.
6. Finney, *Memoirs*, p. 54. On p. 46 Finney said he "could not receive his views on the subject of atonement, regeneration, faith, repentance, the slavery of the will, or any of the kindred doctrines."
7. Finney, *Lectures on Revivals*, p. 83.
8. Ibid.
9. Ibid., p. 141.
10. Wright, *Finney*, p. 190.
11. *Proceedings, Cleveland*, pp. 151-52.
12. Antoinette Brown Blackwell to Weld, June 1879, Weld Family Papers.
13. A. Grimké to Weld and John Greenleaf Whittier, Brookline, Mass., 20 August 1837, Barnes and Dumond, *Letters*, 1:429.
14. S. and A. Grimké to Henry C. Wright, Groton, Mass., 12 August 1837, Ibid., 1:20.
15. A. Grimké to Weld, Groton, Mass., 12 August 1837, Ibid., 1:418.
16. Janis Calvo, "Quaker Women Ministers in Nineteenth-Century America," *Quaker History* 63 (Autumn 1974):78, says that, "Even while arguing for an equal role in the ministry, however, Quakers did not base their arguments on the equality of the sexes. They argued for the right of a woman to be a minister, not for her right to be anything she wished to be." Calvo found no instance in which Quaker women preachers advocated equality of the sexes per se or questioned the role of women in society. She feels that "the ministry provided an available alternative without the necessity of openly or consciously questioning the validity of the traditional role or the unsettling influences of social, from spiritual, equality of the sexes."
17. S. Grimké, *Letters on Equality*, p.4.
18. Ibid., p. 91.
19. Ibid., p. 126.
20. Dieter, "Revivalism and Holiness," p. 52.
21. Hughes, *Fragrant Memories*, p. 16.
22. *Guide to Holiness* 31 (May 1857):135. For similar quotations see Palmer, *Promise*, p. 227; Wheatley, *Palmer*, p. 251.
23. *Guide to Holiness* 31 (May 1857):138.
24. Hughes, *Fragrant Memories*, p. 74.
25. Phoebe Palmer, "Witness of the Spirit," editorial, *Guide to Holiness* 47 (June 1865):137.
26. Ibid.
27. Wheatley, *Palmer*, p. 509. Palmer even wrote a hymn to the Bible, "Blessed Bible, How I Love It!" which Wheatley quotes on p. 625.

28. *Guide to Holiness* 26 (1845):10.
29. Letter, 30 April 1851, Wheatley, *Palmer*, pp. 522, 518.
30. Sarah A. Cooke, *The Handmaiden of the Lord, or Wayside Sketches* (Chicago: S.B. Shaw, Publisher, 1900), p. 72.
31. Roche, *Lankford*, p. 235.
32. Livermore, *Story*, p. 42.
33. Ibid., pp. 141-42.
34. A. Blackwell, *Stone*, pp. 15-16; Hays, *Morning Star*, p. 20.
35. A. Blackwell, *Stone*, p. 59.
36. Ibid., pp. 134-35.
37. Stanton, *Eighty Years*, pp. 21-24.
38. Antoinette Brown to Lucy Stone, 18 March 1848, Blackwell Family Papers.
39. Kerr, *Lady*, p. 54.
40. Antoinette Brown Blackwell, "Reminiscences of Early Oberlin," February 1918, Blackwell Family Papers, Radcliffe College, Schlesinger Library, Cambridge, Mass., p. 4 (handwritten). Brown's article was "Exegesis of 1 Corinthians, xiv., 34, 35; and 1 Timothy, ii, 11, 12," *Oberlin Quarterly Review* 3 (July 1849):358-73. It was preceded by James H. Fairchild, "Woman's Rights and Duties," pp. 326-57. Fairchild was professor of theology and followed Finney as president of Oberlin.
41. Finney, *Memoirs*, p. 5.
42. S. Grimké, *Letters on Equality*, p. 16, See also Sarah Grimké, letter, *Advocate of Moral Reform*, 1 January 1838, pp. 3-5. Shocked subscribers replied in the issues of 1 April, p. 55, and 16 July, p. 108.
43. S. and A. Grimké to Henry C. Wright, Brookline, Mass., 27 August 1837, Barnes and Dumond, *Letters*, 1:436-41; Hannah L. Stickney to S. Grimké, Philadelphia, 30 March 1838, Weld Family Papers.
44. S. Grimké. *Letters on Equality*, pp. 33, 75.
45. Charles Hodge, "West India Emancipation," *The Biblical Repertory and Princeton Review* 10 (1838):603, 604.
46. *HWS*, 1:224, referring to the first national woman's rights convention in Worcester, Mass., in 1850.
47. *HWS*, 1:145-46, referring to the third national woman's rights convention in Cleveland, in 1853.
48. *HWS*, 1:624, referring to an 1855 woman's rights convention in Saratoga Springs, N.Y.
49. *HWS*, 1:647. This time in New York City in 1856 Brown was answering a young theological student who asked the women whether they based their arguments on nature or revelation. The "treatise" referred to was never completed as far as I have been able to determine.
50. *The Proceedings of the Woman's Rights Convention, held at Worcester, October 23d and 24th, 1850* (Boston: Prentiss & Sawyer, 1851), pp. 20-21.
51. Ibid., p. 69.
52. *HWS*, 1:380.

53. Lutz, *Anthony*, p. 48.
54. *HWS*, 2:374. See also Stanton, *Eighty Years*, p. 372.
55. Harper, *Anthony*, 1:77-78.
56. For a list of the defenses I have unearthed, see Appendix.
57. *HWS*, 1:41, 103. Elizabeth Wilson, *A Scriptural View of Woman's Rights and Duties, in All the Important Relations of Life* (Philadelphia: Wm. S. Young, Printers, 1849).
58. See Jerry Wayne Brown, *The Rise of Biblical Criticism in America, 1800-1870* (Middletown, Conn.: Wesleyan University Press, 1969).
59. *Proceedings, Cleveland*, p. 151.
60. Ibid., p. 153.
61. A. Grimké, diary, 24 June 1829, p. 66.
62. *Proceedings, Cleveland*, p. 153.
63. Wheatley, *Palmer*, p. 497.
64. Palmer, *Promise*, p. 354. Palmer here alludes to a new translation of Psalms 68:11, which reads in the KJV "The Lord gave the word: great was the company of those that published it." Today's English Version translates it, "The Lord gave the command and many women carried the news."
65. *HWS*, 1:536-37.
66. Ibid., p. 540.
67. *Proceedings, Cleveland*, p, 164.
68. Ibid., p. 168; *HWS*, 1:142.
69. *Proceedings, Cleveland*, pp. 6, 170.

## CHAPTER FIVE

1. Newberg, "Civil War," p. 108.
2. Ibid., pp. 93, 132.
3. Ibid., pp. 87, 94.
4. Rosell, "Benevolence Empire," p. 49.
5. Richard Carwardine, "The Second Great Awakening in the Urban Centers: An Examination of Methodism and the 'New Measures,' " *Journal of American History* 59 (September 1972):327-40.
6. Finney, *Lectures on Revivals*, pp. 208, 198.
7. McLoughlin, *Revivalism*, pp. 35-36.
8. Newberg, "Civil War," p. 174.
9. "Dr. Beecher and Mr. Beman's Convention on Revivals," *The Christian Examiner* 4 (July and August 1827):357-70; Charles C. Cole, Jr., "The New Lebanon Convention" *New York History* 48 (1950):385-97.
10. Finney, *Memoirs*, p. 214. Nathaniel Sydney Smith Beman was one of the leading New School ministers, pastor of the Presbyterian church in Troy for forty years, where Finney held revivals. He served as a moderator of the Presbyterian

General Assembly in 1831 and led the New School out of that assembly in 1837.

11. Lyman Beecher, *The Autobiography of Lyman Beecher*, Barbara Cross, ed., 2 vols. (Cambridge, Mass.: The Belknap Press of Harvard University Press, 1961), 2:75. Charles I. Foster, *An Errand of Mercy: The Evangelical United Front 1790-1837* (Chapel Hill: The University of North Carolina Press, 1960), pp. 258-59, reports that a Methodist wag in *The Christian Advocate* suggested formation of an "American Society for the Prevention of Woman's speaking and praying at improper times and places" and proposed a fund of $30,000 to send out agents to form auxiliaries and award prizes for the best tract on "The 'impropriety' and indecency of woman's praying before a man."
12. Abel Stevens, *The Women of Methodism: Its Three Foundresses* (New York: Nelson & Phillips, 1866), pp. 161-96.
13. I.D. Stewart, *The History of the Freewill Baptists for Half a Century*, 2 vols. (Dover: Freewill Baptist Printing Establishment, 1862), 1:191-92, 306-91.
14. Weld to A. and S. Grimké, New; York, 26 August 1837, Barnes and Dumond, *Letters*, 1:432-33.
15. Finney, *Memoirs*, p. 178.
16. Asahel Nettleton to John Frost, 13 February 1827, Finney Papers.
17. Bennet Tyler, *Memoir of the Life and Character of Rev. Asahel Nettleton, D.D.* (Hartford: Robins & Smith, 1844), p. 251.
18. Newberg, "Civil War," p. 148.
19. *Letters of the Rev. Dr. Beecher and Rev. Mr. Nettleton, on the "New Measures" in Conducting Revivals of Religion, with a Review of a Sermon by Novangelus* (New York: G. & C. Carvill, 1828), p. 91, as quoted in Newberg "Civil War," p. 148.
20. George Gale to Charles Finney, 11 March 1827, as quoted in Johnson dissertation, p. 110.
21. Timothy Dwight to Charles Finney, March 1831, as quoted in Rosell, "Benevolence Empire," p. 68.
22. Finney, *Lectures on Revivals*, p. 138.
23. *Oberlin Evangelist*, 23 April 1825, p. 68.
24. Robert Samuel Fletcher, *A History of Oberlin College*, 2 vols. (Oberlin: Oberlin College, 1943), 1:291.
25. Ibid.
26. Hays, *Morning Star*, p. 51.
27. Fletcher, *History*, 1:294.
28. Gilson, "Antoinette Brown Blackwell," p. 82; slightly different account on pp. 130-31.
29. Ibid., pp. 82-83.
30. Brown, "Reminiscences," p. 4.
31. Ibid., p. 5.
32. Finney, *Memoirs*, pp. 412-13.
33. Finney, *Lectures on Revivals*, pp. 9, 13, 181, 182, 251.
34. Finney, *Memoirs*, p. 440.

35. One reason why women were not permitted to speak by the Campbellites and Disciples, even though they were revivalist, was that they insisted "where the Scriptures speak, we speak; where the Scriptures are silent, we are silent."
36. Finney, *Lectures on Revivals*, p. 189.
37. Newberg, "Civil War," p. 85.
38. Palmer, *Promise*, pp. v-vi, 113.
39. Lydia Sexton, *Autobiography of Lydia Sexton* (Dayton: United Brethren Publishing House, 1882), pp. 208-9. Sexton (1799-1872) was born 12 April 1799 in Rockport, New Jersey, to a Baptist minister, Thomas Casad, and his wife Abigail Tingley. Her first two husbands, Isaac Cox and Moses Moore, each died accidental deaths within a year of marriage, but she finally lived with her third husband, Joseph Sexton, for fifty years. She migrated to Fairfield, Ohio, near Dayton, then to Jasper County, Indiana, and finally to Spring Hill, Kansas, where she was appointed chaplain to the Kansas State Prison at Leavenworth on 29 January 1870. She was licensed by the United Brethren Church quarterly from 1851-57 and after that as a preacher "for life." Although she was not officially ordained, she appears to have baptized her prison converts and celebrated Communion with them.
40. Sadie J. Hart, "My Experience," *Guide to Holiness* n.s. 6 (April 1869):114-15.
41. Garrison, *Forty Witnesses*, pp. 141-42, 144.
42. Sexton, *Autobiography*, p. 517.
43. A. Grimké to Weld and Whittier, Brookline, Mass., 20 August 1837, Barnes and Dumond, *Letters*, 1:428, 429, 430.

## CHAPTER SIX

1. Beecher, *Autobiography*, 1:191.
2. Tyler, *Nettleton*, pp. 252-53.
3. In the eighteenth century most clergymen were upper-class, wealthy, cultured. The rise of such societies as the American Education Society and others to help pay for the education of clergy in the nineteenth century is just one indication that clergy were being drawn from the lower socioeconomic classes. Suffragists called them "pin cushion ministers" because many of them were educated through the donations of women who did sewing to get the money.
4. Finney, *Memoirs*, p. 45.
5. George Gale, "Autobiography of George W. Gale," 2:47-48, as quoted in Whitney R. Cross, *The Burned-over District* (New York: Harper & Row, 1950), p. 158.
6. "Dr. Beecher and Mr. Beman," *Christian Examiner*, p. 365. Beman moved to amend the motion to add "as heretics, or enthusiasts, or disorganizers, as deranged or mad," all names the Finneyites had been called by the easterners. Edwards then proposed omission of all "epithets," and the amended motion passed.

7. Asahel Nettleton to John Frost, 13 February 1827, Finney Papers, as quoted in Newberg, "Civil War," p. 133.
8. Finney, *Lectures on Revivals*, pp. 75, 94, 117.
9. Hodge, "West Indian Emancipation," p. 604.
10. Finney, *Memoirs*, pp. 45-46, 87-88.
11. Finney, *Lectures on Revivals*, pp. 185, 188-89.
12. Cooke, *Handmaiden*, p. 77.
13. *Beecher-Nettleton Letters*, pp. 99, 89 as quoted in Newberg "Civil War," pp. 146-47, 152.
14. Foote, "Woman's Rights," p. 401.
15. Finney, *Lectures on Revivals*, p. 183.
16. Ibid., pp. 193, 259.
17. Charles G. Finney, *Sermons on Gospel Themes* (Oberlin: E. J. Goodrich, 1876), p. 345.
18. *HWS* 1:167.
19. S. Grimké, *Letters on Equality*, pp. 19-20.
20. Attributed to John Fletcher by Roche, *Sarah Lankford*, p. 127. "The Unction Makes the Minister," *Guide to Holiness* 9 (1846):40.
21. Brown, "Reminiscenses," p. 5 back.
22. S. Grimké, *Letters on Equality*, pp. 102-3.
23. S. Grimké to Weld, New York, 10 March 1837, Barnes and Dumond, *Letters*, 1:373.
24. Palmer, *Promise*, pp. 107, 109.
25. Diary, 10 December 1873, Wheatley, *Palmer*, p. 83.
26. "Letter from Mrs. Palmer," 22 November 1858, *Guide to Holiness* 35 (February 1859):17.
27. Palmer, *Four Years*, pp. 677-78; also in Wheatley, *Palmer*, p. 614.
28. Wheatley, *Palmer*, pp. 631-32.
29. Phoebe Palmer, *Faith and Its Effects: or, Fragments from My Portfolio* (New York: Published for the Author, Joseph Longking, Printer, 1852), p. 290.
30. Wheatley, *Palmer*, p. 614.
31. Foote, "Woman's Rights," p. 406.
32. Palmer, *Promise*, pp. 115, 117.
33. Deborah Peirce, *A Scriptural Vindication of Female Preaching, Prophesying, or Exhortation* (Carmel: Printed for Nathan Roberts, E. Burroughs, Printer, n.d.), pp. 2-6.
34. *HWS* 1:71.
35. See Appendix.
36. Paulina Wright Davis, *A History of the National Woman's Rights Movement, for 20 Years, with the Proceedings of the Decade Meeting Held at Apollo Hall, October 20, 1870* (New York: Journeymen Printers' Co-operative Association, 1871; reprint ed., New York: Source Book Press, 1970), p. 46.
37. D. Dayton, *Discovering*, p. 91.

38. The ordination of the missionary wives is discussed in a series of stories, "Ordination," *Christian Standard*, 15 September 1883, pp. 362-64; 6 October 1883, pp. 387-88; 17 November 1883, pp. 434-36; 24 November 1883, p. 444. See also Sally Smith, "The Ordination of Women in the Christian Church (Disciples of Christ)," paper for Disciple History and Polity, 7 May 1975, Christian Theological Seminary, Indianapolis, Indiana.
39. Della E. Olson, "A Woman of Her Times," *The Evangelical Beacon*, 27 May 1975-2 September 1975.
40. Holiness denominations that ordain women and always have include Assemblies of God, Church of God, Church of God in North America, Church of the Nazarene, Pillar of Fire (founded by the first woman bishop in America, Alma White), Pilgrim Holiness, the Holiness Church, Pentecostal Holiness Church, and the Salvation Army.
41. Weld to S. and A. Grimké, New York, 26 August 1837, Barnes and Dumond, *Letters*, 1:433.
42. S. and A. Grimké to Weld, Fitchburg, Mass., 20 September 1837, ibid., p. 449.
43. S. Grimké, *Letters on Equality*, pp. 188-89. Such Bible schools as D.L. Moody's Moody Bible Institute in Chicago seem to be one of the answers to Grimké's plea. Many of the later women evangelists were trained there.
44. Ibid., p. 100.
45. A. Grimké to Weld, 12 August 1837, Barnes and Dumond, *Letters*, 1:415.
46. J.F. Stearnes, sermon; Hubbard Winslow, sermon, *Report, Boston Female* (1837), pp. 54, 52. Many churches were closed to abolitionists and then to women in particular, whatever their cause. In 1871-72 a Presbyterian, Rev. Cuyler of Brooklyn, was tried by the presbytery for allowing a Quaker preacher, Miss Sarah Smiley, into his pulpit, Lafayette Avenue Presbyterian Church. See Isaac Errett, ed., "Shall Woman Preach?" *Christian Standard*, 16 March 1872, p. 84. It led to the publication of H. Loomis, "May a Woman Speak in a Promiscuous Religious Assembly?" *Congregational Quarterly*, April 1874, and reprinted in pamphlet form. The Brooklyn Presbytery taking refuge in an action by the (Old School) General Assembly of 1837,

    > *Resolved*, That the Presbytery feel constrained to enjoin upon our Churches strict regard to the following deliverance of the General Assembly: Meetings of pious women by themselves for conversation and prayer we entirely approve. But let not the inspired prohibition of the great Apostle as found in his epistles to the Corinthians and to Timothy be violated. To teach and to exhort, or to lead in prayer in public and promiscuous assemblies, is clearly forbidden to women in the Holy Oracles.

    An even more celebrated church trial occurred in 1876 when a Dr. See was tried for admitting a Mrs. Robinson of Indiana and Mrs. E. S. Whitney of New York to his pulpit to speak on temperance. The trial went through the presbytery of Newark, synod of New Jersey, and the General Assembly. See *HWS*, 1:780.
47. Lee, *Five Sermons*, p. 99. This sermon was first published by Luther Lee as *Woman's Right to Preach the Gospel* (Syracuse, 1853), p. 22.

48. Johnson book, p. 167.
49. Lutz, *Anthony*, p, 76.
50. Harper, *Anthony*, 1:167.
51. Frances Willard, "President's Annual Address," *Minutes* (Chicago: National Woman's Christian Temperance Union, 1888), pp. 45-49.
52. Newberg, "Civil War," p. 111.
53. Wheatley, *Palmer*, pp. 619, 633.
54. Maggie Newton Van Cott, *The Harvest and the Reaper, Reminiscences of Revival Work*, with an introduction by Bishop Gilbert Haven, and "Woman's Place in the Gospel," by the Rev. D. Sherman (New York: N. Tibbals & Sons, Publishers, 1877), p. 276. Van Cott (1830-1914) was born in New York City 25 March 1830. She was reared an Episcopalian; her father was a real estate broker. She married Peter Van Cott on 23 January 1848 and had to be asked three times before she would say "obey." Van Cott was sick much of the time and Maggie showed great independence and initiative in running dry-goods and pharmaceutical businesses. She was converted in front of the John Street Methodist Episcopal Church in either 1857 or 1858, during the revival. While making a drug delivery one day she visited the noonday prayer meeting on Fulton Street, got blessed, testified, and was rebuked for it. She began attending Methodist meetings and the Sunday after her husband died in 1866, she joined the church. She had a dream saying "You must preach" in 1868 and was active until her retirement in 1902.
55. William R. Phinney, *Maggie Newton Van Cott: First Woman Licensed to Preach in the Methodist Episcopal Church* (New York: Commission on Archives and History, New York Annual Conference, United Methodist Church, 1969), p. 4, quotes her as declaring in a discussion with her husband and a class leader: "I believe my tongue is my own, John, and I will use it when I please, where I please, and as I please." Gilbert Haven, who spoke at several woman's suffrage conventions and was a friend of the American Woman Suffrage Association, at the end of his introduction to Van Cott, *Harvest*, p. xxvi, said perhaps the church could "offset the demon Woodhull with the saintly Palmer and Van Cott." After all, "it must not let the devil have all the good female speakers."
56. *Notable American Women*, s.v. "Amanda Way," by Clifton J. Phillips; *HWS*, 1:306-12, 328.
57. Wilson T. Hogue, *History of the Free Methodist Church of North America*, 2 vols. (Winona Lake, Ind.: The Free Methodist Publishing House, 1938), 1:344-45. At the church's fourth General Conference in 1874, General Superintendent B. T. Roberts presented a report, for a Committee on Woman's Work, suggesting the adding of a class of ministers having denominational status as "evangelists." They were to be "a class of preachers called of God to preach the Gospel, to labor to promote revivals of religion and spread abroad the cause of Christ in the land; but not called to a pastoral charge or to government in the Church." They were to be licensed by quarterly conferences after due examination, and after four successful years of ministry, could be given a life license. This opened the way for women evangelists. Ibid., 2:176-78, 186.

Although the denomination did not give women full ordination until 1974, Roberts continually agitated for their ordination, authored *Ordaining Women* (Rochester: Earnest Christian Publishing House, 1891), and threatened not to attend another general conference until the denomination acted. Unfortunately he died before he could carry out his threat.

58. Ira Ford McLeister, *History of the Wesleyan Methodist Church of America* (Syracuse: Wesleyan Methodist Publishing Association, 1934), pp. 65, 96-98, 106-7.
59. Sexton, *Autobiography*, pp. 400, 403, 552-53.
60. Donald F. Durnbaugh, "She Kept on Preaching," *Messenger* 124 (April 1975):18-21.

## CHAPTER SEVEN

1. *Panoplist and Missionary Magazine* 10 (1814):1, as quoted in Rosell, "Benevolence Empire," p. 132.
2. Finney, *Lectures on Revivals*, p. 118.
3. Charles G. Finney, *Lectures on Systematic Theology*, ed. James H. Fairchild (New York: George H. Doran Company, 1878), p. 450.
4. Finney, *Lectures on Revivals*, p. 404.
5. Charles G. Finney, "The Pernicious Attitude of the Church on the Reforms of the Age," *Oberlin Evangelist* 8 (21 January 1846):11; D. Dayton, *Discovering*, pp. 20-24, quotes the letter in full because he notes that *Revival Fire*, a twentieth-century reprint of these "Letters on Revivals," prints an entirely different text under this title. Similarly, V. Raymond Edman's *Finney Lives On*, a synopsis of the *Lectures on Revivals on Religion*, under "hindrances to revival" omits mention of "resistance to reform" and "taking the wrong ground on questions of human rights."
6. Charles Finney, "A Seared Conscience," *Oberlin Evangelist*, 28 April 1841, lists "Abolition of Slavery, Temperance, Moral Reform, Politics, Business Principles, Physiological and Dietetic Reform" as issues one cannot disregard.
7. Charles Finney to Theodore Weld, Oberlin, 21 July 1836, Barnes and Dumond, *Letters*, 1:318-19.
8. Finney, "Pernicious Attitude," p, 11; Finney, *Systematic Theology*, p. 223, even appears to advocate outright revolution if a government is unresponsive: "When one form of government fails to meet any longer the necessities of the people, it is the duty of the people to revolutionize. In such cases, it is vain to oppose revolution; for in some way the benevolence of God will bring it about."
9. Johnson book, p. 161, quotes Finney as writing Gerrit Smith: "I am no politician and have for a long time been too disgusted with the political course of things in the U.S. to have any connection whatsoever with either of the political parties," but this does not seem to have discouraged the majority of his followers from being involved.

10. *Guide to Holiness*, April 1869, p. 115.
11. S. Grimké, *Letters on Equality*, pp. 122-23.
12. Ibid., pp. 41, 42, 116, 122.
13. Lumpkin, *Emancipation*, p. viii.
14. Barnes, *Anti-Slavery Impulse*, p. 154.
15. A. Grimké to Jane Smith, 20 January 1837, Weld Family Papers.
16. A. Grimké to George S. Chase, 20 August 1837, Weld Family Papers.
17. Hays, *Morning Star*, p. 107.
18. *Proceedings, Worcester*, p. 21.
19. *HWS*, 1:72.
20. Palmer, *Promise*, p. 148. Wheatley, *Palmer*, pp. 597-98, quoted an 1849 letter that presents an interesting perspective on the class of these women. Said Palmer:

    > I would be careful to be just at the work to which the Master of the household has assigned me, and not be doing the work which I should be paying another to do for me. . . . I know a pious lady to whom the Lord has entrusted a comfortable share of property, and an interesting family, which necessarily require much care. With a feeble state of health, she is so possessed of a literary taste, and a heart inclining her to be variously engaged in doing good, and talents capacitating her nobly for the work. But in view of laying up treasure on earth, she permits herself to bear unaided the cares of her family, while perhaps some poor woman in her neighborhood may be pining in penury, for want of employment. She is consuming her energies in doing the work which God has fitted the other to do for her. May not such, when called to render an account of stewardship, find that there has been a misapproriation of talents?

21. Sexton, *Autobiography*, pp. 342-43.
22. *Report, Boston Female* (1835), p. 39.
23. *HWS*, 1:158.
24. Foster, *Errand*, p. 99. See also John R. Bodo, *The Protestant Clergy and Public Issues* (Princeton, N.J.: Princeton University Press, 1954); Charles C. Cole, Jr., *The Social Ideas of the Northern Evangelists 1826-1860* (New York: Octagon Books, Inc., 1966); Clifford Griffin, *Their Brothers' Keepers: Moral Stewardship in the United States, 1800-1865* (New Brunswick, N.J.: Rutgers University Press, 1960); Joseph R. Gusfield, *Symbolic Crusade: Status Politics and the American Temperance Movement* (Urbana: University of Illinois Press, 1963).
25. Joanna Bethune, *The Power of Faith, Exemplified in the Life and Writings of the Late Mrs. Isabella Graham* (New York: American Tract Society, 1843), pp. 49, 70.
26. Ward Stafford, *New Missionary Field* (New York: J. Seymour, 1817), p. 15.
27. Matthew LaRue Perrine, *Women Have a Work to Do in the House of God* (New York: Edward W. Thomson, 1817), pp. 11, 24.

28. John Carroll Power, *The Rise and Progress of Sunday Schools* (New York: Sheldon & Company, 1863), p. 267.
29. Robert W. Lynn and Elliott Wright, *The Big Little School: Sunday Child of American Protestantism* (New York: Harper & Row, Publishers, 1971), p. 12.
30. Beecher, *Autobiography*, 1:188.
31. Finney, *Lectures on Revivals*, p. xix.
32. Finney, "Pernicious Attitude," p. 11.
33. Immediate abolition was persuasively argued first by Elizabeth Cottman Heyrick in an 1824 pamphlet titled *Immediate, Not Gradual Abolition*, which persuaded the British to adopt that slogan.
34. S. Grimké, *Letters to Beecher*, p. 108.
35. *Report, Boston Female*, pp. 6, 64.
36. Barnes, *Anti-Slavery Impulse*, pp. 24-25.
37. Fletcher, *History of Oberlin*, 1:297-98; Finney's speech was reprinted in the *Oberlin Evangelist*, 21 January 1836.
38. *McDowall's Journal* 2 (December 1834):189.
39. Carroll Smith-Rosenberg, *Religion and the Rise of the American City: The New York City Mission Movement, 1812-1870* (Ithaca: Cornell University Press, 1971), pp. 118-20.
40. Ibid., pp. 103-4.
41. Ibid., p. 131.
42. Keith Melder, "Ladies Bountiful: Organized Women's Benevolence in Early Nineteenth-Century America," *New York History* 48 (1967):245.
43. Hays, *Morning Star*, p. 45.
44. Fletcher, *History of Oberlin*, 1:303.
45. Gilson, "Antoinette Brown Blackwell," p. 144.
46. Cross, *Burned-over District*, p. 237.

## CHAPTER EIGHT

1. Weld to S. and A. Grimké, New York, 10 October 1837, Barnes and Dumond, *Letters*, 1:453. Weld is quoting from a previous letter from Angelina Grimké.
2. Ray [Rachel] Strachey, *Frances Willard: Her Life and Work* (New York: Fleming H. Revell Company, 1913), p. 209.
3. Frances Willard, *Woman and Temperance* (Hartford, Conn.: Park Publishing Co., 1883), p. 451.
4. Frances Willard, *Glimpses of Fifty Years* (Chicago: Woman's Temperance Association, N.J. Smith & Company, 1889), p. 352.
5. Strachey, *Willard*, pp. 211-12. Strachey was Smith's granddaughter and drew heavily on her reminiscences. Smith was the first superintendent of the WCTU's Evangelistic Department.
6. Dieter, "Revivalism and Holiness," p. 136.

7. D. Dayton, *Discovering*, p. 93; A. J. Gordon, "The Ministry of Women," *Missionary Review of the World* 7 (December 1874):910-21.
8. Harper, *Anthony*, 2:588n.; Robinson, *Massachusetts*, p. 146n.; Stanton, *Eighty Years*, pp. 294-95, 303.
9. John W. Smith, *Heralds of a Brighter Day* (Anderson, Ind.: Gospel Trumpet Co., 1955), p. 125, as quoted in D. Dayton, *Discovering*, p. 97.
10. Garrison, *Forty Witnesses*, p. 69.
11. Mary Earhart, *Frances Willard: From Prayers to Politics* (Chicago: University of Chicago Press, 1944), pp. 152, 194.
12. Frances Willard, *Home Protection Manual* (New York: Published at "The Independent" Office, 1879), p. 10.
13. Willard, *Woman and Temperance*, p. 455.
14. Frances Willard, "Presidential Address," *Minutes* (Chicago: National Woman's Christian Temperance Union, 1887), pp. 71-72.

APPENDIX

# Defenses of Woman's Ministry

*An Oration Delivered on the Fourth Day of July 1800 by a Citizen of the United States to Which Is Added The Female Advocate Written by a Lady*. Springfield: Henry Brewer, 1808.

Crocker, Hannah Mather. *Observations on the Real Rights of Women with Their Appropriate Duties Agreeable to Scripture, Reason and Common Sense*. 1818.

Peirce, Deborah. *A Scriptural Vindication of Female Preaching, Prophesying, or Exhortation*. Carmel, N.Y.: Printed for Nathan Roberts, E. Burroughs, Printer, n.d.

Livermore, Harriet. *Scriptural Evidence in Favor of Female Testimony in Meetings for the Worship of God*. 1824.

Major, Sarah Righter. Pamphlet. 1835. Reprinted in Donald F. Durnbaugh, "She Kept on Preaching," *Messenger* (Church of the Brethren) 124 (April 1975):18-21.

Grimké, Sarah M. *Letters on the Equality of the Sexes and the Condition of Woman*. Boston: 1838; reprint ed., New York: Burt Franklin, 1970.

Brown, Antoinette L. "Exegesis of 1 Corinthians, xiv., 34, 35; and 1 Timothy, 11, 12." *Oberlin Quarterly Review* 3 (July 1849):358-73.

Foote, C.C. "Woman's Rights and Duties." *Oberlin Quarterly Review* 3 (October 1849) 383-408.

Mott, Lucretia. "Discourse on Woman," 17 December 1849. Reprinted in Anna Davis Hallowell, *James and Lucretia Mott: Life and Letters*. Boston: Houghton, Mifflin and Company, 1884, pp. 487-506.

Wilson, Elizabeth. *A Scriptural View of Woman's Rights and Duties, in All the Important Relations of Life*. Philadelphia: W. S. Young, Printer, 1849.

Price, Abby. "Women in the Church." *Proceedings of the Woman's Rights Convention, Held at Syracuse, September 8th, 9th & 10th 1852*. Syracuse: Printed by J.E. Masters, No. 26, Malcolm Block, 1852.

Lee, Luther. *Woman's Right to Preach the Gospel*. (A Sermon Preached at Ordination of the Rev. Miss. Antoinette L. Brown, at South Butler, Wayne County, N.Y., September 15, 1853.) Syracuse: Published by the Author, 1853. Reprinted in Luther Lee. *Five Sermons and a Tract*. Edited by Donald W. Dayton, Chicago: Holrad House, 1975.

Philanthropos. "Paul versus Silencing Women." *Una* 1 (December 1853):186-87.

Palmer, Phoebe, *Promise of the Fathers; or, A Neglected Speciality of the Last Days*. Boston: Henry V. Degen, 1859.

Booth, Catherine Mumford. *Female Ministry: or, Woman's Right to Preach the Gospel*. London, 1859; reprinted in expurgated form, London: Morgan & Chase, n.d.; in *Papers on Practical Religion*. London: International Headquarters, 1890; New York: The Salvation Army Supplies Printing and Publishing Department, 1975.

Kellison, Barbara. *The Rights of Women in the Church*. Dayton: Printed at the Herald and Banner Office, 1862.

Brown, O.E. "Women Preachers." *Evangelist*, 24 July 1872, p. 234; 31 July 1872, p. 242.

Sherman, David, "Woman's Place in the Gospel." Preface to John O. Foster, *Life and Labors of Mrs. Maggie Newton Van Cott*. Cincinnati: Hitchcock and Walden, 1872.

Loomis, H. *May a Woman Speak in a Promiscuous Religious Assembly?* Pamphlet of an article from *Congregational Quarterly*, April 1874.

Brown, W.K. *Gunethics; or, The Ethical Status of Woman*. New York: Funk & Wagnalls, 1887. He also wrote a book titled *The Scriptural Status of Woman*.

Black, W.C. *Christian Womanhood*. Nashville: Publishing House of the Methodist Episcopal Church, South; J.D. Barbee, Agent, 1888.

Willard, Frances. *Woman in the Pulpit*. Boston: D. Lothrop Company, 1888.

Godbey, W.B. *Woman Preacher*. Louisville, Ky.: Pentecostal Publishing Co., 1891.

Roberts, B.T. *Ordaining Women*, Rochester, N.Y.: Earnest Christian Publishing House, 1891.

Woolsey, Louisa M. *Shall Woman Preach? or The Question Answered*. Caneyville, Ky.: 1891.

Rishell, Charles W. *The Official Recognition of Woman in the Church*. Cincinnati: Cranston & Stowe; New York: Hunt & Eaton, 1892.

Gage, Matilda Joslyn. *Woman, Church and State*. Chicago: Charles H. Kerr & Company, 1893.

Gordon, A.J. "The Ministry of Women." *Missionary Review of the World* 7 (December 1874):910-21; reprinted as a Gordon-Conwell Monograph, #61.

Sellew, W.A. *Why Not? A Plea for the Ordination of Those Women Whom God Has Called to Preach the Gospel*. North Chili, N.Y.: Earnest Christian Publishing House, 1894.

Franson, Frederick. *Prophesying Daughters*. Minneapolis, Minn.: Johnston and Lundquist's Book and Job Printers, 1896, in German; to be reprinted in English by *The Covenant Quarterly*.

Rees, Seth C. *The Ideal Pentecostal Church*. Cincinnati: M. W. Knapp, 1897.

Willing, Jennie Fowler. "Woman in Gospel Evangelism." *Guide to Holiness* 64 (January 1896).

______. "God's Great Woman." *Guide to Holiness* 67 (December 1897).

______. "Woman and the Pentecost." *Guide to Holiness* 68 (January 1898).

______. "Women under the Pentecostal Baptism." *Guide to Holiness* 70 (February 1899).

Cooke, Sarah A. "Shall Woman Preach the Gospel?" In *The Handmaiden of the Lord*. Chicago: S.B. Shaw, Publisher, 1900, pp. 174-76.

Bushnell, Katharine. *God's Word to Women*. Piedmont, Oakland, Calif.: Published by the Author, n.d.; reprinted by Ray B. Munson, Box 52, North Collins, N.Y., 1976.

White, Alma. *Woman's Ministry*. Zarephath, N.J.: Pillar of Fire Publishers, n.d.

Booth, Evangeline. *Woman*. New York: Fleming H. Revell Company, 1930.

# Bibliography

## Finney's Works

Finney, Charles Grandison. *Lectures on Revivals of Religion*. Edited by William G. McLoughlin. Cambridge, Mass.: The Belknap Press of Harvard University Press, 1960.

______. *Lectures on Systematic Theology*. New York: George H. Doran Company, 1878.

______. *Lectures to Professing Christians*. New York: Fleming H. Revell Company, 1878.

______. *Memoirs*. New York: A.S. Barnes & Company, 1876.

______. "The Pernicious Attitude of the Church on the Reforms of the Age." *Oberlin Evangelist*, 21 January 1846, pp. 11-12.

______. *Sermons on Gospel Themes*. Oberlin: E.J. Goodrich, 1876.

## Works About Finney

Carwardine, Richard. "The Second Great Awakening in the Urban Centers: An Examination of Methodism and the 'New Measures,' " *Journal of American History* 59 (September 1972):327-40.

Cole, Charles C., Jr. "The New Lebanon Convention." *New York History* 48 (1950):385-97.

Johnson, James E. "Charles G. Finney and a Theology of Revivalism." *Church History* 38 (September 1969):338-58.

______. "The Life of Charles Grandison Finney." Ph.D. dissertation, Syracuse University, 1959.

______. "The Life of Charles Grandison Finney." Book manuscript, 1975.

Lobue, Wayne Nicholas, "Religious Romanticism and Social Revitalization: The Oberlin Perfectionists." Ph.D. dissertation, University of Kansas, 1972.

Mattson, John. "Charles Grandison Finney and the Emerging Tradition of 'New Measures' Revivalism." Ph.D. dissertation, University of North Carolina, 1970.

Newberg, Eric Nelson. "The Civil War in Zion: Charles Grandison Finney and the Popularization of American Protestantism during the Second Great Awakening, 1795-1835." Master's thesis, Pacific School of Religion, draft, 1974.

Opie, John, Jr. "Conversion and Revivalism: An Internal History from Jonathan Edwards Through Charles Grandison Finney." Ph.D. dissertation, University of Chicago, 1963.

Rosell, Garth Mervin. "Charles Grandison Finney and the Rise of the Benevolence Empire." Ph.D. dissertation, University of Minnesota, 1971.

Vulgamore, Melvin L. "Social Reform in the Theology of Charles Grandison Finney." Ph.D. dissertation, Boston University, 1963.

Wright, George Frederick. *Charles Grandison Finney*. Boston: Houghton Mifflin Company, 1893.

## Nineteenth-Century Primary Works

American Equal Rights Association. *Proceedings*. New York: H.M. Parkhurst, 1867.

Barnes, Gilbert H., and Dumond, Dwight L., ed. *Letters of Theodore Dwight Weld, Angelina Grimké Weld and Sarah Grimké, 1822-44*. 2 vols. New York: Appleton-Century-Crofts, 1934; reprint ed., Gloucester, Mass.: Peter Smith, 1965.

Beecher, Catharine E. *An Essay on Slavery and Abolitionism, with Reference to the Duty of American Females*. Philadelphia: Henry Perkins, 1837; reprint ed., Freeport, N.Y.: Books for Libraries Press, 1970.

Beecher, Lyman. *The Autobiography of Lyman Beecher*. Edited by Barbara Cross, 2 vols. Cambridge, Mass.: The Belknap Press of the Harvard University Press, 1961.

Blackwell, Antoinette Brown. *The Sexes Throughout Nature*. New York: G.P. Putnam's Sons, 1875.

Bloomer, Dexter C. *Life and Writings of Amelia Bloomer*. Boston: Arena Publishing Co., 1895; reprint ed., New York: Schocken Books, 1975.

Brown, Antoinette L. "Exegesis of 1 Corinthians, xiv., 34, 35; and 1 Timothy, ii., 11, 12." *Oberlin Quarterly Review* 3 (July 1849):358-73.

______. "Original Investigation Necessary to the Right Development of Mind." *Oberlin Evangelist*, 29 September 1847, pp. 156-57.

Brown, Olympia. "Woman's Place in the Church." *The Monthly Religious Magazine* 42 (July 1869):26-35.

Congress of Women. *Papers Read at the Third Congress of Women, Syracuse, October 13, 14 & 15, 1875*. Chicago: Fergus Printing Company, 1875.

Davis, Paulina Wright. *A History of the National Woman's Rights Movement, for Twenty Years, with the Proceedings of the Decade Meeting Held at Apollo Hall, October 20, 1870*. New York: Journeymen Printers' Co-operative Association, 1871; reprint ed., Source Book Press, 1970.

Fairchild, James H. *Elements of Theology Natural and Revealed*. Oberlin: Edward J. Goodrich, 1892.

______. *Oberlin: Its Origin, Progress and Results*. Oberlin: R. Butler, Printer, News Office, 1871.

______."Woman's Rights and Duties." *Oberlin Quarterly Review* 3 (July 1849):326-57.
Foote, C.C. "Woman's Rights and Duties." *Oberlin Quarterly Review* 3 (October 1849):383-408.
Fulton, Justin Dewey. *Woman as God Made Her: The True Woman*. Boston: Lee and Shepard, 1869.
Garrison, S. Olin, ed. *Forty Witnesses*. 1888; reprint ed., Freeport, Pa.: Fountain Press, 1955.
Grimké, Angelina E. *Letters to Catherine E. Beecher, in Reply to An Essay on Slavery and Abolitionism*. Boston: Isaac Knapp, 1838.
Grimké, Sarah M. *Letters on the Equality of the Sexes and the Condition of Woman*. 1838; reprint ed., New York: Burt Franklin, 1970.
Hallowell, Anna Davis, ed. *James and Lucretia Mott, Life and Letters*. Boston: Houghton Mifflin Company, 1884.
Hanaford, Phebe A. *Daughters of America or Women of the Century*. Boston: B.B. Russell, 1883.
Higginson, Thomas Wentworth. *Woman and Her Wishes*. London: John Chapman, 1854.
______. *Women and Men*. New York: Harper & Brothers, 1888.
Hodge, Charles. "West Indian Emancipation." *The Biblical Repertory and Princeton Review* 10 (October 1838):602-44.
"Intelligence: Dr. Beecher and Mr. Beman's Convention on Revivals." *Christian Examiner* 4 (July and August 1827):357-70.
Lee, Luther. *Autobiography*. New York: Phillips and Hunt, 1882.
______. *Five Sermons and a Tract*. Edited by Donald W. Dayton. Chicago: Holrad House, 1975.
______. *Woman's Right to Preach the Gospel*. Syracuse: Published by the Author, 1853.
Livermore, Mary A. *The Story of My Life*. Hartford, Conn.: A.D. Worthington & Company, Publishers, 1897.
______. *What Shall We Do with Our Daughters?* Boston: Lee & Shepard, 1883.
Mahan, Asa. *Autobiography: Intellectual, Moral and Spiritual*. London: T. Woolmer, 1882.
May, Samuel Joseph. *Memoir*. Boston: Roberts Brothers, 1873.
______. *The Rights and Condition of Women; A Sermon, Preached in Syracuse, November 1846*. Syracuse: Stoddard & Babcock, 1846.
Mott, Lucretia Coffin. *Slavery and "the Woman Question."* Edited by Frederick B. Tolles. Haverford, Pa.: Friends' Historical Association, 1952.
"The Oneida and Troy Revivals." *Christian Examiner* 4 (May and June 1827) 242-65.
Palmer, Phoebe. *Faith and Its Effects: or, Fragments from My Portfolio*. New York: Published for the Author, Joseph Longkin, Printer, 1852.
______. *Promise of the Father; or, A Neglected Speciality of the Last Days*. Boston: Henry V. Degen, 1859.

______. *The Way of Holiness*. 50th American edition, New York: Foster and Palmer, Jr., 1867.

Palmer, Walter C. *Life and Letters of Leonidas L. Hamline*. New York: Carlton & Porter, 1866.

Palmer, Walter C., and Phoebe Palmer. *Four Years in the Old World*. New York: Walter C. Palmer, Jr., Publisher, 1870.

Parker, Theodore. *A Sermon on the Public Function of Woman, Preached at the Music Hall, Boston, March 27, 1853*. Rochester: Curtis, Butts & Co., n.d.

Peirce, Deborah. *A Scriptural Vindication of Female Preaching, Prophesying, or Exhortation*. Carmel, N.Y.: Printed for Nathan Roberts, E. Burroughs, Printer, n.d.

Perrine, Matthew LaRue. *Women Have a Work to Do in the House of God*. New York: Edward W. Thomson, 1817.

*Proceedings of the National Woman's Rights Convention, Held at Cleveland, Ohio, on . . . October 5th, 6th & 7th, 1853*. Cleveland: Gray, Beardsley, Spear & Co., 1854.

*Proceedings of the Woman's Rights Convention Held at the Broadway Tabernacle in the City of New York . . . September 6th & 7th, 1853*. New York: Fowler and Wells, 1853.

*Proceedings of the Woman's Rights Convention, Held at Syracuse, September 8th, 9th & 10th, 1852*. Syracuse: Printed by J.E. Masters, 1852.

*Proceedings of the Woman's Rights Convention, Held at Worcester, October 23d & 24th, 1850*. Boston: Published by Prentiss & Sawyer, 1851.

*Report of The Boston Female Anti-Slavery Society . . . Annual Meeting of 1835*. Boston: Isaac Knapp, Printer, 1836.

Richardson, Joseph. *A Sermon on the Duty and Dignity of Woman, Delivered April 22, 1832*. Hingham, Mass.: Jedidiah Farmer, 1833.

Robinson, Harriet H. *Massachusetts in the Woman Suffrage Movement*. Boston: Roberts Brothers, 1881.

Rose, Ernestine. *An Address on Woman's Rights*. Boston: J.P. Mendum, 1851.

Sexton, Lydia. *Autobiography of Lydia Sexton*. Dayton: United Brethren Publishing House, 1882.

Smith, Amanda. *An Autobiography, The Story of the Lord's Dealings with Mrs. Amanda Smith*. 1893; reprint ed., Nobelsville, Ind.: Newby Book Room, 1972.

Stafford, Ward. *New Missionary Field: A Report to the Female Missionary Society for the Poor of the City of New-York and Its Vicinity*. New York: J. Seymour, 1817.

Stanton, Elizabeth Cady. *Eighty Years and More: Reminiscences 1815-1897*. 1898; reprint ed., New York: Schocken Books, 1971.

Stanton, Elizabeth Cady, et al. *History of Woman Suffrage*. 6 vols. Vol. 1, New York: Fowler & Wells, Publisher, 1881. Vol. 2, Rochester: Susan B. Anthony, 1881.

Van Cott, Maggie Newton. *The Harvest and the Reaper*. Introduction by Bishop Gilbert Haven. New York: N. Tibbals & Sons, Publishers, 1877.

Willard, Frances E., and Mary A. Livermore, eds. *A Woman of the Century*. Chicago: Charles Wells Moulton, 1893.

*Woman's Rights Conventions, Seneca Falls & Rochester, 1848*. 1870; reprint ed., New York: Arno Press, 1969.

## Biographies

Bethune, Joanna. *The Power of Faith, Exemplified in the Life and Writings of the Late Mrs. Isabella Graham*. Mew York: American Tract Society, 1843.

Birney, Catherine. *The Grimké Sisters*. Boston: Lee and Shepard, 1885; reprint ed., Westport, Conn.: Greenwood Press, 1970.

Blackwell, Alice Stone. *Lucy Stone: Pioneer of Woman's Rights*. Boston: Alice Stone Blackwell Committee, 1930.

Booth-Tucker, F. de L. *The Life of Catherine Booth: The Mother of the Salvation Army*. 2 vols. London: The Salvation Army Printing Works, 1892.

Chapman, Mary Weems. *Mother Cobb, or Sixty Years' Walk with God*. Chicago: T.B. Arnold, Publisher, 1896.

Dorr, Rheta Childe, *Susan B. Anthony: The Woman Who Changed the Mind of a Nation*. New York: Stokes, 1928; reprint ed., New York: AMS Press, 1970.

Gilson, Mrs. Claude. "Antoinette Brown Blackwell: The First Woman Minister." Cambridge, Mass., Radcliffe College, Schlesinger Library, Blackwell Family Papers.

Gravely, William B. *Gilbert Haven: Methodist Abolitionist: A Study in Race, Religion, and Reform, 1850-1880*. Nashville: Abingdon Press, 1973.

Harper, Ida Husted. *The Life and Work of Susan B. Anthony*. 3 vols. Indianapolis: The Bowen-Merrill Company, 1899, 1898, 1908.

Hays, Elinor Rice. *Morning Star: A Biography of Lucy Stone, 1818-1893*. New York: Harcourt, Brace & World, Inc., 1961.

______. *Those Extraordinary Blackwells*. New York: Harcourt, Brace & World, Inc., 1967.

Hughes, George. *The Beloved Physician, Walter C. Palmer, M.D.* New York: Palmer & Hughes, 1884.

______. *Fragrant Memories of the Tuesday Meeting and "The Guide to Holiness," and Their Fifty Years' Work for Jesus*. New York: Palmer & Hughes, 1886.

Kerr, Laura. *Lady in the Pulpit*. New York: Woman's Press, 1951.

Lerner, Gerda. *The Grimké Sisters from South Carolina*. New York: Schocken Books. 1967.

Lindley, Susan H. "Catharine Esther Beecher: Her Theology and Her Reform Activity." Ph.D. dissertation, Duke University, 1973.

Lumpkin, Katharine DuPre. *The Emancipation of Angelina Grimké*. Chapel Hill: The University of North Carolina Press, 1974.

Lutz, Alma. *Susan B. Anthony: Rebel, Crusader, Humanitarian*. Boston: Beacon Press, 1959.

Phinney, William R. *Maggie Newton Van Cott: First Woman Licensed to Preach in the Methodist Episcopal Church*. New York: Commission on Archives and History, New York Annual Conference, United Methodist Church, 1969.

Roche, John A. *The Life of Mrs. Sarah A. Lankford Palmer*. New York: George Hughes & Company, 1898.

Ruddy, Ella Giles. *The Mother of Clubs: Caroline M. Seymour Severance*. Los Angeles: Baumgardt Publishing Co., 1906.

Suhl, Yuri. *Eloquent Crusader: Ernestine Rose*. New York: Julian Messner, 1970.

Thomas, Benjamin P. *Theodore Weld: Crusader for Freedom*. New Brunswick, N.J.: Rutgers University Press, 1950.

Tyler, Bennet. *Memoir of the Life and Character of Rev. Asahel Nettleton, D.D.* Hartford: Robins & Smith, 1844.

Wheatley, Richard. *The Life and Letters of Mrs. Phoebe Palmer*. New York: W.C. Palmer, Jr., Publisher, 1876.

Willis, Gwendolen B. "Olympia Brown." Racine, Wisconsin, 1960.

Wyatt-Brown, Bertram. *Lewis Tappan and the Evangelical War Against Slavery*. Cleveland: The Press of Case Western Reserve University, 1969.

## Works About Nineteenth-Century Women

Calvo, Janis. "Quaker Women Ministers in Nineteenth Century America." *Quaker History* 63 (Autumn 1974):75-93.

Dayton, Donald W. "Revivalism and Reform: The Experience of Early Oberlin College." Paper presented at Evangelicals for Social Action, Labor Day weekend, 1975.

Dayton, Donald W., and Lucille Sider Dayton. "The Church and the Origins of Feminism," Paper given at conference, "Claiming Our Heritage, Projecting Our Future: 200 Years of Feminism in the Church," Emmanuel United Methodist Church, Evanston, Ill., 11 March 1976.

______. "Recovering a Heritage: Part II. Evangelical Feminism." *Post-American*, August-September 1974, pp. 7-9.

______. "Women as Preachers: Evangelical Precedents." *Christianity Today*, 23 May 1975, pp. 4-7.

Dayton, Lucille Sider, and Donald W. Dayton. "Women in the Holiness Movement." Paper presented to Women's Aldersgate Fellowship and Christian Holiness Association Men at the 106th Annual Convention of the Christian Holiness Association, Louisville, Ky., April 17-19, 1974,

______. "Your Daughters Shall Prophesy: Feminism in the Holiness Movement." *Methodist History* 14 (January 1976):67-92.

Dexter, Elizabeth Anthony. *Career Women of America 1776-1840*. Francestown N.H.: Marshall Jones Company, 1950.

Durnbaugh, Donald F. "She Kept on Preaching." *Messenger* 124 (April 1875):18-21.

Harkness, Georgia. "Pioneer Women in the Ministry." *Religion in Life* 39 (Summer 1970):261-71.

______. *Women in Church and Society: A Historical and Theological Inquiry*. Nashville: Abingdon Press, 1972.

Harrison, Beverly. "The Early Feminists and the Clergy: A Case Study in the Dynamics of Secularization." *Review and Expositor* 72 (Winter 1975):41-52.

Hogeland, Ronald W. "Charles Hodge, The Association of Gentlemen and Ornamental Womanhood: 1825-1855." *Journal of Presbyterian History* 53 (Fall 1975):239-55.

______. "Coeducation of the Sexes at Oberlin College: A Study of Social Ideas in Mid-Nineteenth-Century America." *Journal of Social History* 6 (1972-73):160-76.

______. " 'The Female Appendage': Feminine Life-Styles in America, 1820-1860." *Civil War History* 17 (June 1971):101-14.

James, Edward T., ed. *Notable American Women 1607-1950*. 3 vols. Cambridge, Mass.: The Belknap Press of Harvard University Press, 1971.

Kraditor, Aileen S. *The Ideas of the Woman Suffrage Movement 1890-1920*. Garden City, N.Y.: Doubleday & Company, Inc., 1965.

Lerner, Gerda. "The Lady and the Mill Girl: Changes in the Status of Women in the Age of Jackson." *Mid-Continent American Studies Journal* 10 (Spring 1969):5-15.

Luder, Hope Elizabeth. *Women and Quakerism*. Lebanon, Pa.: Sowers Printing Company, Pendle Hill Pamphlet, 1974.

Melder, Keith E, "The Beginnings of the Woman's Rights Movement in the United States, 1800-1840." Ph.D. dissertation, Yale University, 1964.

______. "Ladies Bountiful: Organized Women's Benevolence in Early Nineteenth Century America." *New York History* 48 (1967):231-55.

Mitchell, Norma Taylor. "From Social to Radical Feminism: A Survey of Emerging Diversity in Methodist Women's Organizations, 1869-1974." *AME Zion Quarterly Review and Methodist History News Bulletin* (April 1975).

O'Connor, Lillian. *Pioneer Women Orators*. New York: Columbia University Press, 1954.

Rossi, Alice, ed. *The Feminist Papers from Adams to de Beauvoir*. New York: Bantam Books, 1973.

Sinclair, Andrew. *The Emancipation of the American Woman*. New York: Harper & Row, Publishers, 1965.

Smith, Sally. "The Ordination of Women in the Christian Church (Disciples of Christ)." Paper, Disciple History and Polity, 7 May 1975, Christian Theological Seminary, Indianapolis, Ind.

Smith-Rosenberg, Carroll. "Beauty, the Beast and the Militant Woman: A Case Study in Sex Roles and Social Stress in Jacksonian America. *American Quarterly* 23 (October 1971):562-84.

Stevens, Abel. *The Women of Methodism*. New York: Nelson & Phillips, 1866.

Thomas, Keith V. "Women and the Civil War Sects." *Past and Present* 13 (April 1958):42-62.

Welter, Barbara. "Anti-Intellectualism and the American Woman: 1800-1860." *Mid-America* 48 (October 1966):258-70.

______. "The Cult of True Womanhood: 1820-1860." *American Quarterly* 18 (Summer 1966):151-74.

## Works on Nineteenth-Century American Church

Ahlstrom, Sydney, *Theology in America*. New York: The Bobbs-Merrill Company Inc., 1967.

Billington, Ray Allen. *The Protestant Crusade*. New York: The Macmillan Company, 1938.

Bodo, John R. *The Protestant Clergy and Public Issues*. Princeton: Princeton University Press, 1954.

Brown, Jerry Wayne, *The Rise of Biblical Criticism in America, 1800-1870*. Middletown, Conn.: Wesleyan University Press, 1969.

Cole, Charles C., Jr. *The Social Ideas of the Northern Evangelists 1826-1860*. New York: Octagon Books, Inc., 1966.

Cross, Whitney R. *The Burned-over District*. New York: Harper & Row, 1950.

Dayton, Donald W. "Asa Mahan and the Development of American Holiness Theology." Paper presented October 1973.

______. "Asa Mahan and the Development of American Holiness Theology." *Wesleyan Theological Journal* 9 (Spring 1974):60-69.

______. *Discovering an Evangelical Heritage*. New York: Harper & Row, Publishers, 1976.

Dieter, Melvin Easterday. "Revivalism and Holiness." Ph.D. dissertation, Temple University, 1972.

Foster, Charles I. *An Errand of Mercy: The Evangelical United Front 1790-1837*. Chapel Hill: The University of North Carolina Press, 1960.

Griffin, Clifford. *Their Brothers' Keepers: Moral Stewardship in the United States, 1800-1865*. New Brunswick, N.J.: Rutgers University Press, 1960.

Hammond, John L. "Revival Religion and Antislavery Politics." *American Sociological Review* 39 (April 1974): 175-86.

Hogue, Wilson T. *History of the Free Methodist Church of North America*. 2 vols. Winona Lake, Ind.: The Free Methodist Publishing House, 1938.

Lynn, Robert W. and Elliott Wright. *The Big Little School: Sunday Child of American Protestantism*. New York: Harper & Row, Publishers, 1971.

McLeister, Ira Ford. *History of the Wesleyan Methodist Church of America*. Syracuse: Wesleyan Methodist Publishing Association, 1934.

McLoughlin, William. *Modern Revivalism*. New York: The Ronald Press Company, 1959.

Magnuson, Norris Alden. "Salvation in the Slums: Evangelical Social Welfare Work, 1865-1920." Ph.D. dissertation, University of Minnesota, 1968.

Marsden, George M. *The Evangelical Mind and the New School Presbyterian Experience*. New Haven: Yale University Press, 1970.

Mead, Sidney. "The Rise of the Evangelical Conception of the Ministry in America: 1607-1850." In *The Ministry in Historical Perspectives*, edited by H. Richard Niebuhr and Daniel D. Williams. New York: Harper & Row, Publishers, 1956.

Neill, Stephen. *The Interpretation of the New Testament 1861-1961*. New York: Oxford University Press, 1966.
Power, John Carroll. *The Rise and Progress of Sunday Schools*. New York: Sheldon & Company, 1863.
Sandeen, Ernest R. *Roots of Fundamentalism 1800-1930*. Chicago: University of Chicago Press, 1970.
Smith, Hildrie Shelton. *Changing Conceptions of Original Sin*. New York: Charles Scribner's Sons, 1955.
Smith, Timothy. *Revivalism and Social Reform: American Protestantism on the Eve of the Civil War*. New York: Harper & Row, Publishers, 1957.
Smith-Rosenberg, Carroll. "Evangelism and the New City." Ph.D. dissertation, Columbia University, 1968.
______. *Religion and the Rise of the American City: The New York City Mission Movement, 1812-1870*. Ithaca, N.Y.: Cornell University Press, 1971.
Stewart, I.D. *The History of the Freewill Baptists for Half a Century*. 2 vols. Dover: Freewill Baptist Printing Establishment, 1862.
Weisberger, Bernard. *They Gathered at the River*. Boston: Little, Brown and Company, 1958.
Welter, Barbara, "The Feminization of American Religion: 1800-1860." In *Clio's Consciousness Raised*, edited by Mary Hartman and Lois W. Banner. New York: Harper & Row, Publishers, 1974.
Zikmund, Barbara Brown. "Asa Mahan and Oberlin Perfectionism." Ph.D. dissertation, Duke University, 1969.

## Works on Nineteenth-Century American History

Barnes, Gilbert Hobbs. *The Anti-Slavery Impulse 1830-1844*. With Introduction by William G. McLoughlin. 1933; reprint ed., New York: Harcourt, Brace & World, Inc., 1964.
Boorstin, Daniel. *The Americans: The National Experience*. New York: Random House, 1965.
Fletcher, Robert Samuel. *A History of Oberlin College*. 2 vols. Oberlin: Oberlin College, 1943.
Gusfield, Joseph R. *Symbolic Crusade*. Urbana: University of Illinois Press, 1963.
Kraditor, Aileen S. *Means and Ends in American Abolitionism*. New York: Random House, 1967.
Schlesinger, Arthur M., Jr. *The Age of Jackson*. Boston: Little, Brown and Company, 1950.
Tyler, Alice Felt. *Freedom's Ferment*. New York: Harper & Row, Publishers, 1944.

# Index

## TITLES IN THE SERIES

# Chicago Studies in the History of American Religion

*Editors*

JERALD C. BRAUER & MARTIN E. MARTY

1. Ariel, Yaakov. *On Behalf of Israel: American Fundamentalist Attitudes toward Jews, Judaism, and Zionism, 1865-1945*
2. Bundy, James F. *Fall from Grace: Religion and the Communal Ideal in Two Suburban Villages, 1870-1917*
3. Butler, Jonathan M. *Softly and Tenderly Jesus is Calling: Heaven and Hell in American Revivalism, 1870-1920*
4. Dvorak, Katharine L. *An African-American Exodus: The Segregation of the Southern Churches*
5. Hardesty, Nancy A. *Your Daughters Shall Prophesy: Revivalism and Feminism in the Age of Finney*
6. Harding, Vincent. *A Certain Magnificence: Lyman Beecher and the Transformation of American Protestantism, 1775-1863*
7. Hewitt, Glenn A. *Regeneration and Morality: A Study of Charles Finney, Charles Hodge, John W. Nevin and Horace Bushnell*
8. Hillis, Bryan V. *Can Two Walk Together Unless They Be Agreed?: American Religious Schisms in the 1970s*
9. Jacobsen, Douglas G. *An Unprov'd Experiment: Religious Pluralism in Colonial New Jersey*
10. Kloos, John M., Jr. *A Sense of Deity: The Republican Spirituality of Dr. Benjamin Rush*

(continued, over)

11. Kountz, Peter. *Thomas Merton as Writer and Monk: A Cultural Study, 1915-1951*
12. Lagerquist, L. DeAne. *In America the Men Milk the Cows: Factors of Gender, Ethnicity, and Religion in the Americanization of Norwegian-American Women*
13. Markwell, Bernard Kent. *The Anglican Left: Radical Social Reformers in the Church of England and the Protestant Episcopal Church, 1846-1954*
14. Morris, William Sparkes. *The Young Jonathan Edwards: A Reconstruction*
15. Pellauer, Mary D. *Toward a Tradition of Feminist Theology: The Religious Social Thought of Elizabeth Cady Stanton, Susan B. Anthony, and Anna Howard Shaw*
16. Potash, P. Jeffrey. *Vermont's Burned-Over District: Patterns of Community Development and Religious Activity, 1761-1850*
17. Queen, Edward L., II. *In the South the Baptists are the Center of Gravity: Southern Baptists and Social Change, 1930-1980*
18. Schmidt, Jean Miller. *Souls or the Social Order: The Two-Party System in American Protestantism*
19. Shaw, Stephen J. *The Catholic Parish as a Way-Station of Ethnicity and Americanization: Chicago's Germans and Italians, 1903-1939*
20. Shepard, Robert S. *God's People in the Ivory Tower: Religion in the Early American University*
21. Snyder, Stephen H. *Lyman Beecher and his Children: The Transformation of a Religious Tradition*

Lewis and Clark College - Watzek Library
BV639.W7 H25 1991 wmain
Hardesty, Nancy/Your daughters shall pro
3 5209 00469 2188